Action Research in P

MW00736922

Today's pressing political, social, economic, and environmental crises urgently ask for effective policy responses and fundamental transitions towards sustainability supported by a sound knowledge base and developed in collaboration between all stakeholders.

This book explores how action research forms a valuable methodology for producing such collaborative knowledge and action. It outlines the recent uptake of action research in policy analysis and transition research and develops a distinct and novel approach that is both critical and relational. By sharing action research experiences in a variety of settings, the book seeks to explicate ambitions, challenges, and practices involved with fostering policy changes and sustainability transitions. As such it provides crucial guidance and encouragement for future action research in policy analysis and transition research.

This text will be of key interest to scholars and students of policy analysis and transition research and more broadly to public administration and policy, urban and regional studies, political science, research and innovation, sustainability science, and science and technology studies. It will also speak to practitioners, policymakers and philanthropic funders aiming to engage in or fund action research.

Koen P.R. Bartels is Lecturer in Management Studies at Bangor University, UK, where he teaches courses in public administration and qualitative research. He has published in leading journals, including *Urban Studies, Environment and Planning C, Public Administration, Public Administration Review*, and *International Journal of Urban and Regional Research*, as well as a book *Communicative Capacity* (2015).

Julia M. Wittmayer works at the Dutch Research Institute for Transitions, Erasmus University Rotterdam, The Netherlands. With a background in anthropology, she is interested in roles of and social relations and interactions between actors in sustainability transitions (governance).

Routledge Advances in Research Methods

Action Research in Policy Analysis

Critical and Relational Approaches to Sustainability Transitions

Edited by Koen P.R. Bartels and Julia M. Wittmayer

LONDON AND NEW YORK

First published 2018 by Routledge

2 Park Square, Milton Park, Abingdon, Oxfordshire OX14 4RN

52 Vanderbilt Avenue, New York, NY 10017

Routledge is an imprint of the Taylor & Francis Group, an informa business

First issued in paperback 2020

Copyright © 2018 selection and editorial matter, Koen P.R. Bartels and Julia M. Wittmayer; individual chapters, the contributors

The right of Koen P.R. Bartels and Julia M. Wittmayer to be identified as the author of the editorial matter, and of the authors for their individual chapters, has been asserted in accordance with sections 77 and 78 of the Copyright, Designs and Patents Act 1988.

All rights reserved. No part of this book may be reprinted or reproduced or utilised in any form or by any electronic, mechanical, or other means, now known or hereafter invented, including photocopying and recording, or in any information storage or retrieval system, without permission in writing from the publishers.

Notice:
Product or corporate names may be trademarks or registered trademarks, and are used only for identification and explanation without intent to infringe.

British Library Cataloguing-in-Publication Data
A catalogue record for this book is available from the British Library

Library of Congress Cataloging-in-Publication Data
Names: Bartels, Koen P. R., editor. | Wittmayer, Julia M., editor.
Title: Action research in policy analysis : critical and relational approaches to sustainability transitions / edited by Koen P.R. Bartels & Julia M. Wittmayer.
Description: Abingdon, Oxon ; New York, NY : Routledge, 2018. | Series: Routledge advances in research methods | Includes bibliographical references and index.
Identifiers: LCCN 2018006782 | ISBN 9781138553828 (hbk : alk. paper) | ISBN 9781315148724 (ebk : alk. paper)
Subjects: LCSH: Action research. | Policy sciences–Research–Methodology. | Social change–Research–Methodology.
Classification: LCC H62 .A51315 2018 | DDC 320.6072–dc23
LC record available at https://lccn.loc.gov/2018006782

ISBN: 978-1-138-55382-8 (hbk)
ISBN: 978-0-367-58946-2 (pbk)

Typeset in Times New Roman
by Wearset Ltd, Boldon, Tyne and Wear

To Vittorio and Lela
In loving memory of my father, Bart Bartels

Contents

Figures

Tables

Boxes

Contributors

Karima Arichi is ad-interim area manager for City District Amsterdam-Oost. She has worked for the Municipality of Amsterdam for over ten years. She has been responsible for developing a learning programme for civil servants in Amsterdam-Oost focused on working alongside newly developing citizens initiatives. As area manager, she oversees relationships between the city-administration and different stakeholders. She is particularly interested in creating settings where civil servants, citizens and other stakeholders can co-create policy and learn together.

Ainhoa Arrona is research facilitator at Orkestra-Basque Institute of Competitiveness and PhD candidate at University of Deusto (Spain). She has worked for several years in an action research project and currently participates on territorial development research projects in collaboration with policymakers. She is writing her thesis on collaborative policymaking and governance in regional development and innovation. Her main interests in this field focus on the policy process, policy analysis, the research-policy nexus, policy learning and governance.

Ander Arzelus joined the Provincial Council of Gipuzkoa in 1980 and has developed most of his career in the President's Cabinet. Among many other responsibilities, he has coordinated strategic initiatives – such as strategic plans and cross-border collaboration projects, the area of studies, and many courses on topics related to Administration. He is currently chief officer of the Cabinet and technical coordinator of the Management Strategy Directorate. He has been actively involved in Gipuzkoa Sarean since it was launched in 2009.

Bálint Balázs is Senior Researcher and Managing Director of the Environmental Social Science Research Group. He has international research experience in the field of sustainable and local food systems, transition to sustainability and policy analysis, as well as public engagement, science-policy dialogues, cooperative research and participatory action research. He is a member of the International Network for Community-Supported Agriculture Research Group and board member of the research network Environment and Society (RN12) of the European Sociological Association.

Dirk Barrez is an independent journalist at PALA.be and an author of non-fiction books mainly on globalization, most recently about transition, and the one before about cooperatives. Previously Barrez worked more than 20 years for the public broadcaster as a journalist and as editor and coordinator of a current affairs programme. He was in 2009 one of the initiators of the Transition Network Civil Society (TNM) in Flanders and he is still an active member.

Koen PR Bartels is Lecturer in Management Studies at Bangor University (United Kingdom), where he teaches courses in public administration and qualitative research. His main research interests are public encounters, social and democratic innovation, urban governance, interpretive and qualitative research, practice theory, and relational philosophy. He has published on these topics in leading journals, including *Urban Studies, Environment and Planning C, Public Administration, Public Administration Review*, and *International Journal of Urban and Regional Research*. His book *Communicative Capacity: Public Encounters in Participatory Theory and Practice* was published by The Policy Press in 2015.

Thomas Block is director of the Centre for Sustainable Development and lecturer of 'Sustainability and Governance' at the Department of Political Sciences of Ghent University. His research focus is on complex decision-making and transition governance, education on wicked issues, future studies, sustainable cities and urban projects. In his research approach, he works from a (nuanced) constructivist epistemology, an interpretative policy analysis framework, a participative research design, and in the framing of sustainability issues as 'political' matter.

Claire Bynner combines a professional background in the field of community participation and governance, with research expertise on neighbourhoods, diversity and social cohesion. Her PhD examined social contact and trust in a super-diverse neighbourhood. She currently works as a Research Associate at the School of Social and Political Studies, University of Glasgow. As a researcher for the What Works Scotland research centre, Claire conducts collaborative action research and leads on place-based approaches to public service reform.

Floriane Clement is currently senior research fellow at INRA, France. Priori to that, she was senior researcher, Nepal country representative and gender focal point at the International Water Management Institute (IWMI), based in Kathmandu, Nepal. Her research is aimed at understanding the gaps between the intentions of natural resource policies and programmes on the one hand, and practices on the ground on the other hand. Her work is rooted in human geography, borrowing concepts, theories and tools from political science, feminist studies and development studies.

Chris Digman is Technical Director at Stantec. He is a Chartered Civil Engineer and Fellow of the Institution of Civil Engineers who has worked for over 20 years in the water and wastewater industry. He is a nationally recognised Technical Leader in the field of Urban Drainage specialising in flood risk management, resilience, pollution control, sewer solid movement and wastewater and stormwater management.

Martine de Vaan is project manager for area development and sustainable innovation at the Dutch Central Government Real Estate Agency. She works on sustainable re-development of (mostly) former military locations, and the national innovation programme for energy neutral buildings. She has been the main driver of several highly ambitious pilots on energy neutral government offices. In 2017 she was rewarded with a tenth position in the election of green professionals – public and private – in the Dutch built environment.

Alison Gardner spent 15 years working in and around English local authorities before being 'set free' by the UK coalition government's spending cuts to pursue her research ambitions. She currently leads the 'slavery-free communities' programme at the University of Nottingham, exploring how we create healthy and prosperous places which are resistant to modern slavery. Action research and appreciative inquiry continue to underpin her collaborative work with communities, civil society organisations and public services.

James Henderson has a background in community-based and participatory research from within the third sector; increasingly focused on community sector organisations, e.g. community development trusts, community social enterprises and community housing associations. He completed an ESRC-funded PhD on community-led anchor organisations at Heriot-Watt University in 2014. He joined the What Works Scotland research programme in 2015 and is pursuing action research on public service reform and further research into community anchors.

Rutger Henneman is a social entrepreneur in urban farming, writer and mover in social movements. He studied International Development Studies at Wageningen University with a minor in Moral Philosophy. Living in Rotterdam (the Netherlands) Rutger is a project manager for GroenGoed in several community gardens. He is also active in several cooperative organizations like Groene Groeiplekken, Groen010 and Warm Rotterdam. Furthermore, Rutger is an editor of webmagazines *Het Potentieel* and *Stadslandbouwtijdschrift*.

Damakant Jayshi is a freelance journalist based in Atlanta, U.S. He is a contributor to the *Nepali Times* weekly in Nepal. Jayshi is a former executive director of Panos South Asia, a media development non-profit with presence in Bangladesh, India, Nepal, Pakistan and Sri Lanka. He is the founder of the fact-checking initiative, South Asia Check. He is a 2007 Nieman Fellow at Harvard University. Jayshi has a Master's in English Literature from the University of Calcutta.

Shivant Jhagroe is a postdoctoral researcher at the Eindhoven University of Technology. In his dissertation (2016), he examined the politics of urban sustainability transitions. Currently, he studies the transformation of domestic energy practices in the context of smart homes and energy technologies. Shivant's research interests include Sustainable Urbanism, Transitions, Environmental Politics, Critical Theory, and Science and Technology Studies.

Liz Jones has over 20 years' experience as a skilled senior policymaker, researcher and partnership manager. She brings extensive policy experience across a wide policymaking and influencing agenda. She has worked in local government, the civil service and the charity sector.

Csilla Kiss works as International Research Engagement and Liaison Officer at the Centre for Agroecology, Water and Resilience at Coventry University (United Kingdom). Her role is to support researchers with international projects and partnerships. She has a strong interest in transdisciplinary and participatory approaches to research.

Martien Kuitenbrouwer is the co-founder of the Public Mediation Programme at the University of Amsterdam – an action-research programme focused upon unravelling public disputes. She is a PhD candidate and part-time lecturer for this topic at the University of Amsterdam as well. She has had a career as an elected policy official for the city of Amsterdam and is now predominantly concerned with research and design of pragmatic interventions for policy disputes that are stuck.

Miren Larrea is Senior Researcher at Orkestra-Basque Institute of Competitiveness and lecturer at the University of Deusto (Spain), University of Agder (Norway) and National Technological University (Argentina). She leads Zubigintza, an action research lab at Orkestra where she conducts long-term AR projects with various regional governments to develop collaborative policy processes. She has published in international journals and books on topics such as action research for territorial development, governance and policy-learning.

Alison McPherson was part of one of the Inquiry Teams of What Works Scotland's action research. No further details are provided for reasons of anonymity.

Erik Paredis is an assistant professor at the Department of Political Sciences of Ghent University, where he is connected to the Centre for Sustainable Development and the Ghent Institute for International Studies. His research interests include the politics of sustainability, the governance of transitions, the role of civil society, the relationship between sustainability and science and technology, and North-South issues of sustainability.

György Pataki is senior researcher for the Environmental Social Science Research Group and associate professor at the Department of Decision Sciences, Institute of Business Economics, Corvinus University of Budapest. His research interest is diverse, started in the field of ethics and economics, moved on to sustainability challenges to business organisations and biodiversity and ecosystem services valuation, currently engaged with social entrepreneurship and social innovation. He is committed to generating actionable knowledge through participatory, community-based research.

Liz Sharp is a Senior Lecturer at the Department of Urban Studies and Planning, Sheffield University, UK. Her research investigates the processes through which the public are engaged in making and implementing environmental (water) policy.

Borbála Sarbu-Simonyi lives on a small farm in the South West of Hungary. Formerly she was active in food sovereignty-related projects with Budapest-based NGO Védegylet (Protect the Future).

Sonja van der Arend, as a researcher of policies, specialises in citizen participation and politics in environmental governance. After completing her MSc, PhD and postdoc at several Dutch universities, she is now an independent writer and researcher under the heading of SenF – serious fiction.

Emma L Westling is a Research Associate at the Department of Urban Studies and Planning, Sheffield University, UK. Her research focuses on water governance and sustainability and she is particularly interested in how knowledge and expertise are negotiated and produced in interdisciplinary teams.

Julia M Wittmayer works at the Dutch Research Institute for Transitions, Erasmus University Rotterdam, The Netherlands. With a background in anthropology, she is interested in roles of and social relations and interactions between actors in sustainability transitions (governance). A specific focus is on the role of research and transdisciplinary engagements as well as research methodologies.

Preface

If you want truly to understand something, try to change it.
(Attributed to Kurt Lewin; quoted in Greenwood, 2015, 200)

Action research is a refuge for social scientists who are dissatisfied with the state of the world and dominant research practices and have a desire to change these (Brydon-Miller *et al.*, 2003). While it still operates in the relative margins of mainstream academia, over the course of 75 years, action research has become a more widespread and accepted approach, as evidenced by nine peer-reviewed journals and several esteemed handbooks and popular textbooks. It is particularly thriving in the fields of education, community studies, development, health and human services, organisational studies, professional development, systems thinking, and rural and regional development (Dick, 2011). Policy analysis and transition research were remarkable absentees in this trend. When we first met in 2012 at the Interpretive Policy Analysis (IPA) conference in Tilburg, we decided we wanted to change this.

We quickly learned we were not alone. Over the past years there has been a notable increase of action research in policy analysis and transition research. We have therefore facilitated a growing community of action researchers in sharing their experiences in panels at the IPA conferences in 2013 (Vienna), 2014 (Wageningen), 2015 (Lille), 2016 (Hull), and 2017 (Leicester) and in the section of the Standing Group for Theoretical Perspectives in Policy Analysis at the European Consortium of Political science Research (ECPR) conference in 2016 (Prague). A total of 28 presentations illustrated how policy analysts and transition researchers had been using action research in contexts as varied as water management, regional welfare systems, prostitution policy, social integration of Roma, animal husbandry, urban governance, climate change, and elementary schools.

Our initial exploration of action research principles, practices, and dilemmas in 2013 led to a symposium in *Critical Policy Studies* about the remarkably similar "double-edged dynamics and outcomes" (Bartels and Wittmayer, 2014: 400–401) across different projects of producing usable knowledge versus facing pressures of instrumentalisation. These insights triggered further reflection in

2014 on what ambitions and expectations we might reasonably hold for trans-forming contemporary crises and how to reconcile these with the possibilities and constraints of coproducing usable knowledge in practice. Our panel discus-sions identified three specific issues to consider in this respect: criticising hege-monic systems, engrained habits, and power relations; dealing with 'uncomfortable selves and others'; and assessing impact and change. Our panel discussions in 2015 led us to tease out criticality and relationality as underlying principles for dealing with these issues. As such, we gradually developed a col-lective understanding of what is involved in action research in policy analysis and transition research. We convened two panels in 2016 about critical-relational action research and developed the outcomes of the group discussions into the guiding framework for this book. In 2017, finally, we brought together the con-tributors to the book to discuss each other's chapters and the overall book project.

Over the years, many people have contributed to making this book a reality. We would first of all like to thank the authors of the chapters and reflections for what has been a very pleasant, instructive, and collaborative process. We are also grateful to the organisers of the IPA and ECPR conferences for their support and to everyone who participated in our panels as presenters and audience. Special thanks go to Richard Freeman, Peter Feindt, Tim May, and colleagues at DRIFT and Bangor Business School for their support over the years. Funding from the European Union allowed one of us dedicated time for the editorial work.[1] We would also like to acknowledge the extremely valuable support from Andrew Taylor and Sophie Iddamalgoda at Routledge. And we would like to especially thank a number of people for the most important, yet undervalued, academic activity: peer reviewing the chapters and providing the authors and us with critical constructive comments: Laurence de Carlo, Jasper Eshuis, Merlijn van Hulst, Noel Longhurst, Derk Loorbach, Stefanie Schmachtel, Sandra Karner, Tamara Metze, Karlijn Schipper, and Hendrik Wagenaar. Finally, and most fundamentally, we would not have been able to create this book without the patience, support and love of our partners Noemi and Han.

Facilitating the development of a community of action researchers in policy analysis and transition research has been an important additional goal of our efforts over the years. We hope the book will serve as a catalyst in this respect, encouraging academics in policy analysis and transition research to use and cul-tivate action research in order to live up to their transformative ambitions. While one might accuse us of using facile rhetoric or giving in to 'presentism', we feel an ever-stronger sense of urgency to address the contemporary sustainability crises we face since we both became parents over the past years. We therefore dedicate this book to our children and their future.

Note

1 Julia Wittmayer would like to acknowledge support from the "Transformative Social Innovation Theory" ("TRANSIT") project, funded by the European Union's Seventh

Framework Programme (FP7) under grant agreement 613169. The views expressed in this book are the sole responsibility of the authors/editors and do not necessarily reflect the views of the European Union.

References

Bartels KPR and Wittmayer J (2014) Symposium introduction: usable knowledge in practice. What action research has to offer to critical policy studies. *Critical Policy Studies* 8(4): 397–406.

Brydon-Miller M, Greenwood D and Maguire P (2003) Why action research? *Action Research* 1(1): 9–28.

Dick B (2011) Action research literature 2008–2010: themes and trends. *Action Research* 9(2): 122–143.

Greenwood DJ (2015) An analysis of the theory/concept entries in the Sage encyclopedia of action research: what we can learn about action research in general from the encyclopaedia. *Action Research* 13(2): 198–213.

1 Introduction

Action research in policy analysis and transition research

Koen PR Bartels and Julia M Wittmayer

> It is our contention that action research ... can come to be a significant methodological tool ... in an emerging focus on public affairs. In fact, a public affairs perspective may prove to be the area of greatest utility for A/R, though such utility will not be realized without application and a great deal of effort.
>
> (Keller and Heatwole, 1976: 193)

There is an emerging consensus that more than ever we are living in dangerous times (Hawking, 2016). Climate change, resource depletion, and large-scale agricultural production are rapidly amounting to an ecological tragedy threatening our very existence. The global meltdown of financial and economic systems and dismantling of welfare states have revealed the perversities and cracks of modern democratic capitalism and continue to generate spiralling regressive effects and inequalities. Increases in mass migration, mental health problems, and political demagoguery are mounting pressure on the solidarity and resilience of societies. In sum, we face a series of political, social, economic, and environmental crises that expose the bankruptcy of hegemonic systems and beg urgent action (Fischer and Gottweis, 2012; Gunnarsson et al., 2015; McKibben, 2015; Stout and Love, 2015; Monbiot, 2016; Raworth, 2017).

Developing effective and sustainable responses to these crises challenges us to reflect on the types and purposes of knowledge needed and, more fundamentally, on the modes of research for generating it. Such research and knowledge need to contribute to sustainability transitions – i.e. long-term processes of change towards more sustainable societies (Grin et al., 2010) – in ways that honour fundamental interdependencies between people and other living and non-living entities and acknowledge the associated knowledge uncertainty, value pluralism, and power inequalities. We therefore propose to adopt a mode of research that (1) generates actionable knowledge, (2) recognises, works with, and strengthens relationships, and (3) critically and constructively transforms hegemonic systems.

In the past, attention has been frequently called to the value of action research for addressing the increasing complexity of our societies, the structural inabilities of public organisations to effectively handle these, and the deterioration of underlying worldviews (Keller and Heatwole, 1976; Comfort, 1985; Reason, 1994; Reason and Bradbury, 2001). Action research involves researchers and other stakeholders ('co-inquirers') in critical and relational processes aimed at collaboratively producing scientifically and socially relevant knowledge and transformative action (Reason and Bradbury, 2001; Greenwood and Levin, 2007; Dick, 2015). Recently, action research has been hailed as a methodology for environmental governance (Van Buuren *et al.*, 2014; Castellanet and Jordan, 2016; Hansen *et al.*, 2016), territorial development (Karlsen and Larrea, 2014), democratic welfare governance (Gunnarsson *et al.*, 2015), and public service reform (Orr and Bennett, 2012). It is also used in participative forms of evaluation (Guba and Lincoln, 1998; Abma, 2004; Edelenbos and Van Buuren, 2005) and in co-production with policy actors, communities and vulnerable groups (Goodson and Phillimore, 2012; Aldridge, 2015; Beebeejaun *et al.*, 2015; Frantzeskaki and Kabisch, 2016; Richardson and Durose, 2016). Its principles can also be found in the surge of transdisciplinary research (Hadorn *et al.*, 2008; Lang *et al.*, 2012; Scholz and Steiner, 2015), Mode-2 knowledge production (Gibbons *et al.*, 1994; Nowotny *et al.*, 2003; Regeer and Bunders, 2009) and post-normal science (Funtowicz and Ravetz, 1993) – all three focusing on increasing the policy-relevance of science.

While Keller and Heatwole claimed in 1976 (p. 193) "that action research … can come to be a significant methodological tool … in an emerging focus on public affairs", to date it was hardly used in policy analysis and sustainability transition research. Calls for adopting it are growing (Fischer, 2004; Wagenaar, 2007; Audet and Guyonnaud, 2013; Bartels and Wittmayer, 2014; Geels *et al.*, 2016) as both fields include a strong normative commitment to developing knowledge that helps to resolve complex societal issues. Policy analysis aspires "to normatively committed intervention in the world of action" (Goodin *et al.*, 2006: 6) by critically interpreting processes of sense-making, argumentation, and negotiation through which policy actors address public problems (Fischer and Forester, 1993; Hajer and Wagenaar, 2003; Fischer and Gottweis, 2012). Sustainability transition research, in turn, aims to better understand sustainability transitions and increasingly sees an active role for researchers in accelerating sustainable development (Loorbach *et al.*, 2017; Geels *et al.*, 2016).

The aim of this book is to highlight this emerging use of action research in both fields and propel it in a specific direction. We explain what it has to offer and demonstrate how it can be engaged in productively by explicating the specific ambitions, challenges, and practices involved with doing action research to foster sustainability transitions through changes in the policy domain. Our core argument is that action research is both critical and relational and that, to productively address the current crises, we need to better engage with their dynamics while (1) negotiating 'the starting point' of the research process, (2) enacting 'multiple roles and relationships', (3) 'addressing hegemonic structures, cultures, and practices', and (4) evaluating 'reflexivity, impact, and change'. Each chapter in this book both illustrates and develops this four-tier guiding framework through accounts of different approaches to 'critical and relational' action research in a variety of geographical and policy contexts.

Before we outline the guiding framework and introduce the chapters, we first highlight key developments in policy analysis and transition research towards action research and provide a brief overview of its critical and relational dynamics.

Developments in policy analysis and transition research

Policy analysis has a longstanding commitment to identifying the best ways of addressing complex public problems and advancing democratic values. Harold Lasswell (1970), one of the founders of the field, called for 'knowledge of and in the policy process' that is problem-oriented, contextual, multidisciplinary, and normatively committed to human dignity (Fischer, 2007). For long, policy analysis was nevertheless dominated by a 'high modernist' approach in which professional experts have the authority and tools to produce objective, technical knowledge of the most optimal decisions (Colebatch, 2006). But over the past decades, critical, deliberative, and interpretive approaches to policy analysis have increasingly drawn attention to the power-laden and argumentative processes through which policy actors strive to influence decisions and find mutually acceptable ways of implementing policies. Grounded in a normative desire to generate critical policy-relevant knowledge, these studies aim to facilitate processes of public deliberation, reflection, and change (e.g. Fischer and Forester, 1993; Hoppe, 1999; Hajer and Wagenaar, 2003; Goodin *et al.*, 2006; Fischer and Gottweis, 2012). While more rationalistic approaches focused on generating objective knowledge and clarifying courses of action for policy actors are still mainstream, it is widely accepted that the "persuasive task of policy making and analysis alike lodges in these dynamics of deciding which puzzle to solve, what counts as a solution, and whose interests to serve" (Goodin *et al.*, 2006, 28).

Despite widespread research-policy interactions (see e.g. Nutley *et al.*, 2003; Hoppe, 2005; Gough and Boaz, 2011), policy analysts struggle to have a sustainable impact. Policy systems are highly complex because they include many interdependent individuals, organisations, communities, and groups, each with their own interests, values, and practices (Keller and Heatwole, 1976). Together, they need to share power and responsibilities, make goals, rules, and structures, and achieve mutual understanding, benefits, and respect (Hajer and Wagenaar, 2003). This implies "a relational conception of knowledge (that is, knowledge understood as a product of an interaction among competing views), [in which] the policy analyst has no privileged position from which to define the issues" (Fischer, 2007: 103) and can only provide temporal, imperfect solutions to complex problems and changing policies. In this light, action research has been identified as an appropriate methodology for policy analysis and is increasingly taken up (Keller and Heatwole, 1976; Fischer, 2004; Wagenaar, 2007, 2011; Mischen and Sinclair, 2008; Bartels and Wittmayer, 2014).

A similar development can be observed in transition research. This emerging interdisciplinary field analyses the objects, dynamics and processes, multiple actors, and governance of long-term radical changes of socio-technical systems and broader societal systems over time periods of 25–50 years (Grin *et al.*, 2010, Markard *et al.*, 2012, Loorbach *et al.*, 2017), particularly emphasising their co-evolution, complexity, and uncertainty (Geels and Schot, 2010; Rotmans and Loorbach, 2010). In terms of normative direction, sustainability has become recognised as an inherently political concept. Loorbach (2014: 53) called for replacing the initial "focus on sustainability in terms of making existing regimes less unsustainable ... by a focus on strategies that facilitate the least disruptive and (economically and socially) costly pathways towards new dynamic equilibria". What sustainability comes to mean, and how it can become meaningful, in a specific time and place, then, is shaped through processes of public negotiation and contestation. Transition research has therefore seen a surge in critical and interpretive approaches emphasising the power, politics, meaning-making, and agency involved in transitions, including attempts to influence change dynamics in specific directions (Hendriks, 2009; Meadowcroft, 2009; Hoffman, 2013; Avelino *et al.*, 2016; Avelino, 2017).

While most transition research focuses on describing, explaining and interpreting transition processes, a focus on more action-oriented approaches has been emerging (e.g. Audet and Guyonnaud, 2013; Geels *et al.*, 2016). Popular in this regard has been 'transition management' as an approach to support sustainability transitions (Loorbach, 2010; Loorbach *et al.*, 2011; Markard *et al.*, 2012). Belying its name, transition management is about organising "an interactive and selective participatory stakeholder searching process aimed at learning and experimenting" (Grin *et al.*, 2010: 140). It aims to facilitate societal learning and innovation by creating spaces in which all actors can participate in exploring and building alternatives (including ideas, practices, and social relations) as well as in challenging and changing the status quo (Loorbach, 2010; Wittmayer *et al.*, 2014). While links between action research and transition research are increasingly strengthened, a systematic understanding of the potential of action research for understanding and supporting sustainability transitions is still missing.

Critical and relational action research

In broadening the space for action research in our fields, we place ourselves on the shoulders of giants, especially those of Peter Reason and Hillary Bradbury (2001), Davydd Greenwood and Morten Levin (2007), and Sara Kindon, Rachel Pain, and Mike Kesby (2007), who have provided comprehensive and accessible overviews of the rich history, wide-ranging scope, and diverse approaches of action research. We define action research as *critical and relational processes through which researchers and their co-inquirers aim to collaboratively produce scientifically and socially relevant knowledge and transformative action*. Action research is not a single approach or methodology, but, as Dick (2015: 441) puts it, "a diverse family of related processes that draw on various methods and tools to achieve change" based on *three shared elements* – action, research, and participation (Reason and Bradbury, 2001; Brydon-Miller *et al.*, 2003; Chandler and Torbert, 2003; Greenwood and Levin, 2007; Kindon *et al.*, 2007; Burns, 2014;

Dick, 2015; Greenwood, 2015) – and grounded in *two underlying principles* – criticality and relationality.

The first shared element, *action*, refers to researchers and co-inquirers doing something together; i.e. they undertake practical activities to change concrete situations. Actively engaging with mundane understandings and practices produces a 'theory of action' about what is going on, should be done, and will (not) work. For instance, *Action Science* (Argyris *et al.*, 1985) constructs and tests theories of action by using the 'ladder of inference' to reveal differences between 'espoused theories' and 'theories-in-use'. Instead, *Appreciative Inquiry* (see Dick, 2004, 426–427; Mischen and Sinclair, 2008, 159–160) harnesses the 'power of positive thinking' by going through the 4-D cycle (discovery, dream, design, and destiny). In yet another variety, *Systemic Action Research* (Burns, 2014; Romm, 2015) engages in 'multiple parallel inquiries' to uncover the web of interconnections between multiple actors and wider systems and outcomes.

Second, *research* implies an emergent and iterative process of collaborative inquiry, action, and reflection that generates deeper understanding and change. This involves both challenging and transforming taken-for-granted assumptions, practices, and relationships as well as jointly adapting research design and methods to situational and emergent needs. Famously, *Cooperative Inquiry* (Heron, 1996) comprises a four-phased cycle of co-inquiry, action, experiential learning, and reflection. *Pragmatic Action Research* (Greenwood and Levin, 2007) has a similar emphasis on ongoing inquiry and redesign, combining the construction of arenas for dialogue with the flexible and responsive use of multi-method techniques.

Finally, *participation* is both an ontological given and ethical norm of action research processes and outcomes. Everyone who participates in a situation or wider system should be included in and committed to authentic and empowering collaboration and results. *Human Inquiry* (Reason, 1994; Reason and Bradbury, 2001) prominently takes a participatory worldview, in which we inevitably participate in co-creating the world through our interactions and, therefore, should enhance the quality of these co-creative processes. *Participatory Action Research* (Brydon-Miller *et al.*, 2011), in turn, strives to combat social injustice by facilitating dialogue in oppressed communities that raises their awareness, self-esteem, and power to use their own knowledge vis-à-vis dominant powers and interests.

Going beyond this conventional overview of the core elements and diversity of action research, a key contribution of this book is to highlight what we have come to understand as a fundamental dynamic between the underlying principles of criticality and relationality.

Action research is founded on a *critical stance* towards injustices, exclusion, and inequalities, or, framed more positively, a commitment to fostering democratic social change (Freire, 2000; Flyvbjerg, 2001; Brydon-Miller *et al.*, 2003; Kindon *et al.*, 2007; Hale, 2008; Brydon-Miller *et al.*, 2011; Greenwood, 2015; Romm, 2015). Following founding father Kurt Lewin's 'collaborative research' (see Dickens and Watkins, 1999), co-inquiry surfaces and deconstructs taken-for-granted assumptions and interpretations to cultivate communities of inquiry and redistribute power. This can create more participatory policy implementation and planning (Harwood and Zapata, 2007; Mischen and Sinclair, 2008) and produce sustainable organisational change (Comfort, 1985; Koliba and Lathrop, 2007). Moreover, fostering what Paolo Freire (2000) calls a 'pedagogy of the oppressed' can raise critical consciousness of oppression and a struggle for liberation in the face of flagrant political-economic inequalities.

This critical stance to the many wrongdoings of the world also challenges dominant conceptions of knowledge and social research engrained in mainstream academic disciplines, values, and practices (Reason, 1994; Kemmis, 2006; Levin and Greenwood, 2011; Bartels and Wittmayer, 2014). While mainstream social research is certainly valuable for analysing, describing, and explaining past and current dynamics, action research "rejects the notion of an objective, value-free approach to knowledge generation in favour of an explicitly political, socially engaged, and democratic practice" (Brydon-Miller *et al.*, 2003: 13). Knowledge is embedded in institutions and discourses that sustain particular constructions of what is normal and desirable as well as whose perspectives and powers are privileged/disadvantaged accordingly. Knowing is thus not a monological process of 'discovering' an external, static reality in which researchers can abstain from any responsibility for it; rather, it is a dialogical process of intervening in actual situations with immediate consequences for who is and who is not affected, included, and empowered (Flyvbjerg, 2001; Wagenaar, 2007; Romm, 2015).

Accordingly, action research implies a *relational worldview* (Reason, 1994; Reason and Bradbury, 2001; Greenwood, 2015), where all living and non-living entities form webs of connection with each other. Following classical pragmatism, critical realism, and General Systems Theory, the focus is not on actors or institutions but on the relationships through which they reciprocally bring one another into being and are nested in wider systems. This means that the world – and our understanding of it – is not individual or fixed but a dynamic, evolving, open-ended process of ongoing collaborative sense-making about, and negotiating of different interpretations, meanings, and courses of action (Greenwood and Levin, 2007; Bartels, 2012; Burns, 2014; Romm, 2015). As Freire (2000: 89) puts it, this process "cannot be reduced to the act of one person 'depositing' ideas in another, nor can it become a simple exchange of ideas to be 'consumed' by the discussants"; it has to be authentic dialogue between "people in their relations with the world" (ibid.: 81).

This relational worldview means that action researchers are interconnected with other people and real-world situations and share responsibility for fostering change. 'Research subjects' become active co-inquirers in the research: they pose questions, co-design processes and methods, offer alternative interpretations, and propose when and how to use co-produced knowledge. 'Researchers', in turn, become active co-shapers of local practices: they carry out work, suggest new views and courses of action, and are personally implicated in projects (Greenwood and Levin, 2007; Light *et al.*, 2011; Bartels, 2012; Wittmayer *et al.*, 2014). As such, they can develop "a mutually understandable discourse … through living together over time, sharing experiences, and taking actions together" (Greenwood and Levin, 2007: 66). Actively building and maintaining relationships is necessary to ensure commitment even when tensions run high. This requires a reflexive attitude towards the positionality, attitudes, assumptions, and expectations of researchers and co-inquirers, including the intimacy and reciprocity of their relationships (Chandler and Torbert, 2003; Shdaimah *et al.*, 2009; Burns, 2014; Greenwood, 2015).

Taken together, criticality and relationality[1] create challenging dynamics for action researchers. Being critical means increasing awareness, questioning, and pushing for transformation of habits, discourses, and power inequalities engrained in hegemonic systems. In turn, being relational implies maintaining trust, shared goals, and commitment as well as pragmatically accepting things for what they are and what is practically possible. So how can action researchers challenge others to change their behaviour and reconstruct their systems without aggravating and alienating them? Or, vice versa, how can action researchers sustain respectful and meaningful relationships and responsively adapt their own understandings and identity without sacrificing their personal integrity and transformative and counter-hegemonic orientation? More often than not, action researchers struggle with co-optation and instrumentalisation of the research to the interests of power holders (Brydon-Miller *et al.*, 2003: 24–25; Bartels and Wittmayer, 2014) and see their democratising and participatory ambitions significantly watered down (Gregory, 2000; Gunnarsson *et al.*, 2015 Hansen *et al.*, 2016).

At the same time, criticality and relationality reaffirm each other and their dynamics can be made productive (Freire, 2000; Romm, 2015). Good relationships are needed for critique to be tolerated and have an effect, while a critical stance is needed for relationships to generate transformative ideas and sustainable practices. Being critical means co-developing transformative action through relational processes of joint inquiry and experimentation. This involves jointly experiencing and critically assessing the situation at hand and considering it not as a fixed, taken-for-granted reality but as a 'reality in process' open to transformation. By communicating dialogically (i.e. without monologically imposing views, depositing knowledge, or enforcing change; Freire, 2000; Wagenaar, 2007), new understandings and courses of action can emerge that an ever-widening circle of people agree to (Bartels, 2012). In other words, improving relationality, in the sense of strengthening the quality of our innate social bonds, means being critically aware of the wider systems, discourses, and relationships within which these are nested.

To conclude, handling the inherently challenging yet potentially productive dynamics of criticality and relationality is fundamental to action research. In the next section, we explain our guiding framework for doing so in policy analysis and transition research.

Guiding framework for critical and relational action research

Our guiding framework is a heuristic (rather than a 'how to' guide) that sensitises action researchers and their co-inquirers to issues, tensions, and possibilities that arise when enacting critical and relational practices in concrete action research settings. Specifically, we propose they engage in ongoing joint reflection on how doing critical and relational action research involves (1) negotiating 'the starting point', (2) enacting 'multiple roles and relationships', (3) addressing 'hegemonic structures, cultures, and practices', and (4) evaluating 'reflexivity, impact, and change'.

The starting point

A defining feature of action research is its aim "to engage with the world *as it is*" (Dick and Greenwood, 2015: 196; emphasis in original) and induce change towards *how it can be* (Avelino and Grin, 2017). The concrete situation, local knowledge, and experienced problems of people form the starting point for transformative change (Freire, 2000). The starting point usually is a convergence of several issues, such as a personal dissatisfaction with mainstream social research and academia (Brydon-Miller *et al.*, 2003), the needs of people implicated in a local situation and their request for help (Schein, 2001), and the desire to strive for a vision of a better future (Reason, 1994). All of these are embedded in specific contexts that, amongst others, embody existing socio-political relations, governance cultures, available knowledge, dominant discourses, and funding opportunities.

Action research is all but a panacea in such complex contexts; rather, a crucial issue is to understand when it is suitable, why, where, and for whom, as well as which specific approach to action research best fits situational needs and contingencies (Mischen and Sinclair, 2008). Moreover, a working understanding of the context and research design should constantly be reflected on, negotiated, and adapted (Keller and Heatwole, 1976: 197; Greenwood and Levin, 2007: 133–134; Loeber, 2007). The starting point will thus in many ways shape the ambitions, practices, and outcomes of action research. The following questions can guide joint reflection about this:

- Who is the problem owner; who asks whom for help; and who is included and excluded?
- How is the research institutionalised, funded, and governed?
- How is openness to critical reflection on relational change safeguarded?
- What is the nature of the local situation and wider context?

Multiple roles and relationships

A popular way to characterise action research is the dictum that it is conducted *with* rather than *for* stakeholders (Reason, 1994; Reason and Bradbury, 2001;

Greenwood and Levin, 2007; Beebeejaun *et al.*, 2015). As we already mentioned, this places action researchers and co-inquirers in complex social, political, ethical, and personal relationships and requires ongoing reflection on their positionality. Greenwood and Levin's (2007: 124–130) notion of the "friendly outsider" goes a long way in dealing with the tensions involved with being simultaneously a collaborative participant in the local situation and a critical observer seeking to change it. However, we suggest that positionality is better understood by considering how action researchers have multiple relationships and roles throughout the process (Pohl *et al.*, 2010; Brydon-Miller *et al.*, 2011). Within the course of an action research project, they can, e.g., act as change agents, knowledge brokers, reflective scientists, self-reflexive scientists, and process facilitators (Wittmayer and Schäpke, 2014).

In practice, such roles overlap in ways that can either be (perceived as) mutually reinforcing or confusing. Their (non-)performance and evaluation depends on how action researchers and co-inquirers negotiate their mutual identities, roles, and relationships in real-time encounters and reflexive moments. This involves dealing with the "identity costs" (Wagenaar, 2007: 323) that action researchers incur when their multiple roles and relationships generate emotionally charged challenges to their presence, ethics, and values. Yet such inherent tensions can also be made productive to developing common ground, mutual trust, and shared actions (Harwood and Zapata, 2007; Shdaimah *et al.*, 2009). For this to happen, joint reflection should explore:

- What would relationships and roles ideally look like?
- Which roles do action researchers actually assume and why?
- How do action researchers relate to others, especially people who are not open to transformative change?
- How can action researchers bear and utilise 'identity costs' involved with their multiple relationships and roles?

Hegemonic structures, cultures, and practices

The critical foundation of action research renders it inevitably normative. There is of course a considerable difference in challenges to the status quo between, e.g., a facilitator of a participatory evaluation (Guba and Lincoln, 1998) and an activist scholar (Hale, 2008). Nevertheless, action research always asserts the impossibility and undesirability of even creating the impression of neutrality (cf. Forester and Stitzel, 1989; Hammersley, 1995). Such explicit normativity directly challenges mainstream social research and academic systems (Levin and Greenwood, 2011) as well as instrumental forms of co-production not committed to transformative change (Campbell and Vanderhoven, 2016).

As action researchers aim to combine a critical approach with practical impacts towards structural change, they cannot escape power struggles, instrumental approaches to knowledge, integrity challenges, bureaucratic proceduralism, and systemic constraints. In fact, it is inevitable when striving to create actionable knowledge (Flyvbjerg, 2001). Action researchers and co-inquirers need to engage with the status-quo because it is here that their actions not only can get diluted and co-opted but also that real transformative impact can occur (Pel and Bauler, 2014). Succumbing to hegemonic pressures or seeking to avoid them altogether will lead action researchers and co-inquirers to fall into the trap of mutually instrumentalising each other and losing sight of transformative aims and potentialities (Bartels and Wittmayer, 2014). The following questions can guide joint reflection:

- How do institutional infrastructures shape the scope for challenging the status quo?
- How is knowledge of the substantive issues at hand negotiated?
- How can engrained habits and power inequalities of hegemonic systems be challenged?
- How can action researchers and co-inquirers prevent instrumentalisation to each other's purposes?

Reflexivity, impact, and change

A distinguishing feature and core ambition of action research is to achieve change. Yet what this means is remarkably difficult to pin down. Theoretical concepts of and personal ambitions for change are inevitably transformed in a messy, resilient practice (Loeber, 2007) in which action researchers are just one of many actors, each with different ideas about the shape and desirability of change. Besides mainstream evaluation of inputs, outputs, outcomes, and impacts, action research emphasises process-impacts such as changes in modes of collaboration, relationships, everyday practices, and worldviews (Campbell and Vanderhoven, 2016; Luederitz *et al.*, 2017). Importantly, such evaluation should increase reflexivity about the process, purposes, problems, and context and lead to more transparent and impactful action research.

Evaluating such impact during and after the research thus requires ongoing and authentic reflexivity (see Finlay, 2002). This can generate learning about system change for sustainability; i.e. a deeper appreciation of the institutional and material contexts and how these can(not) be changed (Beers and Van Mierlo, 2017). In striving for transformative change, action researchers and co-inquirers may come to appreciate small-scale changes as illuminating the path to sustainability transitions (Brydon-Miller *et al.*, 2003: 25; Burns, 2014; Loorbach *et al.*, 2017). The following questions can guide joint reflection:

- How can the scope and timeline of a project be determined?
- What is success or failure; when can we speak of a changed situation or system?
- How can we reconcile discrepancies between ideals of change and what is practically possible?
- What is being learned and changed by being reflexive?

Outline of chapters

Once again, the framework does not provide (or suggest the possibility of) single or final answers; rather, it serves as a heuristic for designing, enacting, and evaluating action research projects in policy analysis and transition research. Each chapter both illustrates and develops several elements of the four-tier framework by reflecting on their contextual practices. To further deepen our understanding, each chapter includes a 'co-inquirer reflection'. Co-inquirers were invited to tell their own story about their motivation for engaging in this kind of research, their relationship with the researcher(s), their biggest challenges, and the impact of the research.

Part I of the book highlights how the glocal sustainability crises we currently face require *actionable* forms of knowledge and research. Emma Westling and Liz Sharp explain why a major interdisciplinary project for clean water in the UK needs 'critical-applied social research' and what tensions this generates. Bálint Balázs and György Pataki demonstrate how unsustainable Hungarian agro-food policy was changed through 'cooperative research'. And Shivant Jaghroe examines how and why counter-hegemonic challenges to neoliberal food and economic (knowledge) regimes emerging from urban gardening in Rotterdam (the Netherlands) benefit from 'transition scientivism'.

Chapters in Part II discuss *heuristics* for engaging in the critical and relational dynamics of action research in policy contexts. James Henderson and Claire Bynner stress the importance of 'cultivating sanction and sanctuary' to sustain spaces for shared learning and pragmatic change in collaborative governance in Scotland. Erik Paredis and Thomas Block reflect on their experiences with negotiating space for 'mild intervention' in a civil society movement committed to sustainability transitions in Flanders. And Ainhoa Arrona and Miren Larrea explain how enacting 'soft resistance' gradually generated institutional change in territorial development in the Basque Country.

In Part III, the final set of chapters share experiences with specific approaches to *doing* critical-relational action research for policy change and sustainability transitions. Alison Gardner reviews the value of using 'appreciative inquiry' for influencing austerity reforms in a British local authority. Martien Kuitenbrouwer explains how 'reconstruction clinics' enabled Dutch stakeholders in moving on from their policy conflicts. Floriane Clement demonstrates how 'audiovisual media' and 'deliberative events' empowered local farmers and influenced environmental change discourse in Nepal. Finally, Sonja van der Arend argues that writing 'policy fiction' of environmental governance in the Netherlands has untapped potential for changing understanding of sustainability policy and practice.

In the concluding chapter, we bring everything together by providing a cross-analysis of the critical-relational dynamics in the chapters and reflecting on what we have learned about the different elements of our guiding framework and the future of action research in our fields.

Outlook

We deem the pursuance of action research in policy analysis and transition research a crucial move for generating effective and sustainable responses to the political, social, economic, and environmental crises we currently face. Action research highlights how criticality and relationality are fundamental to policy change and sustainability transitions and associated research practices. Enacting critical and relational practices in concrete action research settings is a vital way for working out how this inherently challenging dynamic can be made productive to addressing our contemporary crises. Doing so means facing many risks and challenges, especially given the discord between action research and mainstream science, and there remain many unanswered questions to develop action research in our fields. We will turn to all these issues in the conclusion, responding to Keller and Heatwole's (1976: 193) claim that the great potential of action research for our fields "will not be realized without application and a great deal of effort".

Note

1 We have outlined these principles as ideal-typical constructions and discuss their analytical nature and usage in more detail in the conclusion.

References

Abma T (2004) Responsive evaluation: the meaning and special contribution to public administration. *Public Administration* 82(4): 993–1012.

Aldridge (2015) *Participatory research. Working with vulnerable groups in research and practice*, Bristol, The Policy Press.

Audet R and Guyonnaud MF (2013) Transition in practice and action in research. A French case study in piloting eco-innovations. *Innovation: The European Journal of Social Science Research* 26(4): 398–415.

Argyris C, Putnam R and Smith DML (eds.) (1985) *Action science: concepts, methods and skills for research and intervention*, San Francisco, Jossey-Bass.

Avelino F and Grin J (2017) Beyond deconstruction. A reconstructive perspective on sustainability transition governance. *Environmental Innovation and Societal Transitions* 22: 15–25.

Avelino F, Grin J, Pel B and Jhagroe S (2016) The politics of sustainability transitions *Journal of Environmental Policy and Planning* 18(5): 557–567.

Avelino F (2017) Power in sustainability transitions: analysing power and (dis)empowerment in transformative change towards sustainability. *Environmental Policy and Governance*, Online first DOI: 10.1002/eet.1777.

Bartels KPR (2012) The actionable researcher: cultivating a process-oriented methodology for studying administrative practice. *Administrative Theory and Praxis* 34(3): 433–455.

Bartels KPR and Wittmayer JM (2014) Symposium introduction: how usable knowledge means in action research practice. *Critical Policy Studies* 8(4): 397–406.

Beebeejaun Y, Durose C, Rees J, Richardson J and Richardson L (2015) Public harm or public value? Towards coproduction in research with communities, *Environment and Planning C* 33(3): 552–565.

Beers PJ and Van Mierlo B (2017) Reflexivity, reflection and learning in the context of system innovation: prying loose entangled concepts. In: Elzen B, Augustyn AM, Barbier M, and van Mierlo B (eds.) *Agro ecological transitions: changes and breakthroughs in the making*, Wageningen University and Research, 243–256.

Brydon-Miller M, Greenwood D and Maguire P (2003) Why action research? *Action Research* 1(1): 9–28.

Brydon-Miller M, Kra, M, Maguire P, Noffke S, and Sabhlok A (2011) Jazz and the banyan tree: roots and riffs on participatory action research. In: Denzin NK and Lincoln YS (eds.) *The Sage handbook of qualitative research*, Thousand Oaks, CA: Sage, 387–400.

Burns D (2014) Systemic action research: changing system dynamics to support sustainable change. *Action Research* 12(1): 3–18.

Campbell H and Vanderhoven D (2016) *Knowledge that matters: Realising the potential of co-production*, www.n8research.org.uk (accessed 13 November 2016).

Castellanet C and Jordan CF (2016) *Participatory action research in natural resource management. A critique of the method based on five years' experience in the Transamozonica region of Brazil*, London, Routledge.

Chandler D and Torbert B (2003) Transforming inquiry and action. Interweaving 27 flavors of action research. *Action Research* 1(2): 133–152.

Colebatch HK (ed.) (2006) *The work of policy: an international survey*, Lanham, MD, Lexington Books.

Comfort LK (1985) Action research: a model for organizational learning. *Journal of Policy Analysis and Management* 5(1): 100–118.

Dick B (2004) Action research literature. Themes and trends. *Action Research* 2(4): 425–444.

Dick B (2015) Reflections on the Sage encyclopedia of action research and what it says about action research and its methodologies. *Action Research* 13(4): 431–444.

Dick B and Greenwood, D.J. (2015) Theory and method: why action research does not separate them. *Action Research* 13(2): 194–197.

Dickens L and Watkins K (1999) Action research: rethinking Lewin. *Management Learning* 30: 127–140.

Edelenbos J and Van Buuren A (2005) The learning evaluation. A theoretical and empirical exploration. *Evaluation Review* 29(6): 591–612.

Finlay L (2002) Negotiating the swamp: the opportunity and challenge of reflexivity in research practice. *Qualitative Research* 2(2): 209–230.

Fischer F (2004) Professional expertise in a deliberative democracy. *The Good Society* 13(1): 21–27.

Fischer F (2007) Policy analysis in critical perspective: the epistemics of discursive practices. *Critical Policy Studies* 1(1): 97–109.

Fischer F and Forester J (eds.) (1993) *The argumentative turn in policy analysis and planning*, London: UCL Press.

Fischer F and Gottweis H (eds.) (2012) *The argumentative turn revisited: public policy as communicative practice*, Durham, NC: Duke University Press.

Flyvbjerg B (2001) *Making social science matter: why social inquiry fails and how it can succeed again*, Cambridge: Cambridge University Press.

Forester J and Stitzel D (1989) Beyond neutrality: the possibilities of activist mediation in public sector conflicts. *Negotiation Journal* 5(3): 251–264.

Frantzeskaki N and Kabisch N (2016) Designing a knowledge co-production operating space for urban environmental governance – Lessons from Rotterdam, Netherlands and Berlin, Germany. *Environmental Science and Policy* 62: 90–98.

Freire P (2000) *Pedagogy of the oppressed*, New York: Continuum.

Funtowicz SO and Ravetz JR (1993) The emergence of post-normal science. In: Von Schomberg R (ed.) *Science, politics and morality*, Dordrecht: Springer, 85–123.

Geels FW and Schot JW (2010) The dynamics of transitions: a socio-technical perspective. In: Grin J, Rotmans J and Schot JW (in collaboration with) Loorbach, D and Geels FW (eds.) *Transitions to sustainable development; new directions in the study of long term transformative change*, New York: Routledge, 11–104.

Geels FW, Berkhout F and van Vuuren DP (2016) Bridging analytical approaches for low-carbon transitions. *Nature Climate Change* 6: 576–583.

Gibbons M, Limoges C, Nowotny H, Schwartzman S, Scott P and Trow M (1994). *The new production of knowledge: the dynamics of science and research in contemporary societies*, London: Sage.

Goodin RE, Rein M and Moran M. (2006) The public and its policies. In: Moran M, Rein M and Goodin RE (Eds.) *The Oxford handbook of public policy*, Oxford: Oxford University Press, 3–35.

Goodson L and Phillimore J (eds.) (2012) *Community research for participation. From theory to method*, Bristol: The Policy Press.

Gough D and Boaz A (2011) Complexities of making use of research. *Evidence and Policy: A Journal of Research, Debate and Practice* 7(3): 247–249.

Greenwood DJ (2015) An analysis of the theory/concept entries in the Sage encyclopedia of action research: what we can learn about action research in general from the encyclopaedia. *Action Research* 13(2): 198–213.

Greenwood DJ and Levin M (2007) *Introduction to action research: social research for social change*, Thousand Oaks, Sage.

Gregory A (2000) Problematizing participation. A critical review of approaches to participation in evaluation theory. *Evaluation* 6(2): 179–199.

Grin J, Rotmans J, Schot JW, Loorbach D and Geels FW (eds.) (2010) *Transitions to sustainable development; new directions in the study of long term transformative change*, New York: Routledge.

Guba E and Lincoln Y (1989) *Fourth generation evaluation*. Newbury Park, CA: Sage.

Gunnarsson E, Hansen HP, Steen Nielsen B and Sriskandarajah N (eds.) (2015) *Action research for democracy. New ideas and perspectives from Scandinavia*, London: Routledge.

Hadorn GH, Biber-Klemm S, Grossenbacher-Mansuy W, Hoffmann-Riem H, Joye D, Pohl C, Wiesmann, U and Zemp E (eds.). (2008) *Handbook of transdisciplinary research*, Zurich: Springer.

Hajer MA and Wagenaar H (eds.) (2003) *Deliberative policy analysis. Understanding governance in the network society*, Cambridge: Cambridge University Press.

Hale CR (Ed.) (2008) *Engaging contradictions. Theory, politics, and methods of activist scholarship*, Berkeley/Los Angeles, CA: University of California Press.

Hammersley M (1995) *The politics of social research*, London: Sage.

Hansen HP, Steen Nielsen B, Sriskandarajah N and Gunnarsson E (2016) *Commons, sustainability, democratization. Action research and the basic renewal of society*, London: Routledge.

Harwood SA and Zapata M (2007) Creating space for hermeneutics in practice: using visual tools to understand community narratives about the future. *Critical Policy Studies* 1(4): 371–388.

Hawking S (2016) This is the most dangerous time for our planet. *Guardian.* 1 December 2016. www.theguardian.com/commentisfree/2016/dec/01/stephen-hawking-dangerous-time-planet-inequality?CMP=share_btn_link (accessed 9 December 2016).

Hendriks C (2009) Policy design without democracy? Making democratic sense of transition management. *Policy Sciences* 42(4): 341–368.

Heron J (1996) *Co-operative inquiry: research into the human condition*, London: Sage.

Hoffman J (2013) Theorizing power in transition studies: the role of creativity in novel practices in structural change. *Policy Sciences* 46(3): 257–275.

Hoppe R (1999) Policy analysis, science and politics: from 'speaking truth to power' to 'making sense together'. *Science and Public Policy*, 26(3), 201–210.

Hoppe R (2005) Rethinking the science-policy nexus: From knowledge utilization and science technology studies to types of boundary arrangements. *Poiesis and Praxis* 3(3): 199–215.

Karlsen J and Larrea M (2014) *Territorial development and action research. Innovation through dialogue*, Surrey: Gower Publishing.

Keller L and Heatwole CG (1976) Action research in policy analysis. A Rejoinder to Frank Sherwood. *Administration and Society* 8(2): 193–200.

Kemmis S (2006) Participatory action research and the public sphere. *Educational Action Research* 14(4): 459–476.

Kindon S, Pain R and Kesby M (Eds.) (2007) *Participatory action research approaches and methods: connecting people, participation and place*, Hoboken: Taylor and Francis.

Koliba CJ and Lathrop J (2007) Inquiry as intervention. Employing action research to surface intersubjective theories-in-use and support an organization's capacity to learn. *Administration and Society* 39(1): 51–76.

Lang DJ, Wiek A, Bergmann M, Stauffacher M, Martens P, Moll P, Swilling M and Thomas CJ (2012) Transdisciplinary research in sustainability science: practice, principles, and challenges. *Sustainability Science* 7(S1): 25–43.

Lasswell HD (1970) The emerging conception of the policy sciences. *Policy Sciences* 1(1): 3–14.

Levin M and Greenwood D (2011) Revitalizing universities by reinventing the social sciences. In: Denzin NK and Lincoln YS (eds.) *The Sage handbook of qualitative research*, London: Sage, 27–42.

Loeber A (2007) Designing for phronèsis: experiences with transformative learning on sustainable development. *Critical Policy Studies* 1(4): 389–414.

Loorbach D (2010) Transition management for sustainable development: a prescriptive, complexity-based governance framework. *Governance* 23(1): 161–183.

Loorbach D (2014) *To transition! Governance panarchy in the New transformation*. Inaugural lecture. Rotterdam: Erasmus University of Rotterdam.

Loorbach D, Frantzeskaki N and Thissen WH (2011) A transition research perspective on governance for sustainability. In: Jaeger CC, Tàbara JD, Jaeger J (eds.) *European research on sustainable development, Volume 1: Transformative science approaches for sustainability*, Springer: 73–90.

Loorbach D, Frantzeskaki N and Avelino F (2017) Sustainability transitions research: transforming science and practice for societal change. *Annual Review of Environment and Resources* 42(1): 599–626.

Luederitz C, Schäpke N, Wiek A, Lang DJ, Bergmann M, Bos JJ, Burch S, Davies A, Evans J, König A, Farrelly MA, Forrest N, Frantzeskaki N, Gibson RB, Kay B, Loorbach D, McCormick, K, Parodi O, Rauschmayer F, Schneidewind U, Stauffacher M, Stelzer F, Trencher G, Venjakob J, Vergragt PJ, von Wehrden H, Westley FR (2017) Learning through evaluation. A tentative evaluative scheme for sustainability transition experiments. *Journal of Cleaner Production* 169: 61–76.

Markard J, Raven R and Truffer B (2012) Sustainability transitions: an emerging field of research and its prospects. *Research Policy* 41(6): 955–967.

McKibben B (2015) Climate deal: the pistol has fired, so why aren't we running? *Guardian*, 13 December 2015, www.theguardian.com/commentisfree/2015/dec/13/paris-climate-talks-15c-marathon-negotiating-physics (accessed 13 December 2015).

Meadowcroft J (2009) What about the politics? Sustainable development, transition management, and long term energy transitions. *Policy Sciences* 42(4): 323–340.

Mischen PA and Sinclair TAP (2008) Making implementation more democratic through action implementation research. *Journal of Public Administration Research and Theory* 19: 145–164.

Monbiot G (2016) Neoliberalism – the ideology at the root of all our problems. *Guardian*, 15 April 2016, www.theguardian.com/books/2016/apr/15/neoliberalism-ideology-problem-george-monbiot (accessed 24 May 2016).

Nowotny H, Scott P and Gibbons M (2003) Introduction: 'Mode 2' revisited: the new production of knowledge. *Minerva* 41(3): 179–194.

Nutley S, Walter I and Davies HTO (2003) From knowing to doing. A framework for understanding the evidence-into-practice agenda. *Evaluation* 9(2): 125–148.

Orr K and Bennett M (2012) Public administration scholarship and the politics of coproducing academic–practitioner research. *Public Administration Review* 72(4): 487–496.

Pel B and Bauler T (2014) The institutionalization of social innovation: between transformation and capture, TRANSIT working paper Nr. 2. TRANSIT: EU SSH.2013.3.2–1 Grant agreement no: 613169.

Pohl C, Rist S, Zimmermann A, Fry P, Gurung GS, Schneider F, Speranza CI, Kiteme B, Boillat S, Serrano E, Hirsch Hadorn G and Wiesmann U (2010) Researchers' roles in knowledge co-production: experience from sustainability research in Kenya, Switzerland, Bolivia and Nepal. *Science and Public Policy* 37(4): 267–281.

Raworth K (2017) *Doughnut economics: seven ways to think like a 21st-century economist*, London: Random House Business Books.

Reason P (ed.) (1994) *Participation in human inquiry*, London: Sage.

Reason P and Bradbury H (eds.) (2001) *Handbook of action research. Participative inquiry and practice*, London, Sage.

Regeer BJ and Bunders JFG (2009) *Knowledge co-creation: interaction between science and society. A transdisciplinary approach to complex societal issues*, The Hague, RMNO.

Richardson L and Durose C (2016) *Designing public policy for co-production: theory, practice and change*. Bristol: The Policy Press.

Romm NRA (2015) Reviewing the transformative paradigm: a critical systemic and relational (indigenous) lens. *Systemic Practice and Action Research* 28: 411–427.

Rotmans J and Loorbach D (2010) Complexity and transition management. *Journal of Industrial Ecology* 13(2): 184–196.

Schein EH (2001) Clinical Inquiry/Research. In: Reason P and Bradbury H (eds.) *Handbook of action research. Participative Inquiry and practice*, London: Sage, 228–237.

Scholz RW and Steiner G (2015) The real type and ideal type of transdisciplinary processes: part I—theoretical foundations. *Sustainability Science* 10(4): 527–544.

Shdaimah C, Stahl R and Schram SF (2009) When you can see the sky through your roof: Policy analysis from the bottom up. In: Schatz, E (ed.) *Political ethnography: what immersion contributes to the study of politics*, Chicago: The University of Chicago Press, 255–274.

Stout M and Love J (2015) *Integrating process. Follettian thinking from ontology to administration*, Claremont, CA: Process Century Press.

Van Buuren A, Eshuis J and van Vliet M (eds.) (2014) *Action research for climate change adaptation. Developing and applying knowledge for governance*, London and New York: Routledge.

Wagenaar H (2007) Philosophical hermeneutics and policy analysis: theory and effectuations. *Critical Policy Studies* 1(4): 311–341.

Wagenaar H (2011) *Meaning in action. Interpretation and dialogue in policy analysis*, Armonk: M.E. Sharpe.

Wittmayer JM and Schäpke N (2014) Action, research and participation: roles of researchers in sustainability transitions. *Sustainability Science* 9(4): 483–496.

Wittmayer JM, Schäpke N, van Steenbergen F and Omann I (2014) Making sense of sustainability transitions locally. How action research contributes to addressing societal challenges. *Critical Policy Studies* 8(4): 465–485.

Part I

Sustainability crises and actionable knowledge and research

2 Both critical and applied?
Action research and transformative change in the UK water sector

Emma L Westling and Liz Sharp

Introduction

This chapter explores the tension inherent to all action research of achieving both applicability and criticality through the case study of TWENTY65 – Tailored Water Solutions for Positive Impact (TWENTY65), a large interdisciplinary UK water research project seeking to support transformative change in the water sector. Such transformative change is seen as required if resilient water services are to be maintained in the face of climate change impacts, population growth, rising environmental standards and changes in consumer behaviours (e.g. ACT Government, 2014; Defra, 2017). Whereas in the past answers to water questions have been seen as lying in the technical domain, utilities and regulators are increasingly recognising that this transformative change will involve social innovation as well or instead of technical change (e.g. Defra, 2017; Ofwat, 2017). This shift from a focus on water supply to the promotion of environmentally friendly efficient practices is not only a question of learning better how to communicate; changing practices also involves the re-allocation of costs, risks and responsibilities hence raising issues of governance and equity. For such implications to be explicit rather than hidden, much greater engagement between the water sector and social science is required (Sharp, 2017).

Research on transformative change in water management is a particularly challenging field for action research to maintain its criticality because many partner practitioners and researchers are drawn from technical sciences and are predominantly positivist in their approach to knowledge. This challenge may be even more extreme in a UK context where water services are delivered by privately owned monopolies whose perspective on social responsibility is developed in the context of their economic regulator Ofwat (The Water Services Regulation Authority). Moreover, as well as researching social transformation wrought by the water industry, the very process of conducting action research may also be seen as itself constituting (or trying to constitute) something of a transformation in drawing attention to social issues and matters of positionality. In all these senses, the case of action research with UK water companies can be seen as an 'extreme case' (Flyvbjerg, 2001) through which the applicability-criticality tension can be explored.

As argued in the introduction of this book, action research approaches that develop actionable knowledge, recognising and strengthening relationships while maintaining a critical voice, are paramount in supporting sustainability transitions. However, such approaches and the knowledge they typically generate may be in tension with what is primarily valued within a historically technocratic and compliance-oriented UK water sector (Speight, 2015). Our focus in this chapter is therefore on how action research in the water sector can be both critical and applied in order to support transformative change and on where the key tensions lie. Like the editors of this volume we understand action research as necessarily critical, which involves a commitment to challenge unequal or oppressive power relations, to support social justice and progressive politics, to maintain transparency about our own positionality and to be reflexive over the research process. However, whereas the editors understand action research as necessarily 'relational', here our understanding is only that it achieves the lower bar that it is 'applied'. The descriptors, 'relational' and 'applied', both imply a dialogic research process that intervenes in practice; however, in relational research the research subjects are active co-inquirers, whereas this is not necessarily our expectation of applied research. Our understanding of 'action research' as being critical and applied is therefore looser than the understandings of the editors; it encompasses other processes of collaborative social enquiry like 'social learning' (Ison *et al.*, 2013) or 'co-production' (Lövbrand, 2011). To be completely clear, while we agree that action research is ideally relational, we would argue that this relationality might be a hard requirement to meet, perhaps particularly within a field of practice with strong technical research traditions.

Whether relational or applied, practitioners collaborate with researchers to undertake 'action research', using time and energy that is lost from day-to-day activities. Individuals and groups choose to collaborate with researchers because they perceive they have something to gain from the research. All action research therefore needs to be conducted in a way that is mindful of delivering these benefits and maintaining its 'applicability' but this can sometimes be in tension with researchers' desire to be critical.

This chapter draws on the processes of framing and the early development of critical action research within one of the TWENTY65's social science research themes 'Enhancing Water Services through Mobilisation' (Mobilisation). This work involves close interaction with technical colleagues from both academia and from industry. Here, we reflect on this activity, highlighting the tensions we have had to negotiate to maintain action research standards of being both critical and applied. By doing so we explicitly seek to (1) enhance understandings of action research by analysing how criticality and applicability play out in supporting transformative change in the water sector, (2) highlight key areas where criticality and applicability are likely to be in tension in collaborative knowledge production within technical fields and (3) provide insights to support action researchers facilitating critical and applied research as part of interdisciplinary and cross-sector projects. In reflecting on how criticality has been sometimes compromised, but also negotiated and maintained, this chapter builds on previous work concerning the role of reflexivity in collaborative research (West-ling *et al.*, 2014).

Social research on water

In the field of water management, most existing social research falls into one of two traditions: it is either 'critical' or 'applied', but rarely both. Critical social science has been particularly useful in critiquing water management's current norms and processes. Drawing either on political ecology (e.g. Bakker, 2003; Castro and Heller, 2009; Kaika, 2003; Swyngedouw, 2004) or science and technology studies (e.g. Shove, 2003; Stirling, 2006), this work includes insightful analyses about the contemporary history of water governance within a neoliberal society (Bakker, 2003; Swyngedouw, 2004) offering explorations about how different waters are embedded in and reproduce both a physical and social landscape (Linton and Budds, 2014) and examinations of how policies and technological investments play through to the daily practices of individuals (Shove, 2010). The strength of these critical approaches is that they highlight how different waters are constructed and contested by different stakeholders, stressing the values reproduced, and highlighting the connections between policies and daily practices. A significant critique of these approaches, however, is that they are written from an external 'academic' viewpoint and have little opportunity to impact on policy and practice. Insofar as they are perceived at all, such critical social science is indeed seen as 'critical' by water engineers and practitioners, in the sense that it is *critical of them!* For Shove (2010) this is partly a consequence of current traditions of policymaking that expects that science will provide predictions rather than discussing values and hence seeking to shape daily life through physical and institutional design.

Quite separate from these critical investigations, water management also boasts a long tradition of applied social research, most of which is focused on the management of social-ecological (e.g. Folke, 2006; Holling, 1978) or socio-technical (e.g. Brown and Clarke, 2007; Sim *et al.*, 2007) systems. This work has done much to stress the importance of working across different stakeholder groups and hence has demonstrated the crucial role of 'the social' within technical domains. However, while conducted in close contact with practitioners, this work might be argued to be 'uncritical' in the sense that the researchers' positionality is not always made explicit, and the work is often built on an assumption that practitioners and researchers are united around a shared and unambiguous goal. We would also argue that this work is 'applied' but not 'relational', in that it is not necessarily based on a dialogical process of intervening, nor are research subjects usually active co-inquirers in the research.

A small set of work bridges the critical and applied traditions, drawing on critical social science but also working closely with technical practitioners and researchers of water (Browne *et al.*, 2013; Molyneux-Hodgson and Balmer 2014; Pullinger *et al.*, 2013; Westling *et al.*, 2014; Woelfe-Erskine, 2015). Such research builds evidence about the benefits of connecting governance, infrastructural development and everyday practices through a variety of partnerships between the industry and policy makers, advocacy bodies, utility customers and environmental charities. In common with the applied social research discussed above, such work is carried out in close co-operation with practitioners or technical researchers, and hence has real potential to support transformative change in water practices. In terms of their *critical* credentials, all of these works support progressive agendas because they are critiquing and developing environmental aspects of water policy but doing so in a way that is sensitive to social issues such as gender and equality. But these aspects of criticality are probably true of most social research on water. Crucially for us, however, such approaches also recognise the importance and complexities of partnerships as, for example, requiring time and 'translation' when disciplines, sectors or 'lay' and 'expert' divides are breached (Bos *et al.*, 2015; Browne *et al.*, 2013; Medd and Marvin, 2007), while additionally acknowledging the material and active nature of waters. This research can also therefore be seen to be reflexive in recognising the relational challenges experienced when people with different priorities, expertise and values work together towards mutual under-standings, goals and practical outcomes. By encouraging a collective awareness about different values and beliefs, reflexivity has been identified as one route through which some of the difficulties of managing the power dynamics of part-nerships such as those between water utilities and publics, or academics and prac-titioners can be overcome (Lövbrand, 2011; Mackenzie *et al.*, 2012; Phillips *et al.*, 2013; Stirling, 2006; Voß and Bornemann, 2011; Westling *et al.* 2014). In the environmental governance literature, a reflexive approach to governance requires not only that a range of groups come together, but also that they collectively envi-sion a diversity of alternatives to current action modes and strategies (Beck, 2006) and hence acknowledge that there is no universal solution to a problem (Grin, 2006). By stressing the variety of perspectives and highlighting the plurality of available options, action research on water can (and should!) be conducted in a way that is applicable, collaborative and yet still critical!

In order to further explore these different components of action research and to address the aims of this chapter as defined in the introduction, we draw atten-tion to the negotiations and potential tensions between producing knowledge that is critical and applied in specifically asking: (1) How can critical action research influence transformative change in the water sector? (2) What are the main ten-sions or issues in seeking to influence change underpinned by a critical approach? What is the role of the action researcher in technical research pro-jects? These questions are discussed through the case of the Mobilisation Research Theme, introduced below.

Case study context

'Mobilisation' is one of two social-science-led research themes included in the TWENTY65 project. TWENTY65 is a £3.9 million (5 million Euro) research project that seeks to work towards 'clean water for all' in the next 50 years through research to be conducted between 2016 and 2021. Six UK universities and over 70 water-related partners are committed to identifying and developing 'disruptive innovations' that will enable the transformation of the water sector. The project is also truly interdisciplinary, including academics from Civil Engineering, Management, Geography, Planning, Mechanical Engineering and Chemical Engineering. Unusually it combines engineering, physical sciences and critical social science.

In the TWENTY65 proposal it was explained that *mobilisation initiatives* 'support water stakeholders in changing their actions in order that collective water services can be delivered more efficiently and/or with reduced impact'. 'Stakeholders' refers, in this instance, to citizens/water users, who are also the companies' customers, who might be mobilised directly or indirectly to change their water practices. For example, dog walkers might be asked to report pollution or fly-tipping instances, residents may be asked to save water, or restaurants may be asked to review their procedures for disposing of waste oil. This distinguishes mobilisation initiatives from participation processes, which stimulate citizens' engagement for the purposes of influencing the water companies' decisions. Of course, many mobilisation initiatives may also involve elements of participation (and vice versa), but in this project a choice was made to focus on initiatives that are primarily concerned with mobilisation.

The context for the mobilisation work package is water organisations' default *technical* response to water challenges. Cultural/behavioural routes to address problems are only considered if the technical solutions do not work. However, in the face of a Victorian pipe system, user disengagement with water, anticipated water scarcity and flood risk from climate change, and population growth, it is recognised that current levels of water services will be hard to deliver in the future through technical solutions, and that the latter will come with a considerable environmental and financial cost. Mobilisation initiatives offer an alternative route to action that might be both more environmentally benign and cheaper. Mobilisation initiatives are already employed in some fields of water management practice – most notably to address water shortages and to deal with issues like Fats, Oil and Grease (FOG) in sewers (Ofwat, 2011). But the limited evidence available about the initiatives suggests that they are of mixed quality and have yielded mixed successes (e.g. Knamiller and Sharp, 2009; Medd and Chappels, 2008; Sharp *et al.*, 2015). Most pertinently, water utilities seeking to develop mobilisation initiatives have nowhere to go for good practice, there is no systemisation or record keeping about when mobilisation is employed and when not, and there are no standard processes of evaluation for mobilisation initiatives. In this respect mobilisation initiatives contrast strongly with areas of innovative practice in technical fields (for example, regarding leak detection) in which innovations are developed with researchers and data gathering about their efficacy is a high priority.

The overall aims of the Mobilisation Research Theme are to increase the quality of *all* water mobilisation initiatives to be as good as today's best, to broaden the scope of areas in which mobilisation is considered and to ensure that the evaluation of initiatives becomes standard practice enabling learning across the board. These ambitions are to be achieved through mapping the nature and extent of mobilisation initiatives, and by using case studies to explore ideas about 'good practice' in this field. The fact that mobilisation initiatives have not been 'mapped' before is because the framing of 'mobilisation' as one set of related initiatives is new. By mapping water mobilisations, we are pointing out that the practices of mobilising publics to (variously and for example) save water, dispose of FOG responsibly or report pollution incidents are not so different. Through this research, we expect to not only identify and connect the individuals undertaking this work, but also to empower them to raise questions within their organisation about the choices made in relation to when and whether mobilisation is considered as an appropriate means of action. In terms of best practice, we expect to raise questions about what constitutes effective mobilisation, in particular, examining whether mobilisation contributes to a change in service levels and for whom, and whether environmental or social inequality is challenged or reinforced through the changes.

In order to contribute to these debates, in combination with the TWENTY65 project's collaborative nature and commitment to transforming water practice, an action research approach was adopted. Although our definition of action research is 'looser' than that of the editors, it still enables and supports the 'Mobilisation' research that develops theory to examine practical action with practitioners, to produce critical and applied knowledge (Reason and Bradbury, 2008, p. 1). In addition, by using a research project as the starting point, we offer a different aspect of action research, which often focuses on researchers working with practitioners 'in the field' to co-produce knowledge. Although water practitioners are involved in the research project, the analysis in this chapter primarily considers the negotiations taking place between researchers from different academic disciplines within TWENTY65. These technical researchers are our co-inquirers, and coordinate the interaction of the whole project with water practitioners; as critical social scientists developing and maintaining validation and support from technical researchers is an important first step to transforming the water sector more broadly. To address the questions initiated in the introduction, the analysis below draws on the processes of bid design as well as negotiations currently taking place at the project's Management Board Meetings (four times a year involving academics to discuss Research Themes' progress), and associated Research Theme update meetings with the TWENTY65's Project Manager, Leadership Board Meetings (twice a year involving Water Industry leaders, their consultants, UK water partnerships representatives) and the Strategic Board Meetings (once a year, involving leaders from non-water utilities (e.g. waste sector) and regulators). Negotiations analysed in this chapter also extend to those taken place in the planning and performing of TWENTY65 events, such as the Annual Water Conference and Thought Leadership Club meetings (TLCs), both processes supporting the wider generation of research ideas and efforts to address water's grand challenges. In addition, one of the authors is part of the TWENTY65 'Hub' that meets weekly and coordinates a series of interactive meetings (e.g. TLCs and the Annual Conference) developing and bringing forward a research agenda, through which (it is hoped) further disruptive innovations can be identified, developed and funded. In the next section, three key issues from our experience in the Mobilisation Research Theme in seeking to produce critical and applied knowledge that supports transformative change in the water sector is identified and discussed.

Three challenges for action research on water

Issues of translation and integrity

As critical social scientists, we are constantly asked to simplify our research process or outcomes (in particular our language) sometimes to the point where our messages are changed. Such problems are common in interdisciplinary science or engineering-led projects where social science often is assumed to take the same form as or fit into more positivist framings of knowledge (Pohl, 2005; Popa *et al.*, 2015) In our case, the term 'mobilisation' has for example caused difficulties amongst engineering academics and project partners. Project partners were not used to the concept in relation to public and customer engagement and would rather see us talking about engagement or participation. However, 'mobilisation' was chosen because it refers to a particular type of initiatives, which, as explained earlier, seek to influence public practices, rather than, for example, collecting public views about water services to influence the practices of the water provider. Despite the clear contribution that mobilisation can make to the TWENTY65 goal of achieving 'clean water for all' it was decided centrally to change the terminology referring to this theme on the website. Perhaps due to the challenge of explaining the difference between mobilisation and participation, the Mobilisation Research Theme is now defined as *'Understanding the potential for public engagement to improve water services'*. While this terminology *might* be accurately interpreted to mean 'mobilisation' initiatives, it is more likely to be loosely understood to include public participation as well as mobilisation. While the website's detailed description does include a definition about mobilisation, it is nevertheless the case that decisions about how the TWENTY65 project headlines the Mobilisation Research Theme should include considerations of what those undertaking this specific research want to communicate. For us, the definition and 'creation' of 'mobilisation' offers new ways of understanding public engagement in the water sector and hence is a central part of our contribution to knowledge. Simply interchanging the term with a concept with a different meaning (in this case engagement) downgrades our knowledge. This is not a simple matter. What is the appropriate balance between something that can be easily understood by partners, and something that incorporates social science language and hence requires partners to engage with our research at a different level? This dilemma is indeed present in the Mobilisation Research Theme, but it is also one that the project as a whole constantly needs to come to terms with. Hence, it is important for researchers to balance the need for integrity with being collaborative and mindful of partners' potential limited experience of their field of expertise. It is noteworthy, moreover, that being aware and mindful of the potential confusion that could arise from our communicated messages also encourages us to consider language and concepts very carefully, which has the potential to sharpen and clarify the purpose of our research to others but also to ourselves.

Issues of integrity extend beyond language and also include the process and outcomes of critical research that are often at risk of being compromised. Our technical research colleagues and the different project advisory boards are likely to look for immediate evidence of 'activity' in terms of data collection and in delivering 'evidence' about mobilisations. For example, when presenting at the project Leadership Board meeting that convenes twice a year and includes representatives from the UK water industry, their consultants and water partnerships, one attendee highlighted the lack of £-signs assigned to demonstrate the value of mobilisation initiatives. This comment clearly undermined the importance of the research theme, suggesting that its impact was not seen as useful if it could not be directly integrated to UK water utilities' business plans by for example demonstrating reduced costs for water companies through changing public water practices (e.g. reduced water consumption compared to costs involved in building another reservoir to meet demand). The implication was that monetary costs would be more useful knowledge than an analysis of how water utilities currently work with publics to support transformative change in the water services. Countering this perspective involved stressing the highly context-dependent nature of any monetary evaluations of policy options (while also being aware that cost-benefit analysis was neither our interest nor our expertise). Our experiences here are far from unique but do align with policymaking traditions expecting single objective answers (e.g. Shove, 2010; Stirling 2010). This example also illustrates how there is a constant balance to be found in terms of when to deliver and what to deliver, and when to intervene or let things pass. A similar dilemma has been reported by Stirling (2010) in relation to providing policy advice that is plural and conditional rather than presenting single definitive recommendations more commonly adopted in policy. In Stirling's case however, the negative comments were not necessarily communicated by the policy maker herself, who turned out to be quite enthusiastic, but the people around her. This situation highlights that there may be interpretations made by others or even ourselves about what 'type' of science is likely to be seen as legitimate or applicable and how it should be presented, which may not always turn out to be accurate in practice. Hence, we would argue that staying true to your own research and how it is conducted, and at the same time being clear about how it can be useful in practice and contribute to change becomes crucial for action research to have an impact.

In relation to the Mobilisation Research Theme, criticality is maintained through the use of existing social science literature to systematically develop new and different modes of practice that could transform elements of social life with potentially positive and progressive social outcomes. It also seeks to be critical because its investigation explores and reveals the implicit values in the way the mobilisation initiatives are developed and implemented and enables debate about the nature of best practice. Further, criticality plays an important role not least when it comes to evaluation of mobilisation initiatives. A particular concern at present is that because of the complete lack of knowledge of such initiatives, existing evaluation processes are focused on achieving instrumental goals, e.g. funding for the next initiative. While such evaluations are often necessary, more comparative data and reflexive input from practitioners could provide a more effective basis for co-creating knowledge about water mobilisation that is both critical and relational.

Further, in terms of maintaining our criticality within the project, it will also be important to make progress on the broader networking aspirations of the Research Theme. One response has been to develop a strategic network of social science researchers of water that had its first meeting immediately following the TWENTY65 Annual Conference in April 2017 with the second planned for April 2018. The aim of the first workshop was to address the questions "What does social science currently bring to the discussion about water challenges?" and "What could social science offer that has not been there?" The workshop concluded that 'Collaborative Interpretive Research on Water' has an important emergent role helping water utilities to design and manage their ongoing dialogues with their publics. Such a network of critical social scientists would also have an important role in pushing forward the transformation of the water sector to become more welcoming to critical social science knowledge and expertise, and hence contribute to a more environmentally and socially progressive set of water services.

An important aspect to highlight in relation to research integrity is that many of the social scientists and engineers in TWENTY65 have collaborated before and the project ideas in the bid came from an established interdisciplinary water centre (Sheffield Water Centre). Established trust therefore eased the negotiation of process and outcomes for the project. In addition, the relationships within the group may help 'sell' critical social science to (sometimes) unreceptive water practitioners and policy makers. If engineering academics that are highly respected amongst water practitioners openly support social science, it adds credibility to our knowledge and expertise. In addition, the water sector's increasing recognition of the importance of working in partnership with publics to address water related challenges (e.g. Ofwat, 2017) has led many individuals working on water services to express commitment to social agendas, including addressing issues of inequality. Indeed, it is clear that those seeking to work with the Mobilisation Research Theme from water utilities are committed to promoting mobilisation as means to socially and environmentally progressive actions. Having confidence that the people you are working with share your values certainly provides a level of comfort and trust that makes it possible to conduct the research effectively as well as maintain relationships.

Issues of applicability

The second challenge concerns the applicability component of our research and action research in general, and expands beyond the immediate project and project partners to include departmental colleagues and wider social science research. Mobilisation might be seen as something of a 'Trojan horse' for critical social science and in producing knowledge that seeks to be both critical, applied and to some extent relational, we need to constantly justify how the design, process and outcomes of the research is influenced, on the one hand by our critical stance, and on the other, by its applied or relational ambitions. Within the Department of Urban Studies and Planning, for example, criticality and a commitment to social justice are highly esteemed. Reviews on draft research outputs stress the need for theoretical inputs to be clear and for critical messages to be honed and focused. Showing these colleagues the more applied and relational aspects of our research where knowledge is co-produced with practitioners could risk being viewed as having compromised our 'external' critical role as researchers. However, theorising or conducting analysis about certain phenomena is also a form of acting and intervening in the collaborative process that holds normative commitments to how participation (in our case mobilisation) should be performed (Chilvers and Kearne, 2016: 281). So, theorizing too inevitably intervenes in the 'cycles of world making' (Jasanoff, 2004: 12). By offering something that the water companies genuinely regard as useful while maintaining a critical voice, we argue that social science's seat at the water management research table is more fully secured.

The focus on mobilisation means we are concerned with initiatives that 'ask' publics to act to improve water services. Such initiatives would be critiqued from a political ecology perspective as potentially manipulating the public to undertake work that should be provided by the state (or the utility under the oversight of the state). A concern might be that what begins as a voluntary initiative has the potential to 'creep' into the mainstream, and services that were once provided by the state are delegated to 'community', and service levels then vary according to people's willingness and ability to volunteer or pay. Though we have some sympathy with the critique, it is not useful to apply such a comment in a sweeping way across water services. The critique certainly raises important 'critical' research questions that need to be investigated in the process of examining mobilisation initiatives including who initiates, who is invited, who benefits, and who is responsible for ensuring change happens? However, investigating these questions is a different position from making judgements about the inherent nature of all mobilisation initiatives. We consider such generalisation inappropriate because although these initiatives may not have been used systematically to date, if developed with a caring ethos, we believe that these initiatives have the potential to provide a more socially aware and cheaper water service that reduces environmental impacts and hence delivers value to everyone. In addition, it is not useful to view water management as a zero-sum game. For example, both households and utilities can take action to waste less water. Transformative change to address complex sustainability issues takes place at both structural and individual levels (Whitmarsh *et al.*, 2010) and hence it is not a question of needing action by one party or the other: we need action by both. Through critical social science being in dialogue with technical water research and practice (rather than isolated from), opportunities arise to highlight and critique the social justice implications that research and practice protagonists assume to be sustainable. In this light, critical action research could be crucial in supporting transformative change contributing to a more environmentally and socially progressive water sector.

Issues of influence

For action research to influence transformative change in the water sector, there is an issue of integration. In other words, how to move from critical social science being acknowledged as important to being acted upon in policy and practice. In the UK water sector, it is increasingly recognised that social science holds an important place in influencing water management and other technical fields, as demonstrated through the discussion of engagement in government policies (e.g. Defra, 2016) and regulation (e.g. Ofwat 2016a, 2016b, 2017) but also in terms of research funding agendas. It is for example widely understood that the grand challenges of water require the physical and engineering sciences to collaborate with wider expertise, including social sciences (e.g. Sofoulis, 2015). The UK Engineering and Physical Sciences Research Council (EPSRC) that awarded funding to the TWENTY65 project hence required that social sciences formed a part of the proposal, which resulted in two out of eight Research Themes being social-science-led. However, less acknowledged in these forums are the likely challenges faced when producing knowledge underpinned by different ontologies (Connelly and Anderson, 2007; Sofoulis, 2015) and when generating outcomes of value for a range of actors including academics (e.g. engineers and social scientists), practitioners and policy makers. In the case of the TWENTY65 project, it was initiated by the Sheffield Water Centre (SWC), an interdisciplinary research network with a core of research on urban water issues. Although bringing together people from a range of academic disciplines (including engineering and social sciences) the group has been awarded significant funding over the last 15 years from EPSRC, and the critical mass of expertise in the group have engineering backgrounds, including the Principal Investigator of TWENTY65. In this respect, the TWENTY65 project is an example of where social science is included and recognised as an important part of a project, but the overall project lead comes from engineering which has implications for how knowledge is interpreted and valued. For example, when demonstrating important outcomes from the project to wider partners, technical solutions tend to dominate.

On the other hand, the TWENTY65 project itself and its first Annual Conference held in April 2017 provides an example of the increasing attention to social science in the water sector. The conference was a two-day event seeking to bring the water sector together including different academic disciplines, and water-related organisations. In total, 142 people attended the conference of which 56 were academics and 86, policy makers, practitioners, or from SMEs/ the voluntary sector. The second conference day's plenary (the role of public engagement in Water Management) and associated discussions were dedicated to social science, while 'social' conference sessions were also available through the rest of the day. The fact that other project members agreed to allocate a full half day plenary session to social 'solutions' indicates a shift away from purely technocratic solutions to water management, historically dominating the field, to a more socially aware sector which appreciates the importance of contributions from social science in order to deliver 'clean water for all'. The socially orientated keynotes and conference sessions caused lively debates and were also those most appreciated by the conference attendees expressed through the post conference evaluation survey. According to the TWENTY65 Project Manager, the significant social science content of the conference was the one thing that made the conference unique and strongly contributed to the conference success. The TWENTY65 conference brought the water sector together through including different sectors, but more importantly perhaps, it provided a unique space for discussing or at least starting to highlight the challenges of how to integrate critical social science into water management. For example, in the Plenary Session on 'The role of public engagement in Water Management' the discussant Zoe Sofoulis (2017) highlighted the frustration of, that although social science is recognised as crucial in order to deliver a sustainable and resilient water service, such research is not underpinning innovation in water management. This issue relates to the broader tension of why social scientists (or critical action researchers) are rarely included in water decision making given the increased pressure from regulators for water utilities to work with, influence and understand their publics. How critical and relational action research could aid water management and therefore provide practical outcomes becomes a central question. Or in relation to Shove's (2010) point about policymaking being more modest about what it can do and more aware of what it produces, how could water decision-making evolve to be ready for influences from critical approaches to knowledge?

In order to begin to address these issues, an important starting point for the Mobilisation Research Theme, would be to identify and team up with practitioners and policy makers that are passionate about a more socially orientated water future, and through those networks promote change. We already have contact with a series of individuals who might be viewed as 'engagement champions' in the water sector: senior members of staff in water companies or consultancies who are committed to the use of mobilisation and participation initiatives as part of the delivery of sustainable and equitable water services. Added to these senior staff, the key informants for our Mobilisation research are practitioners employed as community engagers and change-makers within the water industry. It should be noted that at present this set of workers is not organised together and is relatively less engaged with water research than their technical equivalents, probably because of the technical emphasis of most water research to date. Though not all will be trained in social science, the activities of these enablers mean that they are already supportive of an agenda concerned with more attention to public needs and perspectives in water practices. Providing crucial contacts and sources of information for the Mobilisation Research Theme, effectively they constitute a core and growing constituency of on-the-ground workers and demonstrators of water-related community engagement, who may in the future rise to take on senior roles. By understanding these workers, but also training/supporting them, by drawing them into research and by making their work more visible through publications, the Mobilisation Research Theme has the potential to help constitute and build a new practitioner community, and hence to aid the integration of social perspectives more fully into water practices. Furthermore, by building networks among other critical social researchers of water such support can increase in quantity and depth. In the future an increased volume of water-related action research, particularly research that is able to be genuinely 'relational' working with practitioners to develop and implement innovative mobilisation initiatives, has the potential to help build the identity and confidence of the social practitioners of water, and hence support the sector's wider transformation.

Conclusion

This chapter has enhanced understandings of action research in technical fields by illustrating how criticality and applicability play out in the interdisciplinary research project TWENTY65 which seeks to support transformative change in the water sector. Specifically, we have highlighted three areas of tension between these goals. First, issues of translation and integrity concern how social science research is presented and discussed. Our experience stresses the need to negotiate and compromise, remaining attentive to the way that terminology will be heard and understood, while also maintaining the need to challenge boundaries. Second, under the 'issue of applicability' we explained how we selected a research topic that would secure social sciences' seat at the research table, while still allowing critical action research to be carried out. The broader lesson here is the need to respond to current issues and concerns within the technical field, but to utilise theory and reflexivity to maintain a critical perspective. Third, under the subtitle 'issues of influence' we have discussed the processes of moving beyond recognition of social research to the utilisation of social knowledge within the technical field. Here, we argued the need for critical action researchers to cultivate allies both within research and with practice.

As is apparent, our identification of these issues does not mean that we believe that such projects should be abandoned. On the contrary, we have argued that critical action research is particularly suitable for working in technical fields such as water management that involve environmental and infrastructure governance (other examples may include energy, housing and transport). This is because these fields have a significant impact on our social lives and our environment, and yet are dominated by technocratic decision making and have very limited democratic or social justice input. Water users' marginal involvement in decision-making about the water sector's regulation, priorities and future aims, together with their psychological distance from the centralised water supply and disposal systems which many have come to take for granted, is an equally serious issue threatening the water sector's sustainability as the deteriorating infrastructure and climate change that are so frequently highlighted.

While there is existing critical social science exploring these fields, it tends to operate from outside the area of practice and not work in conjunction with practitioners and scientists grappling with contemporary challenges. This is not surprising given the contrasting ontologies between the fields (Sofoulis, 2015). Critical action research projects hence provide a crucial opportunity to present social science perspectives and arguments outside the 'normal' context for social science, supporting greater attention to ethical, justice and environmental concerns within water management. As is illustrated by the TWENTY65 example, a significant and useful route for such critical action research is through collaborative research projects with engineering/natural scientists, also intent on transformative change. Crucially, we would argue that it is only through critical and applied action research that more socially sensitive perspectives associated with critical social science can enter into dialogue with technical decision makers and innovators to push forward more socially and environmentally progressive futures.

Acknowledgements

The authors acknowledge the financial support provided by the UK Engineering and Physical Sciences Research Council via Grant EP/N010124/1. They also thank Caroline Wadsworth, Julia Wittmayer, Koen Bartels, Ainhoa Arrona, Miren Larrea and one anonymous reviewer for helpful comments on earlier drafts.

References

ACT Government (2014) ACT Water Strategy 2014–44 – Striking the balance. Australian capital territory, Canberra, 2014.

Bakker K (2003) *An uncooperative commodity: privatizing water in England and Wales*, Oxford: Oxford University Press.

Beck U (2006) Reflexive governance: politics in the global risk society. In: Voß J-P, Bauknecht, D and Kemp R (eds.) *Reflexive Governance for Sustain-able Development*, Cheltenham: Edward Elgar Publishing Limited, pp. 31–56.

Bos JJ, Brown RR and Farrelly MA (2015) Building networks and coalitions to promote transformational change: insights from an Australian urban water planning case study. *Environmental Innovation and Societal Transitions* 15: 11–25.

Brown RR and Clarke JM (2007) Transition to water sensitive urban design: the story of Melbourne, Australia, Report No. 07/1, Facility for Advancing Water Biofiltration, Monash University, June 2007.

Browne A, Pullinger M, Medd W, and Anderson B (2013) *Patterns of water: resource pack*, Lancaster, UK: Lancaster University.

Castro JE and Heller L (2009) *Water and sanitation services: public policy and management*, London: Earthscan.

Chilvers J and Kearne M (2016) Remaking participation – towards reflexive engagement. In: Chilvers, J. and Kearne, M. 2016 (eds.) *Remaking participation science, environment and Emergent Publics*, Oxon: Routledge.

Connelly S and Anderson C (2007) Studying water: reflections on the problems and possibilities of inter-disciplinary working. *Interdisciplinary Science Reviews* 32: 213–232.

Defra (2016) Creating a great place for living enabling resilience in the water sector. Policy Paper.

Defra (2017) The government's strategic priorities and objectives for Ofwat September 2017. Presented to Parliament pursuant to section 2A of the Water Industry Act 1991.

Flyvbjerg B (2001) *Making social science matter: why social inquiry fails and how it can succeed again*, Cambridge: Cambridge University Press.

Folke C (2006) Resilience: the emergence of a perspective for social–ecological systems analyses. *Global Environmental Change* 16: 253–267.

Grin J (2006) Reflexive modernisation as a governance issue, or: designing and shaping re-structuration. In: Voß J-P, Bauknecht, D and Kemp R (eds.) *Reflexive governance for sustain-able development*, Cheltenham: Edward Elgar Publishing Limited, pp. 57–81.

Holling CS (ed.) (1978) *Adaptive environmental assessment and management*, New York: John Wiley and Sons.

Ison R, Blackmore C and Iaquinto BL (2013) Towards systemic and adaptive govern-ance: exploring the revealing and concealing aspects of contemporary social-learning metaphors. *Ecological Economics* 87: 34–42.

Jasanoff S (2004) The idiom of co-production. In: Jasanoff S (ed.) *States of knowledge: the co-production of science and social order*, New York: Routledge, 1–12.

Knamiller C and Sharp L (2009) Issues of trust, fairness and efficacy: a qualitative study of information provision for newly metered households in England. *Water Science and Technology: Water Supply* 9(3): 323–331.

Kaika M (2003) Structural continuities and institutional change in water management. *European Planning Studies* 11(3): 283–298.

Linton J and Budds (2014) The hydrosocial cycle: defining and mobilizing a relational-dialectical approach to water. *Geoforum* 57: 170–180.

Lövbrand E (2011) Co-producing European climate science and policy: a cautionary note on the making of useful knowledge. *Science and Public Policy* 38 (3): 225–236.

Mackenzie J, Tan P-L, Hoverman S and Baldwin C (2012). The value and limitations of participatory action research methodology. *Journal of Hydrology* 474: 11–21.

Medd W and Marvin S (2007) Strategic intermediation: between regional strategy and local practice. *Sustainable Development* 15(5): 318–327.

Medd W and Chappells H (2008) From big solutions to small practices: bringing back the active consumer. *Social Alternatives* 27(3): 44–49.

Molyneux-Hodgson S and Balmer AS (2014) Synthetic biology, water industry and the performance of an innovation barrier. *Science and Public Policy* 41(4): 507–519.

Ofwat (2011) Push, pull, nudge: how can we help customers save water, energy and money?

Ofwat (2016a) Water 2020: our regulatory approach for water and wastewater services in England and Wales – overview.

Ofwat (2016b) Ofwat's customer engagement policy statement and expectations for PR19. Policy Statement.

Ofwat (2017) Tapped In – from passive customer to active participants. Commissioned report, Corporate Culture Group.

Phillips L, Kristiansen M, Vehviläinen M and Gunnarsson E (eds.) (2013) *Knowledge and power in collaborative research – a reflexive approach*, New York: Routledge.

Pohl C (2005) Transdiciplinary collaboration in environmental research. *Futures* 37(10): 1159–1178.

Popa F, Guillermin M and Dedeurwaerdere T. (2015) A pragmatist approach to transdisciplinarity in sustainability research: from complex systems theory to reflexive science. *Futures* 65: 45–56.

Pullinger M, Browne A, Anderson B and Medd W (2013) *Patterns of water: the water related practices of households in southern England, and their influence on water consumption and demand management*, Lancaster, UK: Lancaster University. Downloadable from www.escholar.manchester.ac.uk/uk-ac-man-scw:187780.

Reason P and Bradbury H (2008) Introduction: inquiry and participation in search of a world worthy of human aspiration. In: P. Reason and H. Bradbury, eds. *The SAGE handbook of action research: participative inquiry and practice*, London: Sage, 1–10.

Sharp L, Macrorie R and Turner A (2015) Resource efficiency and the imagined public: insights from cultural theory. *Global Environmental Change* 34: 196–206.

Sharp L (2017) *Reconnecting people with water*, London: Earthscan.

Shove E (2003) *Comfort cleanliness and convenience*, London: Berg.

Shove E (2010) Beyond the ABC: climate change policy and theories of social change. *Environment and Planning A* 42(6): 1273–1285.

Sim P, McDonald A, Parsons J and Rees P (2007) Revised options for UK domestic water reduction: a review. University of Leeds WaND Briefing Note 28.

Sofoulis Z (2017) Plenary Session: the role of public engagement in Water Management. TWENTY65 Annual Conference 2017. Manchester 4–5 April.

Sofoulis Z (2015) A knowledge ecology of urban Australian household water consumption. *ACME* 14(3): 765–785.

Speight V (2015) Innovation in the water industry: barriers and opportunities for US and UK utilities. *WIREs Water* 2(4): 301–313.

Stirling A (2006) Analysis, participation and power: justification and closure in participatory multi-criteria analysis. *Land Use Policy* 23: 95–107.

Stirling A (2010) Keep it complex. *Nature* 468: 1029–1031.

Swyngedouw E (2004) *Social power and the urbanization of water: flows of power*, Oxford: Oxford University Press.

Voß J-P and Bornemann B (2011) The politics of reflexive governance: challenges for designing adaptive management and transition management. *Ecology and Society* 16(2): 1.

Westling E, Sharp L, Rychlewski M and Carrozza C (2014) Developing adaptive capacity through reflexivity: lessons from collaborative research with a UK water utility. *Critical Policy Studies* 8(4): 427–446.

Whitmarsh L, O'Neill S and Lorenzoni I (2010) Climate change or social change? Debate within, amongst, and beyond disciplines. *Environment and Planning A* 43: 258–261.

Woelfe-Erskine C (2015) Rain tanks, springs, and broken pipes as emerging water commons along Salmon Creek, CA, USA, *Acme* 14(3): 735–750.

Co-inquirer reflection

Chris Digman, MWH

My experience in the UK and abroad (as well as from discussing with colleagues and reading global literature) shows that engineering can only go so far to resolve and address the challenges that we face today. For example, such challenges include how we manage surface water to reduce flooding and pollution or how we manage the solids loads in the drainage network and arriving at wastewater treatment works. Essentially, our desire to 'build' our way out of problems has or is coming to an end. Therefore, how we engage and mobilise a change in people's actions is fundamental. I believe this cannot be done through engineering and technology alone (although they will still play their part). However, it will be through using various social science techniques and learning to mobilise individuals and communities.

I have been involved with research for nearly 20 years and have a visiting role at the University of Sheffield. I have seen the important role social science has had through the Pennine Water Group and now the Water Centre, therefore it was a natural place and opportunity to engage further.

My relationship is positive and engaging with the researchers. Whilst time is often the biggest constraint, I find it very helpful to spend time and learn from the knowledge and experience of the social science researchers. I feel comfortable to ask open questions and not be constrained to formalised meetings. This I hope is a two-way benefit that not only helps develop my thinking but also theirs. I actively seek to work with the team on research projects, as well as more practitioner/delivery-focused projects and raising awareness of the team's work with bodies responsible for managing water.

There were three key challenges encountered during the research:

1   **Language:** Both water engineers and social scientists use different language. This can be a blocker at times but resolved through clarification and open discussion. This is critical as many of the terms used by each other have very specific meanings and can be misinterpreted.
2   **Time to learn and engage more:** This is important to ensure more and more that this different field of science is brought into engineering and help to solve the problems we face. Without the time and effort spent, opportunities can be missed. This also applies to providing support to develop the

research as well as the white papers. A possible alternative model to bring in the expertise needed to develop papers and work on projects periodically would be to complete short sprints when people come together that focus on delivery as much as discussion.

3   **Making progress as quick as desired:** This is not about having an output per se, but more likely having visibility of progress (which may also have been made, but missed by myself).

The learning from the research has supported my thinking and discussions within the water industry. It has provided an opportunity for me to see that we need to tackle today's and tomorrow's problems through multiple and overlapping lenses. The learning has also helped me to understand that mobilisation is necessary and that it's not just about engagement or behaviour change. Whilst this forms part of the approach, it's about the active action and participation of people and communities. Such approaches may also help deal with a reliance on a centralised system currently in place in the UK, and how by raising the awareness of water could achieve multiple benefits.

By having this greater visibility of the thinking and thoughts of what will help this possible journey take place, it is enabling discussions and putting forward alternative ways to address the challenges in water industry business plans currently being developed.

3 Cooperative research for bottom-up food sovereignty and policy change

Bálint Balázs and György Pataki

Introduction

In recent years local food systems and short food supply chains (SFSCs) have moved into the centre of attention in the EU policy arena (Kneafsey *et al.*, 2013). However, patterns and processes of local food system development in transition countries are different from the experiences of the US or Western Europe (Kiss *et al.*, 2008; Balázs, 2012; Jehlička and Smith, 2011). Local food entered the public discussion as a specific policy domain in the wake of several EU-funded research projects. These often pointed out the urgent need for targeted financial and public support (e.g. exemptions from food safety regulations) and support for labelling, promotion and collective marketing (Karner and Chioncel, 2010; Schermer *et al.*, 2010).

Growing up in a green district of Budapest in the 1970s and 1980s, both of us enjoyed playing all day in a garden full of cherry trees and vegetables, eating wild sorrel for lunch and coming home only for dinner. Family stories highlighted everyday practices of food self-provisioning, exchange or processing, for example grandma carrying the garden produce and buckets of roses to a downtown farmers' market for selling. These formative experiences informed our choices to study at the Institute for Nature Conservation and Landscape Management at St. István University in Gödöllő, where ecological economists and environmental sociologists introduced us to the world of collaborative economies and community agriculture. Over the past decade we have worked to develop the Environmental Social Science Research Group (ESSRG), and we took part in the work of Védegylet (Protect the Future), a civil society organisation (CSO) promoting environmental protection and natural and cultural diversity. Our personal dissatisfaction with mainstream 'objectivist' styles of academic research gave rise to our reflexive approach to foster change (see e.g. Balázs *et al.*, 2005), and our aim to give voice to marginalised farmers (e.g. Balázs *et al.*, 2009; Bodorkós and Pataki 2009), and pushed us in the direction of cooperative research. Through these experiences we developed a critical but constructive approach, which requires multiple roles during this research process (Wittmayer and Schäpke, 2014).

As the economic situation for small-scale farming worsened over the course of the transition years of the 1990s, activists of Védegylet and practitioners in the Hungarian food movement decided to work to transform current regulations for local food systems. They faced several questions that were not entirely new to food sovereignty struggles. We saw in their struggles the potential for cooperative inquiry, conducted by civil activists of CSOs together with professional researchers, to contribute to policy change enhancing economic conditions for small-scale farming in Hungary. We started to work with them as 'co-researchers', and jointly formulated our research question examining how current policies shape the development of alternative agro-food systems; and we also considered how collaborative research by CSO activists and academic researchers might contribute to transforming the policy field for alternative agri-food initiatives. This article is a reflection on the progression and outcomes of this type of cooperative research, conducted in the interests of bottom-up food sovereignty and policy change.

Policy making has traditionally relied on expert organisations, and our domain has not had experts who could create actionable policy-relevant knowledge. Agricultural policy makers implemented stakeholder engagement only by inviting big business interests into decision making. The lack of appropriate institutionalisation processes that could represent small-scale food production became clear. Transparency and accountability have been lacking in most policy processes, allowing power plays and manipulation to come to the fore. EU-level projects, on the other hand, have usually pressed for participatory, collaborative research on alternative agro-food networks.

This chapter presents, at both the substance and process level, an inspiring policy experiment showcasing how the incremental transformation of a national scale food system might be achievable on the national scale. The next section, on our methodological approach, discusses the components and prospects for cooperative research in the local food policy domain. The third section, on the research context, details the controversies surrounding institutional transformations in the agro-food domain, with particular regard to top-down and bottom-up engagement around food sovereignty in Hungary and its initial successes. The fourth section gives an overview of our case study, emphasising our participatory process for policy change built on cooperative research. Our fifth, reflective section goes back to our original research question and presents our analysis of the consensus-building exercise in bringing together stakeholders for envisioning alternative agro-food systems in Hungary. It also shows how agency has been created to regain a voice for food sovereignty in a cooperative research setting. The conclusion argues that, by building a robust network of CSO partners and food communities from the bottom up, the process has had some preliminary success in meeting diverse stakeholders' expectations and becoming a positive example of policy change.

Methodological approach

We have long advocated participatory action research in rural development (Balázs *et al.*, 2005, 2009; Bodorkós and Pataki, 2009; Málovics *et al.*, 2012).

Therefore, our disposition has been actively self-reflective: sympathetic but critical towards an otherwise urgent – an urgency exacerbated by the economic crisis – sustainability issue in the food system. This pushed and prepared us to cooperate with food producers and activists on numerous projects at the national, regional and global levels. The Food Sovereignty movement established a network in Hungary in 2012, and we actively facilitated the engagement of CSOs in it as knowledgeable partners, and initiated links with international organisations and initiatives. We have benefited from the financial support of an EU-level cooperative research project on alternative agro-food networks (Karner and Chioncel, 2010). We paired up as professional researchers with activists of Védegylet, an ecopolitical organisation active throughout the research process. Our equal partnership was based on shared interests and mutuality, while seeking to bring favourable outcomes for the local food movement in Hungary and foster socially desirable types of agri-food innovation. Our methodological approach was, therefore, a normative choice that brought to the table the issues of accountability, power plays, domination and inequality, and attempted to practise research as an empowering bottom-up process engaging multiple actors and incorporating their needs.

We understand cooperative research as a type of action research that is, to follow the formulation of Peter Reason, aiming for research with and for people rather than on people (Reason, 1994). Cooperative research was first introduced as a new paradigm in science policy, based on an expert workshop of the European Commission (Stirling, 2006). It has entirely different roots from other action research approaches, inasmuch as it originates in the Social Studies of Science or Science and Technology Studies tradition. It is promoting a radical move towards *democratising "science governance"* by envisioning a genuinely transdisciplinary research and innovation process around politically controversial themes (Irwin, 2008) – in our case, the acknowledgement of smallholder farming as an agent of agro-food systems. Practically, it implies that in cooperative research we are invited to leave the comfort zone of our academic research habits, primarily by building up a new form of the research process, which involves both researchers and non-researchers in a close cooperative engagement (Stirling, 2008). Cooperative research stems from a motivation to address matters that are important to people and involve practitioners in creative actions for change – to do things better. In line with all qualitative research, cooperative inquiry concerns revising our understanding of the world; but, beyond deep understanding, it aims to transform current practices. Cooperative research gives priority to a transformative inquiry, i.e. participants change their ways of being and doing and relating to the world (Reason, 1994).

Epistemologically, cooperative research calls for treating all types of knowledge equally by integrating scientific, textual, expert and scholarly knowledge with other types of practice-based embodied knowledge. It incorporates values from outside the realm of science, by experimenting with new research methods, tools and concepts. This integration in the process of knowledge production can uncover reliable and actionable knowledge located between the realms of scientific and non-scientific knowledge. In other words, cooperative research builds upon an 'extended epistemology' involving multiple types of knowing (both theoretical and practical knowing) and different knowledge forms (both scientific and local knowledge). Consequently, it pairs up diverse types of knowledge holders in the research process as co-researchers. Being co-researchers means that all actors are involved in all research decisions, from the design and carrying out of the inquiry, through making sense and drawing conclusions and, most importantly, in initiating actions and exerting influence on the substantive subject matter or domain of the research (Karner and Chioncel, 2010).

Bottom-up engagement, often referred to as upstream engagement (Stirling, 2006), is a core component of cooperative research arrangements. It emphasises the need for co-designing the framework of research processes and incorporating knowledge holders' interests, needs and values. Cooperative research shares a 'participative worldview' with other types of action research: 'human beings are engaged in co-creating their reality through participation' (Reason, 1994: 324). Affected people need to participate in knowledge production relating to matters of high societal relevance; otherwise, the knowledge created will bear no substantive meaning to them. Actionable knowledge is a result of an inclusive process of production, in which knowledge will be owned and usable at the same time. The process of cooperative inquiry will consequently be a democratic, shared process, responding to collective interests and concerns.

In sum, we summarise the promises of cooperative research in the following three points:

- *Knowledge integration.* Cooperative research is helpful in integrating different kinds of knowledge. In this way, it provides theoretical insights anchored in real stakeholder needs, the evidence base for policy change and valuable experiences for civic advocacy.
- *Upstream engagement.* Cooperative research enables a process that gives voice to knowledge holders or their representatives who have been systematically left out of policy processes. The upstream engagement of actors engenders the formulation of efficient policy networks.
- *Shaping the policy agenda.* Cooperative research can contribute to opening up the participatory policy processes to meaningful dialogue and identify entry points for incorporating the value frames of the widest range of knowledge holders. In a sense, cooperative research may substitute for missing capacities on the government side, helping provide an evidence base for policy change.

Our primary aim in the cooperative research presented here was to arrive at a common problem-framing and, subsequently, to bring in the potential to initiate meaningful policy change through co-creating evidence and knowledge of a transformative potential regarding the agro-food policy domain in Hungary.

Research context

As for institutional transformations, since the Second World War, several dramatic turnarounds or forced regime changes have been distinctive in the agro-food domain. The 1945–1948 land reform, collectivisation by 1962, compensation and privatisation in the 1990s, and the Europeanisation and late self-organisation since left only a marginal role for prosperous, bottom-up organic developments in the sector.

Looking at the Hungarian agro-food sector from a socio-technical systems viewpoint, one can see a dual (bipolar) economy: an overwhelming large-scale agro-industry and service providers on the one hand, and a disproportionately high number of fragmented small producers and organisations on the other. Small farms control less than a fifth of the land; and, despite the government's stated goal to increase it, the number of small-scale farmers is decreasing (Balázs, 2012). Land privatisation starting after the political transition in the early 1990s led to enormous unemployment in the rural regions, amidst an extreme concentration and polarisation of land. The intensity is reaching a feudal level: only 5 per cent of the population has agricultural land, and only a fraction of these holdings are larger than one hectare.

The farm structure, economic viability, profitability and competitiveness of the Hungarian agri-food sector have long been established themes and concerns for mainstream scholarly investigations and discourses. We find much evidence that market acquisition by sizeable foreign food companies directly targeted the food processing industries, involving significant foreign direct investment in the agro-food sector. Given the collapse of Hungary's export markets in the former Eastern Bloc and widespread corruption involving both domestic players and foreign investors, enterprises in the agri-food sector were often privatised at fire-sale prices. Many of them have been subsequently liquidated by the new owners,

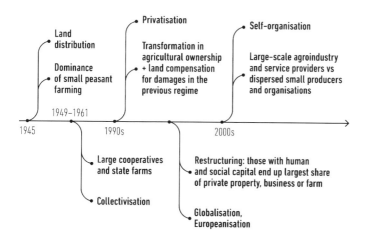

Figure 3.1 Institutional transformations in the Hungarian agro-food system.

who were often interested only in acquiring market share for imported products. After only ten years of transition, foreign ownership in the Hungarian food processing sector exceeded 60 per cent (Jansik, 2000).

For the most part, the country's agri-food sector also lost out in the EU accession process (from 2004) (Jámbor and Sirone Varadi, 2014). Today Hungary's trade balance in agri-food products with the EU-15 is negative, despite the country's agro-ecological potential and traditional role as a food producer. Part of this is explained by weaknesses in Hungarian agri-food export competitiveness, as the sector failed to adapt to changes in demand in its reconfigured export markets (Juhász and Wagner, 2013). Price and quality competitiveness of lower-priced cereal and oilseed commodities show relative potential in this respect.

The change of government in 2010 led to a complete institutional transformation in line with an ethnocentric–protectionist political agenda. This development provided a window of opportunity for the policy reform initiative promoted by the local food movement in Hungary. The policy process initiated by the *New Agricultural and Rural Development Strategy 2020* (Ministry of Rural Development Hungary, 2012), also referred to as 'The Constitution of Rural Hungary', pressed for a proportionately much higher allocation of resources for the development of local food systems as a primary tool for domestic economic development.

Small-scale farming, a vulnerable sector worldwide, has become a politically controversial topic in Hungary. Since the 'retail revolution' (privatisation of the food retail sector to the benefit of foreign capital) in Central and Eastern European countries happened extremely fast (Dries *et al.*, 2004), it resulted in additional difficulties for small-scale farmers attempting to join new food distribution channels from which they were excluded. However, the active and conflict-generating government policy directly targeting large, foreign-owned supermarket chains ('Crisis tax', 'Plaza stop', 'Sunday retail ban') has not engendered much public support and did not lead to significant improvement. Political autonomy, social self-organisation and mobilisation for collective action have all been wholly usurped in the semi-autocratic political arena, limiting any civic control function. Thus, the food sovereignty movement in Hungary is scattered, and more focused on developing alternative niches than on political action (see e.g. Balázs *et al.*, 2015).

In this context, farmers' associations and civil society organisations play an important role in supporting and engaging small-scale family farmers and forging paths towards international cooperation, as with the peasant movement of La Via Campesina (LVC).[1] The National Association of Hungarian Farmers' Societies and Co-operatives (Magyar Gazdakörök és Gazdaszervezetek Szövetsége), hereafter Magosz, registered with the European Peasant Organisation (CPE), which later joined LVC.[2] Following the Hungarian peasant revolt of 1997, new demonstrations started in 2005–2006. Farmers objected to the agricultural policy that favoured large industrialised farms and capital investors. Magosz mobilised 790 tractors to block roads in 14 counties in Hungary. With more than 40,000 members in more than 800 member societies (local farmers' circles and farmers cooperatives), Magosz's resources come from member fees. Magosz organised a petition in 2005 demanding the reassessment of the agricultural framework in favour of Hungarian smallholder farmers. A position which also reflected public dissatisfaction with global capitalism and neoliberalism, gained broad support from the rural and urban population as well as solidarity expressions from foreign civil organisations. Three weeks of negotiations between representatives of the government and the coalition of farmers' organisations gave rise to self-organisation – led by Magosz, the farmers' coalition included 11 other organisations.[3] Being independent of party politics, the coalition was able to successfully shape the political discussion with the government on 39 jointly identified targets.

With the decline of the traditional Smallholders Party (Független Kisgazda-, Földmunkás- és Polgári Párt), which lost its seats in the national assembly in 2002, the political significance of Magosz gradually increased, ultimately yielding five seats in the national assembly at the 2006 elections in strategic partnership with Fidesz. Magosz went from being a farmer's resistance movement to institutionalisation as a political actor; it did not seek to transform itself into a party, but it maintained a policy dialogue with parliamentary parties as a members-based farmers' organisation. The President of Magosz has been Vice President of the Hungarian National Assembly since 2010. The main aim of Magosz, supporting family farming, has become the slogan of the government, and the ruling party has also co-opted the policy goal of increasing the competitiveness of small-scale family farmers. The agro-food policy of the ruling government as developed by Magosz is based on the unity of agriculture and rural development, aiming at reconnecting agro-food production, processing and sales.

Magosz has created and championed a politically feasible food sovereignty agenda in Hungary, and thematised the media interest in and public understanding of agri-food systems. Magosz has been successful, for example, in promoting the economic independence of Hungarian farmers and their right to development, especially in the political game around the expiration of the land moratorium. It campaigned, at least in its rhetoric, to stop foreign land speculation, land grabs and pocket contracts, and to ensure that rural farmers have access to and gain increased control over agricultural land. The farmland reorganisation program – called 'Land to Farmers' – initiated the leasing and distribution of 250,000 ha of state-owned farmlands managed by the National Land Management Fund Organisation (NFA). Simultaneously, a special loan program was developed by the state-owned Hungarian Development Bank (MFB) to help farmers buy state-owned farmland, subject to a 20-year ban on resale and encumbrance as well as the state's right to repurchase. This all indicates that Magosz has chosen to channel farmers' claims into the decision-making mechanisms through the program of the ruling party. By repeatedly renewing (in 2006, 2010 and 2015) its strategic partnership with the party, Magosz has managed to induce a supportive environment through top-down engagement processes (Juarez *et al.*, 2015).

Bottom-up initiatives for food sovereignty and related struggles for food justice, the right to food, civic food networks and food commoning have been initiated by grassroots organisations.[4] Such organisations have also supported farmers' free self-organisation in their fight for their rights, but they are in only occasional contact with La Via Campesina (LVC) and Magosz. The Nyéléni Europe Forum, held in August 2011 in Krems, Austria, also initiated the bottom-up engagement of farmers and other civil society groups for food sovereignty. A practice network of civic organisations has been created in Hungary to support food sovereignty, and the activists in Védegylet, our 'co-researchers', took a decisive role in its organisation. The more than year-long preparation process for the Food Sovereignty Forum, and the meeting itself, led to social learning and new links between national and international organisations. For many participants of the Forum, mostly from Eastern European countries, it was their first chance to learn about the concept of food sovereignty and understand the vision and strategies for reorganising the way our society relates to food and agriculture.

This first European Forum was, controversially, initially planned by Géza Varga, former Magosz member, to take place in Hungary in 2011. Once a Hungarian rural development pioneer, trained at the Schumacher College, he established the first Hungarian ecovillage with a 300 ha organic farm, Galgafarm, in Galgahéviz, then introduced the concept of food sovereignty to Hungary. Varga later became a representative of the radical nationalist party (Jobbik) in the

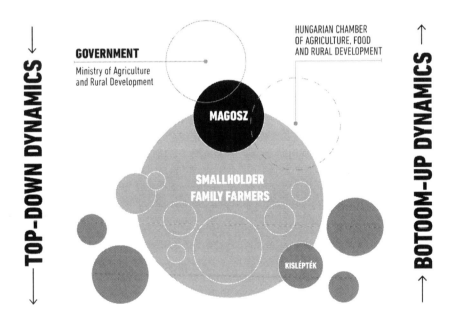

Figure 3.2 Actors Map – Hungary: Magosz and other civic organisations in the interest representation of Hungarian smallholder farmers.

Hungarian parliament, from 2010 to 2014. The steering group of the Forum, including ECVC representatives, ultimately decided to hold the event in Austria, because of Varga's political activity in Jobbik. The preparation process for the Forum took more than a year, allowing civil society organisations from across Europe to map out and organise their national networks. Although the network did not remain a strong working formation after the forum, these organisations continue to re-connect and support each other for different occasions, events and issues.

As the effects of the economic crisis revitalised interest in the viability of small-scale farming, food self-provisioning and related narratives, the civil efforts towards the reform of the smallholder decree (Smallholder Decree, 52/2010) benefited from a supportive political, media and public context. We see similarities with the international efforts of LVC to promote food sovereignty and small-scale food producers. As LVC had already done, Hungarian CSOs soon realised that 'farmers and food producers have been trapped with a sole outlet for their production, forcing them to accept an unacceptable marginal reward for their product', and became convinced of the need for 'supportive food safety rules and local food infrastructure for smallholder farmers' (cited by Juarez *et al.*, 2015: 58).

While top-down and bottom-up engagement efforts for food sovereignty have both faced significant internal controversies around participation, representation and how to relate to the political arena, their central narratives show considerable overlap, and they share entry points into mainstream policy discourses on local food and small-scale farming. The developments related here created a window of opportunity for policy change; recognising this opportunity, we embarked on the joint mobilisation of activists and researchers in a cooperative research framework.

The cooperative research case

Our case study was part of the project "Facilitating Alternative Agro-Food Networks – Stakeholder Perspectives on Research Needs" (FAAN), funded within the 7th EU Framework Programme. The consortium consisted of teams from five research institutions and five civil society organisations in Austria, France, the UK, Poland and Hungary. It utilised the close cooperative engagement of a team of academic research partners and civil society organisations (CSOs) active in the food sovereignty movement in setting up the project concept, the implementation of research activities and the dissemination of the results. This continuous engagement extended from forming the research design through carrying out research activities to generating policy recommendations.

As with all action research, this cooperative inquiry was carried out in cycles of action and reflection. The close cooperative engagement of pairs of CSOs and academic partners reached its high points at project consortium meetings, which enabled partners to enjoy a space for reflection involving more actors and their experience. All reflection workshops and all actions were organised and carried out in a close collaboration between academic and CSO partners. The timeline of the Hungarian case can be briefly summarised as follows:

2008–2009:   Problem-focused research to collect issues of high relevance to practitioners. Research methods: qualitative interviews with small-scale farmers and experts in the sector; document analysis. *Output: problem catalogue and policy recommendations.*

2009:   Petition started by Védegylet to create a bottom-up network for food sovereignty in Hungary. *Output: 51 participants recruited to support the smallholder decree policy reform.*

March 2009:   Press release to mobilise support for policy reform. *Output: media attention.*

April 2009:   Campaign to gather online contributions from citizens groups.

April 2009:   Workshop on the future visions of the local food system in Hungary. *Output: text of smallholder decree policy reform.*

May 2009:   Completion and consolidation of the policy reform text. *Output: final text handed over to the ministry.*

2010:   Comparative analysis of cooperative research cases in partner countries. *Output: policy report on case studies of alternative agro-food networks in the EU (in English), and policy brief on the significance of alternative food systems in Hungary (in Hungarian).*

Cooperative research (CR) involves working together and supporting each other through research. It can help in the self-organisation of food advocacy and facilitate positive social interaction. By identifying stakeholders that have the most to lose but carry the least power to influence policy, this CR setting helps to break out of indifference, and encourage cooperation in food governance. Our cooperative research project also revealed that local communities can no longer defend their rights to food, and that local food systems need support to thrive in a global food system that works well for everyone, in diverse ways.

The need for bottom-up networking for food sovereignty was another central insight from the cooperative research. Beyond tailored policy solutions, CSOs wanted a process which guarantees openness to diverse forms of knowledge in shaping policy. Stakeholder involvement therefore aimed at enhancing the sense of ownership and ensuring buy-in to policy change. The transparency of such a process required that we organised negotiations in informal meetings with grass-roots activists. The research itself created a strong evidence base by including the diverse voices of farmers who were directly affected by the lack of appro-priate regulation and adequate food governance.

The first phase of the project in 2008–2009 was a state-of-the-art analysis of processing and marketing in the small-scale farming sector, based on stakeholder interviews and document analysis. As a result, a problem catalogue was created, with policy proposals as solutions. In the initial phase of the cooperative research we divided tasks: Borbála researched policies linked to the smallholder decree

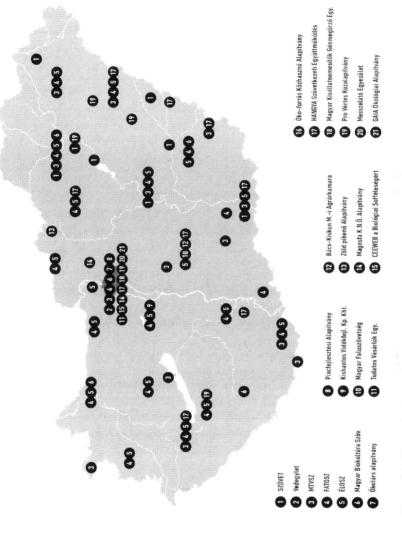

Figure 3.3 Players in the participatory research and policy process.

1 SZÖVET
2 Vedegylet
3 MTVSZ
4 FATOSZ
5 ÉLOSZ
6 Magyar Biokultúra Szöv.
7 Ökotárs alapítvány

8 Piacfejlesztési Alapítvány
9 Kishantos Vidékfejl. Kp. Kht.
10 Magyar Faluszövetség
11 Tudatos Vásárlók Egy.

12 Bács-Kiskun M.-i Agrárkamara
13 Zöld pihenő Alapítvány
14 Magosfa K.N.Ö. Alapítvány
15 CEEWEB a Biológiai Sokféleségert

16 Öko-forrás Közhasznú Alapítvány
17 HANGYA Szövetkezeti Együttműködés
18 Magyar Kisállatnemesítők Génmegőrző Egy.
19 Pro Vértes Közalapítvány
20 Messzelátó Egyesület
21 GAIA Ökológiai Alapítvány

by mapping the complex web of legislation relevant to smallholders in Hungary; Csilla and Bálint examined local case studies of alternative agro-food networks, while Anna created photo essays on farmers markets and later engaged in interviewing with Magosz (see the reflection article in this volume). The results informed a bottom-up networking effort for food sovereignty started by Védegylet and Szövet (Alliance for the Living Tisza). These groups began the process of signing a declaration with food movement actors.

Together, they issued a press release on the policy problem and solutions on 25 March 2009, initiating the effort to reform the smallholder decree. The network organised public discussions, and the media conducted numerous interviews with the advocates. We also initiated a crowdsourcing phase during the spring of 2009 to collect textual contributions from interested stakeholders, mostly online. After we finished summarising all the results from these public consultations, on 30 April 2009 the research group held a workshop at the Corvinus University of Budapest on visions of agro-food systems and suggestions for modifications of the decree. CSOs and previous interviewees (altogether 27 people) convened to explicitly talk about mutual interests and give impetus to the policy reform. The consolidated text was presented in May and handed over to the ministry.[5]

The cooperative research project uncovered the obstacles to the implementation of the actual policy change. In the case of the smallholders' decree, it became apparent that central legal and regulatory elements have been predefined by food hygiene standards and best available technologies (e.g. that rabbit meat must be checked by a local vet). The budgetary concerns of institutions have demarcated many elements of the regulation and, in reality, it was being implemented according to the whims of local authorities. This resulted in ad hoc decisions. Much of the lack of clarity around the local food issues emerged from the fact that the necessary expertise was lacking. The messiness of institutional responsibility, inadequate human resources at local authorities, a lack of capacity to harmonise among different government departments, and the constant institutional reforms since the EU accession probably all played a role here. Unexpectedly, some elements of the regulation (e.g. on slaughterhouses) turned out to be directly or indirectly defined by the EU accession contract. Although the research produced an interesting comparative analysis of the experiences of different EU countries, there proved to be insufficient space for using examples from other nations. Many of the relevant practices originated from before the EU accession. Thus, they were more a remnant than a precedent. Finally, and least surprisingly, the lack of representation of small-scale farming interests in policy planning also meant that regulations such as the Good Hygiene Practice have not been tailor-made for smallholder produce (Karner, 2010).

The scenario workshop, as part of the cooperative research process, helped to identify possible scenarios for alternative agro-food systems. A nominal group technique gave stakeholders the chance to work on their own and then create their collective visions; the same technique was used to jointly assess the three scenarios they created (Karner and Chioncel, 2010). In practice, the workshop followed the style of a stakeholder dialogue. We mainly invited the powerholder stakeholders, but also representatives of marginalised smallholders. Still, the consensus building was not easy. In an introductory activity, all participants introduced themselves and their interests in and perspectives on food systems. The critical policy issues identified in the research were debated within an extended circle of practitioners to co-analyse and co-validate these findings. As a final move, we invited all stakeholders to participate in an interactive exercise to create visions for the future (see Table 3.1 with the elements of three agri-food scenarios). As co-researchers, our main process-level intention was to

Table 3.1 Visions of alternative food networks

Localisation – community-based food systems

Predominantly local stakeholders provide food through direct sales
Produce reaches consumers through the shortest possible route using minimal transport and storage
Food self-provisioning at the household level
Family farming and micro-enterprises
Farmers' cooperatives take over the role of traders, thereby keeping the added value from local processing, marketing and sales
The dominant proportion of food is from alternative agro-food systems
Local municipalities play a decisive role in developing local food systems
Peri-urban operations and regional cooperation
Selling groups help producers to engage with manufacturers
Local authorities actively support the relocalisation of public food
Innovative businesses support the reconnection of consumers and producers

---

Globalisation – commodity-based food systems

Multinationals and investors take over regional and local food provisioning
Proprietary brands take over the role of social linkages between producers and consumers
Agri-business dominates the national economy
Mid-sized and large companies dominate production
Supermarkets and retail become the most influential players in the food economy
Food provisioning is most often realised through home deliveries
The role of alternative agriculture is marginal, while direct sales become only a hobby
Alternatives become economically unviable
Even the personal relations of farmers and producers are excluded

---

Diversity/hybridisation – food commoning

Diverse stakeholders cooperate in multi-stakeholder settings of food provisioning
Local and regional supply is dominated by small-scale producers, family farms and small enterprises
Self-provisioning is coupled with a market-based quality food supply
Food export is served by manufacturers' cooperation; specialised agro-industrial enterprises
Local and regional markets supply small-scale and non-local produce through the cooperation of small-scale farmers and big businesses in processing and transport
Public food catering provides a significant demand for local quality food

---

demonstrate to the policymakers and policy planners that there exists a meaningful collaborative social technique to enjoy openly sharing knowledge with others who are also enthusiastic about quality food supply.

In general, rural development and agro-food policy planning in Hungary lack deliberations on long-term opportunities and future orientations (Korompai *et al.*, 2017). Therefore, it is hard to connect short-term planning exercises to grounded perspectives (Bodorkós and Pataki, 2009). The above scenarios themselves do not create a comprehensive vision on future food provisioning, but build on differentiated and opposing (global-local, quality and high-tech) aspects.

Reflecting the food scenarios produced by the World Economic Forum (WEF), Hungarian stakeholders reached a consensus about the need to transform current food governance. Possibilities for such a transformation are getting more and more attention in public discourses (Balázs *et al.*, 2016). Different relations to the dominant economic system (localisation, globalisation, hybridisation) point to different pathways: community-based or commodity-based food systems and food commoning. It is also apparent that technological innovation does not inevitably dominate and is not wholly unavoidable. Climate change and population growth are not integral parts of these relatively short-term scenarios. Most importantly, a quick switch on the demand side is a vital structuring element. A stark differentiation between economic integration and separation has also emerged from the visions. The globalisation scenario is similar to the 'survival of the richest' scenario by WEF, built on a socially unjust global economy. It is close as well to the 'limitless consumption' WEF scenario, in which negative externalities of the food system increase. The hybridisation scenario offers the globalisation of local alternatives and the localisation of best global food provisioning patterns. It is more or less the same as the eco-efficiency scenario by the Belgian Consensus, or the 'open sustainability' WEF scenario, built on closely connected markets and resource efficiency. The localisation scenario has been built on a strong local economy, and therefore appears similar to the 'local is the new global' WEF-scenarios and the 'decommodification' and 'food-self-provisioning' scenarios by the Consensus Project (see World Economic Forum, 2017; Bauler *et al.*, 2011).

Reflections on hegemonies and impact

Mainstream research has extensively demonstrated the economic vulnerability of farmers and their lack of capacity to actively participate in policy processes; our cooperative research project had to confront these issues too. Our case pointed out that CR for the benefit of small-scale farming can build up agency and create a voice for the food movement in Hungary. It is true that Hungarian farmers are not pro-active; or, as an activist expressed it: 'mobilising them for an issue which, in fact, would support them is a real miracle'. They have neither the time nor the capacity and lack the communication channels to promote themselves. Due to the current low margin between market prices and the amount of investment, smallholder farming is unable to support itself. In sum, activists require extra resources for advocacy, and a CR framework provided a helpful foundation.

The lack of independent and collective agency on the part of farmers has contributed to a controversial role switch. Historically, going back over a century, urban intellectuals have played a leading and inducing role in agrarian movements.[6] Already during the EU accession, individual expert efforts shaped the law harmonisation process; luckily, these experts soon discovered the strategic importance of building up a more supportive legal framework for farmers. In our case, a cooperative network of qualified legal experts, researchers, activists and practitioners started to collaborate with smallholders to collect and interpret necessary information about issues hindering farmers in producing, processing and selling their products. These extended peer and stakeholder networks promoted the reception of our research findings, which thus better reached policy circles.

During this process, explicit and implicit forms of social agency have been created, such as the ability to organise and mobilise for a common cause, share know-how and experiences, and develop a coherent community and a joint agenda. During our meetings and workshops, we primarily needed to fuse expectations and clarify the motivational and operational differences between the team members. Co-creation in such a setting also required mutual recognition and acceptance of knowledge, interests and value differences (see Table 3.2). Mutual understanding for us meant positive social interactions that enable spaces for a shared and sympathetic attitude to each other, so that co-researchers can reinforce each other's role instead of hindering the collaboration. Furthermore, in this type of work (and especially during the process of developing the new smallholder decree), a division of labour became unavoidable. Co-researchers asked for a collection of policy practices from other countries that can help small-scale farmers with marketing and sales. Local practitioners adapted the collection, and civil society organisations then asked for the help of legal experts in introducing their suggestions and arguments for the consideration of political decision makers. This policy link proved to be decisive: beyond the mutual understanding of researchers and activists, we managed to operationalise a method of creating meaningful engagement with the policymaking process.

In essence, the whole process depended on how researchers and practitioners managed to co-create informal spaces for supporting each other through research: mutual visits in each other's offices, joint interviews, coffee with activists and representatives of the grassroots. The consortium meetings provided further spaces for reflection and feedback sessions. During these sessions, we honestly but appreciatively reflected upon the moments of difference and integration. This attitude helped us take stock of our learning experiences and the possible interventions they indicated. For our self-reflection, it was helpful that we kept a cooperative research diary for project notes and process-relevant observations. Based on these reflections, we re-designed the research from time to time to be more relevant to practitioners and policy change.

Table 3.2 Co-creation by activists and researchers

Cooperative (action) research phase	Collaboration modes between CSOs and researchers	Type of actionable knowledge	Reflection phase
Preparatory meetings and workshops	exchanging expectations on the process clarifying collaboration capabilities and actors' roles	focus on change and fusion of potential contributions clarification of the need and place of reflective and self-reflective phases	defining and creating a sense of ownership of the outputs building a systematic and mutually meaningful process
Problem-focused research	organising qualitative interviews and document analysis in activist-researcher pairs holding workshops to process and analyse interviews	identification of issues of high relevance to knowledge holders problem catalogue and policy solutions	extending (opening up) the policy understanding of the issue
Petition started by Védegylet	involving a practitioner as knowledge broker issuing a joint declaration that hooks in food movement actors utilising a bottom-up network with stakeholders involved in varied professional and informal events	identification of change agents – participants who support the smallholder decree policy reform	summarising central insights from the network building
Press release	coordinating email exchanges with various stakeholders to endorse the policy reform ideas co-designing an advocacy campaign launched by the CSOs	support, acknowledgement and media attention assured buy-in the campaign to gather online contributions from citizens groups	fostering public understanding and acknowledgement of small-scale farmers issues evaluating media interviews
Workshop on the future visions of the food system in Hungary	identifying stakeholders and crowdsourcing information	the urgency of food governance a shared understanding of the text of the smallholder decree policy reform	completing and consolidating the policy reform text transmitting the final text to the ministry
Comparative analysis of CR cases in partner countries	division of labour in data processing and analysis	co-designed policy brief on the significance of the issue	producing a policy report on case studies of alternative agro-food networks in the EU

The mixture of farmers' lack of capacity, researchers' traditional role repertoires and grassroots food activism was not a natural one, and required flexibility in the process design. The cooperative research project needed to gradually and organically become more and more invitational to a growing number of participants. Reflection phases in the process were necessary to reach flexible outcomes. The resulting collaborative network has very elastic rules of internal and external governance, primarily triggered by occasional connections with decision makers, mostly upon critical policy issues. Activist or researcher partners as co-researchers mostly shared the role of process facilitator, and this arrangement was well received by stakeholders during the various phases of the collaboration.

Outreach events and green niche initiatives facilitated the building of a further component of social agency. Activists began developing personal experiences in international arenas (e.g. the International Year of Family Farming, the Nyéléni Europe Forum for Food Sovereignty, Erasmus projects), and could be of significant help in inducing further transformation in Hungary. Over the course of the cooperative research, we have also seen a growing number of activists and practitioners engage in challenging or protesting the mainstream food systems from their own alternative niches. Some organised food banks or food aid projects; others created their eco-agri-food initiatives, consumer awareness-raising campaigns, home restaurants (Lakásétterem – www.lakasetterembudapest.hu) or slow food events (www.slowfood.hu), in addition to similar community-based food projects, all of which, in their limited outreach, demonstrated the resistance of the dominant food system to radical change. This phenomenon points to the often-neglected role of the consumer-citizens: any transformative change in the Hungarian agro-food sector can only occur if there is a robust demand by the broader society for local produce and artisanal origin products.

Such initiatives and events also enabled social actors to explore and identify policy innovations and discover successful ways of supporting sustainable agriculture and food production. Participating in such networks or at international fora could be a primary occasion for getting involved and engaging in dialogue about smallholder-related issues, as well as observing well-functioning collaboration among organisations from other countries.

An essential outcome of the cooperative research project was the introduction of a process that led to an advocacy campaign launched by 53 CSOs for the modification of the smallholder decree. The results successfully shaped several legal modifications. The decree for small producers incorporated all of the issues relating to small-scale production, manufacturing, hygiene, trade, control and certification. The first regulation adopted by the Hungarian Ministry of Agriculture and Rural Development jointly with the Ministries of Health and Social Affairs and Employment in 2006 (Nr. 14/2006, II.16) was explicitly created to loosen food hygiene conditions, but only for natural persons producing and selling products in small quantities. The 2010 amendment to the regulation increased the permitted selling quantities, and allowed small-scale producers living in any part of the country to sell their products in the capital. The 2010 decree is more favourable for small farmers and enables them to take full advantage of the continued use of traditional methods at any stage of the production, processing or distribution of food, as specified by the regulations on food hygiene.

Parallel to this achievement, the Public Procurement Act, which previously hampered local sourcing through the prevalence of the lowest price principle, has also been amended (Act CVIII of 2011 on Public Procurement). Farm products such as cold foodstuffs and raw cooking materials, fresh and processed vegetables and fruits, milk and dairy products, cereals, bread and bakery products, honey, eggs and horticultural plants are now exempt from the procurement process up to the EU threshold limit. As a result, much more flexible local food sourcing became possible.

Finally, to help direct sales, the local farmers' markets came under regulation with the 2005 Trade Law, enabling small-scale producers (kistermelők) to sell their produce within the county, or in a 40 km radius of the market, or in Budapest. Further regulations in 2012 redefined the required legal procedures to start a market, mandating a simplification of the notification process and of the hygienic restrictions. Administrative burdens on small and family farm businesses are still very high (with obligations to issue an invoice, pesticide-use logbook, sales logbook, manufacturing data sheet, documentation of the cold chain, and so on) (Benedek and Balázs, 2016).

In essence, the top-down policy processes under the framework of the New Agricultural and Rural Development Strategy 2020 opened a window of opportunity for long-neglected reform initiatives coming from the alliance of civic food networks. Exemptions and flexibility rules have been introduced successfully, according to the production method and sales contexts, favouring local food systems and direct marketing. Hungarian policymaking proved to be willing to answer the call phrased by the actors of the originally bottom-up local food movement. The Hungarian Rural Development Programme launched a thematic sub-programme on the development of local food systems and short food chains to contribute to the implementation of the Multiannual Financial Framework 2014–2020 of the EU.

Conclusions on criticality and relationality

A primary lesson from our cooperative research project on the level of substance is that a transformative agency that could create a new narrative on food democracy is not inherently linked to any of the actors. It can rather be traced in the linkages, the trust-based relations, of multiple actors. Neither government actions nor business or grassroots innovations alone can have transformative agency. The project highlighted that only by connecting these different actors and pathways for reform can we spark lasting food systems transformation. CR has built up elements of this linkage.

An additional realisation is that it is not enough any more merely to critique the mainstream food system and agri-food practices; what is needed is to co-create visions of prospective or emerging alternative and practices. Therefore, we assisted in building a co-created bank of evidence and knowledge base, which proved a potent source for policy change in the Hungarian food policy domain. Practices have changed towards more collaboration in research, civic activism and policymaking. Cooperative engagement has influenced the academic and CSO partners involved, contributed to a change in the social movement for sustainable food systems in Hungary, and resulted in a specific policy change for improving economic opportunity for smallholder farmers in Hungary.

The cooperative inquiry established a capable and dynamic approach for institutionalising collaborative engagement between academic researchers and CSO practitioners when there is a common concern, and shared interests and co-responsibility to change existing practices and structures. The open and inclusive process of knowledge generation, led by a team of academic and CSO partners, gained legitimacy in the eyes of other civic organisations, and, eventually, in the policymaking domain. The partnership of academic and CSO actors successfully utilised the window of opportunity to make a dent in the existing hegemonic structures of the Hungarian agro-food policy domain.

In particular, CR proved to be helpful in incorporating different systems of knowledge into the knowledge generation process. In this way it gave voice to small-scale farmers who have been systematically left out of previous policy processes. It taught us that vulnerable groups such as small-scale farmers do not even have proper representation. The jointly planned interviews with them and scenario exercises with all other stakeholders provided an evidence base for civic advocacy by creating new arguments for meaningful dialogue with authorities and policy planners. The scenarios exercise on the level of substance was not a revelation; on the process level, however, the visions imply that local food is a real entry point for most stakeholders to think about the future of the agro-food system. The cooperative research project also pointed out the deficiencies in food governance in Hungary: the research and the advocacy campaign process substituted for missing capacities on the government side and helped to provide an actionable evidence base for policy change. The process uncovered how the EU regulatory framework could be best approached by local stakeholders to protect local food system developments. The upstream engagement of local actors empowered and supported the bottom-up civic advocacy network to represent the interests of marginalised stakeholder groups; while never a smooth or unambiguous process, the net result was measurably positive for Hungarian smallholders, both procedurally, building democracy, and substantively, reforming policy.

Acknowledgement

This chapter is based on research carried out as part of the Facilitating Alternative Agro-Food Networks: Stakeholder Perspectives on Research Needs (FAAN) and Transformative Social Innovation Theory (TRANSIT) projects, both funded by the European Union's Seventh Framework Programme (FP7). The authors are grateful to the co-researchers in these projects: Csilla Kiss, Bori Simonyi and Anna Korzenszky.

Notes

1 Founded in 1993, LVC is an international movement of peasants, with 186 member organisations in over 70 countries, and fights for agrarian reform within the framework of food sovereignty.
2 The Confédération Paysanne Européen, was created in 1986, and as initiated by 18 organisations from 11 countries, including both countries that later became EU members and others that didn't. In 2008, CPE decided to join the global movement LVC, and changed its name to European Coordination of La Via Campesina (ECVC). Thus, ECVC is an umbrella for peasant organisations wanting to join the work of LVC.
3 Fiatal Gazdák Magyarországi Szövetsége – AGRYA (Hungarian Association of Young Farmers), Magán-Erdőtulajdonosok és Gazdálkodók Országos Szövetsége (National Association of Private Forest Owners and Managers), Magyar Bérkilövő és Független-Vadásztársaságok Országos Szövetsége (Association of Independent Hunting Organisations), Magyar Kertészek Egyesülete (Association of Hungarian Gardeners), Magyar Termelői Értékesítő és Szolgáltató Szervezetek/Szövetkezetek Együttműködése – HANGYA (Association of Producer and Sales Cooperatives), Mezőgazdasági Gazdasági Társaságok Szövetsége (Association of Agricultural Cooperatives), Magyar Parasztszövetség (Hungarian Peasant Union), Magyar Erdőgazdák Szövetsége (Association of Hungarian Foresters), Magyar Kis- és Középbirtokosok Egyesülete (Association of Small- and Medium-Sized Farms) and Biokultúra Egyesület (Association of Organic Farmers).
4 These include e.g. the Kisléptékű Termékelőállítók és Szolgáltatók Országos Érdekképviseletének Egyesülete – hereafter Kisléptét (National Association of Interest Representations for Small-Scale Producers and Service Providers), Védegylet, Szövet (Alliance for the Living Tisza), Tudatos Vásárlók Egyesülete (Association of Conscious Consumers), Greenpeace Hungary, and Magyar Természetvédők Szövetsége (Association of Hungarian Nature Defenders – the Hungarian branch of Friends of the Earth).
5 The final policy proposal can be accessed here: www.foodlawment.hu/downloads/kistermelok.pdf (in Hungarian).
6 A predecessor of Magosz was established in 1896 by Count Sándor Károlyi, the pioneer of Hungarian cooperatives and unions, and the agriarian Marxist uncle of Mihály Károlyi, the 'red Count', Prime Minister and President of the short-lived First Hungarian Republic in 1918–1919.

References

Balázs B (2012) Local food system development in Hungary. *International Journal of Sociology of Agriculture and Food* 19(3): 403–421.
Balázs B, Pataki G and Lazányi O (2016) Prospects for the future: community supported agriculture in Hungary. *Futures* 83: 100–111.
Balázs B, Bela G, Bodorkós B, Milánkovics K and Pataki G (2005) Preserving bio- and socio-diversity through Participatory Action Research. *Living Knowledge: International Journal of Community Based Research* 5: 11–13.
Balázs B, Bodorkós B, Bela G, Podmaniczky L and Balázs K (2009) Multifunctional farming and survival strategies in the Borsodi floodplain. In: A Piorr and K Müller (eds.) *Rural landscapes and agricultural policies in Europe*. Berlin and Heidelberg: Springer, 285–305.
Balázs B, Bertényi G, Králl A, Pintér L and Strenchock L (2015) Green niche-innovations in the Hungarian agro-food system. *Pathways Project*.
Bauler T, Mutombo E, van Gameren V, Paredis E, Crivits M, Boulanger P-M, Lefin A-L and Ruwet C (2011) Construction of scenarios and exploration of transition pathways

for sustainable consumption patterns. Final Report Phase 2. Brussels: Belgian Science Policy.

Benedek Z and Balázs B (2016) Current status and future prospect of local food production in Hungary: a spatial analysis. *European Planning Studies* 24(3): 607–624.

Bodorkós B and Pataki G (2009) Local communities empowered to plan? Applying PAR to establish democratic communicative spaces for sustainable rural development. *Action Research* 7: 313–334.

Dries L, Reardon T and Swinnen JF (2004) The rapid rise of supermarkets in Central and Eastern Europe: implications for the agrifood sector and rural development. *Development Policy Review* 22(5): 525–556.

Irwin A (2008) STS perspectives on scientific governance. In: Hackett EJ (ed.) *Handbook of science and technology studies*, Cambridge, MA: MIT Press, 583–607.

Jámbor A and Sirone Varadi J (2014) 10 years of EU membership: winners and losers in the agri-food sector of the new member states. In: European Association of Agricultural Economists (EAAE) International Congress, Ljubljana, Slovenia, 26–29 August.

Jansik C (2000) Foreign direct investment in the Hungarian food sector. *Hungarian Statistical Review* 78: 78–104.

Jehlička P and Smith J (2011) An unsustainable state: contrasting food practices and state policies in the Czech Republic. *Geoforum* 42(3): 362–372.

Juarez P, Balázs B, Trentini F, Korzenszky A and Becerra L (2015) WP4 Case study report: La Via Campesina. TRANSIT Deliverable 4. Grant agreement no. 613169.

Juhász A and Wagner H (2013) An analysis of Hungarian agri-food export competitiveness. *Studies in Agricultural Economics* (Budapest) 115(3): 150–156.

Karner S (ed.) (2010) Local food systems in Europe: case studies from five countries and what they imply for policy and practice. FAAN report. Graz: IFZ.

Karner S and Chioncel N (2010) The co-production of knowledge about alternative agrofood networks: experiences of involving civil society organisations (CSOs) in 'cooperative research'. Paper for Workshop 'Cooperative Research with CSOs for sustainable development: reflecting on experience'.

Kiss Cs, Simonyi B and Balázs B (2008) Alternative agri-food networks in Hungary. Policy environment and socio-historical context. In: Vadovics E and Gulyás E (ed.) *Sustainable consumption in Hungary, conference proceedings*, Budapest, Hungary: Corvinus University, 76–84.

Kneafsey M, Venn L, Schmutz U, Balázs B, Trenchard L, Eyden-Wood T and Blackett M (2013). Short food supply chains and local food systems in the EU. A state of play of their socio-economic characteristics. JRC Scientific and Policy Reports no. 25911 EN. Joint Research Centre Institute for Prospective Technological Studies, European Commission.

Korompai A, Szabó M and Nováky E (2017) Supporting the absorbent national rural development planning by scenarios. *European Countryside* 9(3): 416–434.

Málovics G, Mihók B, Szentistványi I, Balázs B and Pataki Gy (2012) Participatory action research for local human rights – the case of Roma minority in Szeged, South-Hungary. In: Renn O, Reichel A and Bauer J (eds.) *Civil society for sustainability: a guidebook for connecting science and society*, Bremen: EHV, 149–170.

Reason PE (1994) *Participation in human inquiry*, Thousand Oaks, CA: SAGE Publications.

Schermer M, Renting H and Oostindie H (2010) Collective farmers' marketing initiatives in Europe: diversity, contextuality and dynamics. *International Journal of Sociology of Agriculture and Food* 18(1): 1–11.

Smallholder Decree No. 52 of 2010 of the Ministry of Agriculture and Rural Development on the conditions of food production, processing and marketing by small-scale producers. Available from: www.fao.org/faolex/results/details/en/c/LEX-FAOC114670/

Stirling A (2006) From science and society to science in society: towards a framework for co-operative research. Project Report. European Commission Directorate General for Research.

Stirling A (2008) 'Opening up' and 'closing down' power, participation, and pluralism in the social appraisal of technology. *Science, Technology, and Human Values* 33(2): 262–294.

Wittmayer JM and Schäpke N (2014) Action, research and participation: roles of researchers in sustainability transitions. *Sustainability Science* 9(4): 483–496.

World Economic Forum (2017) *Shaping the future of global food systems: a scenarios analysis*, Geneva: World Economic Forum.

Co-inquirer reflection

Csilla Kiss and Borbála Sarbu-Simonyi

In this article, we reflect on the insights into effective university-CSO partnerships of the FAAN project in which we participated a decade ago. One of us, Csilla, now works in a group called People's Knowledge (www.peoplesknowl edge.org) at the Centre for Agroecology, Water and Resilience at Coventry University (UK) where we think critically about participatory and engaged research. The other, Borbála, has become an organic farmer, running a small-scale agro-tourism business in southwestern Hungary.

Both authors became involved in FAAN as community workers at Védegylet, a Hungarian non-profit organisation advocating for sustainable food systems. Both took part in different capacities: Borbála researching policies linked to the smallholder-decree; Csilla examining alternative agro-food networks (AFFNs) as case studies. ESSRG invited us to become their CSO counterpart in the project, presented as cooperative research, which was a new concept for us. This configuration was intended to ensure that research addresses the needs of grass-roots organisations and is socially more relevant.

We accepted the invitation because we were already engaged on the project's themes and had established a relationship of trust with ESSRG researchers. We had collaborated previously and we shared a vision of the importance of active citizen engagement in shaping food and agriculture systems along food sover-eignty and agroecology principles.

Examining the researcher-CSO dynamic

The project was initiated by the researchers who took the strategic decisions at the consortium level, including the choice of research questions. These focused on the links between policy and practice and, specifically, on AFFN develop-ment strategies. Researchers had ultimate responsibility for analysing findings across countries, and ensuring these fitted into a coherent scientific framework. They also selected the research methods. This posed a challenge for us as we were unfamiliar with the methodological options available. At the European level, mechanisms and tools for collective learning were introduced through focused conversations at consortium meetings and by maintaining a cooperative research diary for project notes and process-relevant observations by researchers.

At the time the relevance of these means for iterative learning were less obvious for the two of us.

At the national level, partners' tasks were complementary. As the Hungarian CSO counterpart, we selected specific national policies for investigation. Our academic-CSO research team agreed that the smallholder-decree was critical and that bottom-up mobilisation for amending the decree in favour of smallholders was gaining momentum. As CSO partners we also had a say in the choice of AFFNs selected as local case studies. We contacted these networks after the project began. Moreover, we could choose the research tasks that we felt most comfortable with and wanted to be involved in at the national level. However, partly because of the focus on changing the decree, we paid less attention to collective learning cycles within our CSO-academic research team in Hungary. With hindsight, journaling and regular meetings to share and co-analyse our findings as we went along – in terms of content and process – would have been beneficial. This would have given the whole research team an integrated view of how our research on policy and local case studies was unfolding and connected and, if necessary, to take collective decisions on re-aligning research with emerging priorities, including those of grassroots organisations.

CSO outcomes: advocacy and learning

Prior to FAAN, Védegylet and other CSOs were already engaged in analysing the policy environment affecting small farmers in Hungary, advocating in their favour, and supporting grassroots initiatives on sustainable food systems. The project fed into this process, strengthening our efforts. It provided additional resources for more structured and focused research as part of a wider program. It helped us navigate a complex web of legislation impacting smallholders in Hungary. The research deepened our knowledge, allowing us to highlight existing contradictions and identify critical issues to address. It enabled us to bring together a wider network of civil society and farmers' organisations, professional bodies and governmental agencies, to facilitate focused debates and collectively craft a set of recommendations – backed by research findings – to amend the smallholder-decree.

If we were to start again this research and learning process, we would revise our involvement in several ways. We would look more into what cooperative research entails and discuss this approach in-depth at the outset with the academic research partner and grassroots organisations. We would seek to include grassroots organisations in the project design process and discuss research questions with them. Broadening our vision of social impact beyond the aim of amending the smallholder-decree, we would also seek to collectively identify key cycles in the research process when collective learning, including the co-production of knowledge, co-interpretation and co-validation of research findings, can take place. We would strive to put these principles into action extending the iterative action-reflection cycles to all co-inquirers, CSO and academic, and at all levels: grassroots, national and European.

In conclusion, this cooperative research was mutually beneficial, strengthened the inquiry and led to important outcomes. Our active participation in and support to grassroots initiatives enabled us to facilitate researchers' access to AFFNs as case studies. At the same time, scientific backing appeared to increase our credibility in the eyes of policymakers, adding political weight to our ongoing advocacy. The collaboration was imperfect, as most projects are, but led to important outcomes for the academics and CSOs involved, as well as for some grassroots initiatives. The process of reflecting, debating and sharing these dynamics are a critical part of improving practices and developing robust and effective approaches to cooperative and participatory research. In this respect various traditions and approaches (PKEC, 2017; Tuhiwai Smith, 2012) can be useful for researchers in academia and CSOs to deepen participation, decolonise methodology and address uneven power dynamics.

Acknowledgements

Csilla is grateful for discussions with Iain MacKinnon, Colin Anderson, Michel Pimbert and Tom Wakeford from CAWR on participatory processes in research. Their insights have helped to inform her reflections on the FAAN project and the framing of this article.

PKEC [People's Knowledge Editorial Collective] (eds.). (2017). Everyday Experts: How people's knowledge can transform the food system. *Reclaiming Diversity and Citizenship Series*. Coventry: Coventry University. Available from: www.coventry.ac.uk/everyday-experts.

Tuhiwai Smith, L. (2012). Decolonising methodologies: research and Indigenous peoples. Zed Books, London.

4   Transition scientivism

On activist gardening and co-producing transition knowledge 'from below'

Shivant Jhagroe

Introduction: producing transition knowledge

Since the early 2000s, different knowledge regimes have emerged to address the impact of climate change, ecological deprivation and socio-economic inequality. 'Transition knowledge' has recently gained popularity in diagnosing current crises and understanding how sustainable transformative change might occur in various domains (Markard *et al.*, 2012). Developing transition knowledge was not only an intellectual but also an instrumental endeavour. The Dutch department of Housing, Spatial Planning and Environmental Protection authorised a study to explore how contemporary environmental concerns around biodiversity, climate change and acidification could be addressed through efforts for systemic change (cf. Kemp and Rotmans, 2009). The scholars, who explored these issues were supported in developing applicable frameworks, ultimately to understand and govern 'system innovations' and 'transitions' directed at tackling a number of environmental concerns. The intersection between academic endeavours and real-world policy concerns turned out to be fruitful, especially in the domains of energy, agriculture and mobility. The role of academic transition knowledge is not neutral (Kern, 2009). As Shove and Walker (2008: 1014) argue, transition management is not simply about "dynamic evolution" and "selection" but concerned with "boundary making and definition". Transition knowledge has been translated and applied in significantly differing contexts. As Audet (2014: 14) shows, there are opposing transition discourses that refer to transformative change in the field of global environmental politics, most notably: (1) a "radical-ecocentrist transition discourse"; and (2) a "managerial-technocentric transition discourse". Even though both discourses are committed to similar concerns, their procedures and technical tools differ widely.

Producing whose transition knowledge?

The ways in which transition knowledge is (co-)produced and employed is particularly interesting in the context of activist bottom-up transition initiatives around decarbonisation and de-growth. Here, it seems, there are clearly different ways of operationalising and utilising the notion of transition knowledge, compared to academic transition concepts as developed and applied via policy-science networks. Practices of mediation between academic transition research and more activist bottom-up knowledge are typical starting points for engaged scholarship and action research (Geels *et al.*, 2016). So far, action research in the context of sustainability transitions has done important work to disclose why the performative role of the researcher, as a participatory co-producer of knowledge, is critical in challenging hegemonic systems and experimenting with alternative systems of production and consumption. Action researchers play a key role as 'epistemic brokers' or 'epistemediators' (Wiek, 2007), in mediating between different forms of knowledge and perspectives. Knowledge negotiation and co-production is crucial in the context of transformative niche-regime dynamics. In negotiating different knowledge claims, there is a politics and inherent normativity that requires further exploration.

The objective of this contribution is to examine how action research can play a role in accommodating and co-producing counter-hegemonic knowledge. Importantly, I argue, this moves beyond action research as a broker that "acknowledges multiple ways of knowing and incorporates normativity and ethics" (Wittmayer and Schäpke, 2014), but acknowledges that knowledge regimes are inherently unequal and hierarchical, justifying more critical forms of knowledge (co-)production (Schostak and Schostak, 2008; Kemmis *et al.*, 2013). To clarify, I do not disagree with work done in the field of transition informed action research, but I problematise and build on the aspect of knowledge mediation and co-production. Transition research as well as action research share – at least potentially – a deeply critical quality that seeks to dismantle hegemonic knowledge regimes and experiment with more sustainable and socio-environmentally just forms of knowing and acting. The guiding question of this chapter is formulated as follows: *how can action research co-produce counter-hegemonic knowledge in the context of sustainability transitions?*

The chapter is structured as follows. Section 2 briefly reviews literature in the fields of transition research and action research, zooming in on how they deal with hegemonic and counter-hegemonic knowledge. It discusses how both transition and action research can indeed be understood as a form of counter-hegemonic knowledge (co-)production. Section 3 builds on these insights and proposes a heuristic, which is called *transition scientivism*. Transition scientivism is presented as a navigational tool for action research practices aimed at (co-)producing counter-hegemonic knowledge. This action research approach reframes four roles of researchers described by Wittmayer and Schäpke (2014): knowledge broker, change agent, reflective scientist and self-reflexive scientist. This new heuristic allows for more critical forms of transformative action research centred on knowledge (co-)production against the grain by 'radicalising' action researcher's roles to some extent. Section 4 presents my action research practices and how hegemonic and counter-hegemonic knowledge is negotiated in an initiative of Transition Towns Rotterdam (The Netherlands) called the Gandhi-garden. It illustrates my action research work with sustainability-inspired citizens, who criticise hegemonic food and economic (knowledge) regimes, and who explore and employ alternative forms of knowledge. Section 5 then returns to the transition scientivism heuristic to reflect on my roles as a critical action researcher. Here, the difference becomes clear between acting as transition scientivist or engaging in more pragmatic and consensus-oriented relational action research. Section 6 concludes with some reflections on the strengths and weaknesses of transition scientivism.

This chapter combines the relational and critical framework (as outlined in the introductory chapter) by foregrounding two key dimensions, namely challenging hegemonic knowledge and multiple roles and relationships of the action researcher. Regarding the underlying critical-relational framework, it becomes clear that critical action research aspects are linked to my focus on the 'counter-hegemonic', whereas the relational action research aspects resonate with embedded (co-)production of alternative knowledge.

Counter-hegemonic traits in transition research and action research

Hegemonic power and knowledge production go hand in hand. As for instance illustrated by Michel Foucault, the 'criminal' and the 'insane' are figures that have been produced by specific forms and processes of problematising, isolating and knowing them. This knowledge production process allows for governable subjects. A different example is 'statistical knowledge' about 'the population', which has been invented and employed in the nineteenth century to address (urbanisation) issues of mortality, hygiene and economic welfare. One could argue that the same holds for producing knowledge about 'energy markets', 'traffic flows' and 'consumer behaviour'. These types of knowledge are not neutral or a priori, but (re)produced via specific ways of defining, categorising and calculating social life (cf. Foucault, 1980). Therefore, calling into question such hegemonic forms of knowing, radically disrupts ways of knowing, classifying and calculating certain phenomena. It goes against the grain of 'normal' knowledge production, either economic, social or scientific knowledge. At the same time, 'counter-hegemonic' knowledge production can reinvigorate forgotten knowledge and 'counter-memory', or experiment with hegemonic knowledge by subverting and rearticulating it (Howarth, 2010). Producing counter-hegemonic knowledge thus is a double movement, it is critique on 'normal' knowledge, and experimentation with 'alternative' knowledge.

Counter-hegemonic transition research

In the domain of 'normalised' academic transition knowledge (expressed in Transition Management, Strategic Niche Management, Multi-Level-Perspective and Technological Innovation Systems, cf. Markard *et al.*, 2012), specific types of knowledge about systemic change are highlighted, revolving around technical, social and governance issues. Some critics have noted that dominant transition theories, such as Transition Management, fit into existing post-political, consensus-driven collaborative learning over struggle and conflict (Shove and Walker, 2008; Kenis *et al.*, 2016). Dominant transition theories seem to avoid transition analysis in terms of critical analysis of power struggles. However, transition research *can* be understood as inherently critical (Jhagroe, 2016). As mentioned by scholars that explore the critical potential of transition theory, it can be considered critical "in the sense that it aims to interrogate the dominant social structures of its time, and to envisage alternative development paths in cases where these dominant structures are held to be undesirable, or un*sustainable*" (Pel *et al.*, 2016: 453). Similarly, Geels mentions that critical theories do resonate with aspects of transition ontologies and key concepts, given its emphasis on power, conflict and struggle. Referring to classical critical scholarship, Geels notes that:

> Hegelian Marxists such as Gramsci (1932) argued that stability of the status quo not only comes from economic domination and state coercion, but also from 'hegemony', ideology and belief systems that make existing structures look 'natural' and prevent the emergence of new (class) consciousness.
>
> (Geels, 2010: 501)

In order to pursue alternative social and economic systems, strategic power struggles and coalitions are crucial in transition processes. Even though 'critical transition research' seems to be a quite marginal(ised) strand of transition research, a number of scholars utilises more critical concepts, methods and vocabularies that highlight regime/niche struggles associated with unequal distributions of power and legitimacy (Avelino *et al.*, 2016). Critical traits within academic transition knowledge can be traced in the field of bottom-up transitions and grassroots innovation. For instance, as Scott-Cato and Hillier (2010) argue, even though the global Transition Towns movement does not employ classical 'class analysis', they still pursue socio-ecological relations outside economic regimes and self-regulatory forms of finance (e.g. alternative currencies) and food (e.g. permaculture). The critical quality here refers to the persistent believe that "small acts of resistance and micro-transformation can destabilise macro systems and effect transformation of the system as a whole" (Scott-Cato and Hillier, 2010: 880). Similarly, Barr and Pollard (2017) unequivocally advocate that grass-roots transition initiatives can be understood in more critical terms than many societal and socio-technical transition scholars do, namely in terms of anti-capitalist and environmental activism underlying particular local spaces of transition.

This has implications for how we conceive of 'transition knowledge'. Regarding the role of transition knowledge in the domain of bottom-up transformations, some actors even call for "a complete overhaul of the existing institutions, while others call for their transformation or partial conservation at both local and higher levels (involving political engagement and academic research)" (Demaria *et al.*, 2013: 201). The intersection of political engagement and academic research is crucial for an engaged and critical action research in the domain of sustainability transitions.

Counter-hegemonic action research

Transition knowledge production via critical inquiry of contemporary systemic challenges and struggles resonates with the ambitions of action research (Ravetz, 2006; Wittmayer and Schäpke, 2014; Wittmayer *et al*. 2014). This is not the place to extensively review different traditions of action research. The most useful forms of action research in this context are *critical* (participatory) action research and *systemic* action research (Schostak and Schostak, 2008; Kemmis *et al*., 2013; Burns, 2007; Ison, 2017). Critical action research is highly valuable as it takes a bolder stance. As Kemmis, McTaggart and Nixon state (2013: 6):

> Critical participatory action research (…) rejects the notion of 'objectivity' of the researcher in favour of a very active and proactive notion of *critical self-reflection* – individual and collective self-reflection that actively inter-rogates the conduct and consequences of participants' practices, their under-standings of their practices, and the conditions under which they practice, in order to discover whether their practices are, in fact, irrational, unsustaina-ble or unjust.

It becomes clearer that this particular type of action research, as a methodo-logical basis, resonates with the engaged and critical quality of transition research. Complementing, critical action research, I argue, a more systemic mode of action research can transcend the risk of an *in situ* fixation. As Ison notes, "action research is transformed into systemic action research whenever those involved act, or strive to act, with epistemological awareness" (Ison, 2017: 283). Epistemological awareness, here, refers to the fact that "within systemic action research the 'researcher' understands and acts with awareness that they are part of the researching system of interest under co-construction, rather than external to it" (ibid.). Again, this more systemic-relational framing of action research as a research practice embedded in and co-producing systemic relations, can be linked to the systemic understandings of sustainable transformative change in transition research. Importantly, it adds to critical action research the more systemic dimension and reflexivity associated with transition research practices, without adhering to a consensus-oriented and deliberative orientation.

In sum, both transition research and action research have points of contact in terms of their critical traits that highlight challenging hegemonic systems of knowledge production, while staying open for experimentation and alternative forms of knowing.

Transition scientivism: a heuristic for counter-hegemonic knowledge (co-)production

Transition scientivism, as I conceive it, is a navigational tool for action research practices that (co-)produces counter-hegemonic knowledge. It builds on the insights discussed above from critical transition research and critical (and systemic) action research. It is instructive to more specifically build on current work in the field of transition informed action research, particularly, four roles of action researchers in the context of sustainability transitions, as described by Wittmayer and Schäpke (2014): 'knowledge broker', 'change agent', 'reflective scientist' and 'self-reflexive scientist':

1   *The knowledge broker*: the researcher accommodates different perspectives and knowledge claims aimed at an inclusive process and "solutions-oriented research" (ibid.: 488).
2   *The change agent*: as a change agent, the researcher accommodates experimentation and learning while trying to "to motivate and empower participants" (ibid.: 488–489).
3   *The reflective scientist*: this 'traditional' scientific role relates to producing "scientific knowledge in accordance with the quality criteria of their disciplines" (ibid.: 487–488) within the boundaries of scientific disciplines and academia.
4   *The self-reflexive scientist*: the researcher reflects on his/her own performative actions and normativity therein. The embeddedness of the researcher, as a co-knowledge producing subject, implies being "part of the dynamic that one seeks to change" (ibid.: 489).[1]

Whereas the role descriptions outlined by Wittmayer and Schäpke (2014) are very valuable and instructive, I argue that these descriptions tend towards advocating 'solution-oriented research'. Especially, challenging dominant structures and pursuing counter-hegemonic alternatives, seem to be represented to a lesser degree in solution-oriented and pragmatic action research. Critical scholarship go hand in hand with systemic critique and democratically informed academic activism (or scientivism). In terms of action research, knowledge production should always be an activity 'against the grain', i.e. countering hegemonic forms of knowledge and power. Calling into question dominant knowledge/power regimes implies foregrounding marginalised and silenced forms of sensing and knowing, e.g. system definitions, economic relations, methods for calculating environmental value. Below, the four roles are reframed and translated into more critical roles that more directly resonate with *critical* transition and action research.

Counter-hegemonic knowledge (co-)production via four roles

As any form of participatory action research, counter-hegemonic knowledge is produced together with other participants in very specific ways; in particular physical settings in conversation with each other, while discussing social issues, having a drink and just 'hanging out'. In other words, there are four concrete ways in which counter-hegemonic knowledge (co-)production can be understood, linked to the four roles briefly presented above.

A knowledge broker 'becomes' a counter-hegemonic knowledge broker. This shift is informed by the idea that knowledge regimes and claims are ordered hierarchically. Given that a scholarly ethics does not suggest only accommodating "multiple ways of knowing" (Wittmayer and Schäpke, 2014: 488), but justifies in particular marginalised and counter-hegemonic forms of knowing, the role of a knowledge broker is about a particular type of knowledge (co-)production. That is to say, counter-hegemonic knowledge (co-)production is not about including 'all perspectives equally', but especially challenging hegemonic perspectives and rendering visible, audible and knowable marginalised voices. This Rancière inspired ethics (Von Eggers, 2013) emphasises disrupting and subverting an unequal epistemic order that downplays the 'unheard, unseen and unknown' (degrowth economics, non-human suffering, underpaid and overworked sweat shop workers).

The role of a change agent moves into the direction of a more radical change agent. In concert with reframing the first role, a more radical change agent politicises issues deemed important by participants (such as clean air, social inequality and liveable spaces) addressing them in wider institutional and public settings. Even though this role description is more in line with how Wittmayer and Schäpke (2014) conceive of change agency than the role of knowledge broker, the 'radicalness' highlights problematisation instead of solution seeking. As Marcuse (2009: 194) argues, researchers that play a role as radical change agents should seek to: (1) *expose* (analysing and communicating root problems); (2) *propose* (working with the affected and oppressed to come up with programmes and strategies for change); and (3) *politicise* (clarifying the political implications of what was exposed and proposed). These activities can be related to the role of a 'non-radical change agent', but the addition of 'radical' basically underscores the focus on politicisation and emancipation, urging solution-driven notion like 'trust' and 'consensus' to take a backseat. This might be at the expense of being relational or pragmatic vis-à-vis dominant knowledge claims as an action researcher, but that is not the underlying aim of transition scientivism.

The role of the reflective scientist here does not merely conform to disciplinary norms as outlined by his/her peers. Quality criteria of any academic discipline have normalised over the years. As long as these 'quality criteria' allow for counter-hegemonic knowledge (co-)production, this would be no concern to me. However, often scientific quality in academia suggests that scholars are objective or abstain from 'becoming political' via the scientific method, as advocated by "positivist hegemony" operating in most social sciences (Wyly, 2010). Rather, a reflective scientist, in accordance with a transition scientivist starting point, engages in critical discussions with his/her peers about the extent to which prevailing research questions, concepts and (analytical) methods reproduce hegemonic (social, economic and political) knowledge. A more radical researcher, then, also experiments with counter-hegemonic forms of doing knowledge production, supported by a sense of urgency regarding the plethora of crises and particular critical theories and methods (Schostak and Schostak, 2008).

As a self-reflexive scientist, the normative agency of the researcher is acknowledged and reflected upon. Instead of mapping and reflecting on one's subjective interventions, e.g. employing a 'mirror metaphor', I think self-reflections are worthwhile, but can also be uncritical. Critical self-reflection adds critique by reflecting on how the 'I' was involved particularly in counter-hegemonic forms of writing, interviewing, conceptualising, observing, participating, reading, etc. This implies that instead of merely mapping and acknowledging the researcher's normativity (e.g. regarding the realisation of sustainable and just spaces), critical self-reflection assumes that the researcher already has assumed a normative stance, i.e. counter-hegemonic knowledge production in the domain of sustainability and socio-economic models, and that this specific normativity is being monitored and reflected on. Importantly, such a stance does not suggest an *a prior* format that is being pursuit, rather, there is much space for self-learning (Rauschmayer *et al.*, 2011). However, and taking seriously the feminist slogan that 'the personal is political', it also refers back to the individual researchers' own 'private life' that can be transformed in various ways in relation to the researcher's 'professional life'.

The Gandhi-garden in Rotterdam: gardening with a mission

After having presented the transition scientivism framework, this section presents an action research account of transition practices associated with the Gandhi-garden in Rotterdam. It particularly focuses on the types of activist activities and forms of knowledge Gandhi-gardeners employed. The empirical materials for this action research account are derived from policy documents, semi-structured interviews with different stakeholders and participatory observations (in 2013 and 2014, as part of my PhD research, see Table 4.1 and 4.2 for a list of interviews and field notes).

Situating Transition Towns Rotterdam

The Gandhi-garden is an urban community project that can be situated in the wider context of Transition Town (TT) Rotterdam. TT is a global movement that seeks to innovate and reinvent contemporary social and ecological life in various

Table 4.1 Reframing roles for the transition scientivist

Role of action researcher	Pragmatic action researcher	Transition scientivism
Knowledge broker	*Including all perspectives equally*	*Foregrounding marginalised perspectives*
Change agent	*Emancipating participants by building trust pragmatically*	*Emancipate participants by politicising issues*
Reflective scientist	*Confirm the quality criteria of academic discipline*	*Challenge quality criteria of academic discipline*
Self-reflexive scientist	*Reflecting on own normative position*	*Reflecting on own counter-hegemonic research practices*

ways. The TT movement emerged in the early 2000s in the United Kingdom (UK). A number of UK initiatives started the first TT's (e.g. Kinsdale in Ireland, Brixton and Totnes in England). Since 2006, more and more TT's emerged inside and outside UK, with about 400 projects by late 2011 and over 2500 Transition initiatives in more than 40 countries in 2013.[2] Each initiative is unique in terms of its thematic focus, specific concerns and strategy, even though there are suggestions and tips to start 'your own TT' and even obtain an 'official TT status'.[3]

The TT initiative of Rotterdam began in the spring of 2009, when a number of people got together and talked about the emerging idea of "Transition Towns". As one of them put it: "Transition Town Rotterdam started with some beer on a balcony" (Interview TA). They discussed what Rotterdam was confronted with in terms of economic and environmental concerns and social deprivation. This small group then invited others whom they deemed interested to share and develop some ideas and set up projects addressing these challenges.[4] Among the participants were people affiliated with ecological associations and "environmentalist organisations". This group was inspired by the ideas of TT Totnes, tying in with more "local concerns". TT Rotterdam presents itself on the website as follows:

> Transition Town Rotterdam is a network of people and initiatives that cooperate in order to change Rotterdam into a healthy, resilient and lively city, hand in hand and neighbourhood by neighbourhood; a city that lives balanced with local natural resources; a resilient city that can absorb economic shocks; a city where everyone can feel at home in a local community and local nature; a city where children can inhale healthy air; learn how healthy food is produced and know that later they can provide their local community with life by honourable and meaningful work; in short, a city that sets an example for others and gives hope for the future.[5]

This somewhat romantic picture is linked to a strategy that combines "head, heart, hands". The combination of these aspects ensures cognitive and strategic thinking (head: diagnosing and reflecting on climate change, peak oil, resilience), while having a specific normative and affective orientation (heart: positive visions and celebrate), and a hands-on approach (hands: think global act local, bottom-up).[6] The group was backed by the local district government *Deelgemeente Noord* (Interview TB). The first initiative of TT Rotterdam was to create a small eco-friendly area in Rotterdam (at the *Bergwegplantsoen*) to engage in urban gardening with local residents and children, some of whom were physically challenged. Together, they have been growing herbs, plants, vegetables and fruit trees[7] (Interview TA; Interview TC; Municipality of Rotterdam, district North, 2014: 15).

Since 2009, a number of new initiatives have been taken up under the umbrella of TT Rotterdam. In total, eight gardens were created in Rotterdam including the Gandhi-garden (in Dutch: *Gandhituin*), a website was launched, biking tours along various urban gardens were organised for outreach purposes (Interview TD), movie nights and courses were organised, as well as local festivals and markets.[8]

The Gandhi-garden in Rotterdam

The *Gandhi-garden* is located in the North of Rotterdam near Rotterdam's belt highway (A20). As of 2011, the Gandhi-garden was supported by and legally anchored in a foundation, the Peace-Foundation (in Dutch: *Vredestichting*). Ever since, the Gandhi-garden welcomed everyone who wanted to work, harvest, cook, eat, relax and talk together. The Gandhi-garden website clearly articulates an additional vision:

> Furthermore, we provide extra space for people that need the land, and working on the land and its fruits, the most. In the future [after 2011, SJ], parts of the garden should provide space for reintegration projects, educational projects and the food bank.[9]

This ambition is directly informed by the work of Gandhi, as the initiators of the garden challenge the dominant economic order of the Netherlands and the Western world: "Only in an economy of exclusion, greed and overconsumption is there scarcity, poverty, extraction of natural resources and climate change".[10]

The Gandhi-garden presents itself as an urban community garden with a *social* ambition. The TT trinity of head, heart and hands illustrate this. In social terms, the "head" refers to the garden as an educational centre that offers courses and lessons to address e.g. poverty, urban gardening, economic approaches and ethical conduct. The "heart" frames the garden as a centre of life that welcomes all people, centre-stages gratitude and celebrates the bounty of nature. The "hands" articulate the garden in terms of working on the land (among other things) and donate vegetables and fruits to the needy (this also covers heart). Furthermore, the foundation is a quite formal structure that accommodates the garden (in terms of finances, official agreements, etc.), but everyone is considered as equal and decisions are taken democratically. Many, if not all, participants of the garden activities (a highly diverse group of people) accept the overall vision of the garden, are ecologically conscious and eat organic and local whenever possible.

Activism and solidarity via the garden

In order to understand what is at stake for many Gandhi-gardeners,[11] it should be clear that most activities are based on, or related to, critique of and alienation from dominant social, economic and cultural systems. This might sound abstract, but for most people I met this could not be more concrete.

A nice example of activism can be illustrated by my participation in the globally orchestrated March Against Monsanto 2013 (MAM).[12] This march was

Figure 4.1 Images of some Gandhi-garden activities.

organised near Rotterdam and took place in many cities in the Netherlands. It was co-organised by a number of people related to TT Rotterdam. This was an exciting experience, as people from all kinds of organisations joined the march (Fieldnote D). The police-escorted protest was directed against Monsanto, a big multinational that sells modified and patented seeds and plants. Many TT participants are critical of the practices and methods of Monsanto to commodify and control forms of life. Social outrage seems to flare up whenever Monsanto, for example, sues farmers that have "their seeds" on their land as a result of wind or moving cattle. Labelling life through property and capitalist greed were fiercely criticised, next to the selling of harmful chemical products by Monsanto. During the march, I was approached by what seemed citizen journalists to explain why I joined the March on camera. For me, this was a symbolic moment to choose between abstaining from actual visible and media involvement, and being fully engaged in the material activist practice I supported. Quite instinctively I decided to answer some of their questions, about why I believed it was important to speak out against Monsanto's profit-boosting practices and its impact on humans (poor farmers, polluted spaces) and non-humans (plants and crops). Interestingly, not all Gandhi-gardeners agreed with articulating social critique and protest as a strategy. Some argued that this was "the old world" and "old energy". Instead, attention should be focused on "positive" things (Interview TT). This incongruity symbolised an implicit disagreement about how 'radical' one should be and what types of strategies were considered as productive (Fieldnote F). Such discussions were sometimes held online, on Facebook's comments area. Interestingly, one of these discussions was about the "radicalness" of Professor Rotmans (my PhD supervisor) and the extent to which he advocated for a technology-based economy instead of a more "radical community based" transition. More symbolic forms of protest seemed to be less problematic, such as throwing 'seed bombs' on an old railroad. Such so-called "guerrilla" gardening events were organised with some action groups (Interview TE). Other types of critique and politicisations that were shared were more general and unapologetic critiques against capitalism, mass consumerism, the excessive use of material goods, and throwing away of food and material products. I spoke with many participants about their critiques (e.g. Fieldnote C; Fieldnote D; Fieldnote E; Fieldnote F). Some of them were generic and intuitive (Interview TF; Interview TG; Interview TT), while others were more intellectual and analytical (Interview TA; Interview TD; Interview TE; Interview TH; Interview TI). Despite these differences, they agreed on the socio-economic and environmental problems we face today. An interesting remark of one Gandhi-gardener was that "people are addicted to society", referring to the socio-psychological problem of materialist consumer culture (Fieldnote H). Gardening in this context was considered a symbolic form of resistance that improves one's health at the same time, indicated by the remark that "no gardener is fat, only their bosses are" (Fieldnote L).

In all instances, the suffering of people, animals, eco-systems and even 'the entire world' was considered worth fighting for. Solidarity with marginalised people and lives was (symbolically) expressed by e.g. donating produce to food banks. Elderly, children and disabled people were sometimes actively involved in gardening activities in order to seed, sow, cook and eat together (Interview TA; Interview TJ; Interview TP). This way, social solidarity with different social groups was cultivated. Similarly, many of the Gandhi-gardeners stretched their solidarity to trans-local and geopolitical struggles, such as poor distant farmers or Palestinian youth (Fieldnote G). The garden participated in an exchange project with Palestinian children from Gaza to pay attention to the importance of trees and nature (which has a significantly different meaning in Rotterdam than in Palestine). Interestingly, in their private lives, some participants were confronted with their activities by their families and friends e.g. why would you be vegetarian? Or, why do you do yoga? Despite these marginalisations, these people still explain their ideas and try to convince others why it seems important to e.g. safe energy or eating less meat (Interview TG; Interview TH). During my field work, I was also confronted with my own conduct, as I often used a car to drive to the Gandhi-garden. I live in The Hague and public transportation implied much longer travel times. This was something I struggled with as a (sometimes lazy) action researcher, as one Gandhi-gardener suggested that using a car was quite "a luxury" (Fieldnote M).

Transition knowledge 'from below' and alterative inspiration

I was regularly struck by the ways in which abstract concepts and transcendent forces were mobilised and referred to by many participants. For many Gandhi-gardeners, philosophy, spiritualism and energetic forces seemed to be a fruitful ground to diagnose social problems, to make sense of the world around them and "fuel" their passion for specific projects, initiatives and practices. In a number of instances, inspirational sources were not shared by everyone and were understood more pragmatically by others. Instead of mobilising explicit legal categories or political ideals, I picked up many inspirational sources. Many types of experience and knowledge were mobilised, not only a transition narrative of "peak oil and climate change", but also critical references to Gandhian thought, car-use, urban smog statistics, Karl Marx, Rousseau, ecological systems thinking, Sufism, Krishna consciousness, druid philosophy and other sources of knowledge (Fieldnote O).[13]

Gandhi's legacy and philosophy were particularly foregrounded. This was evident during a Gandhi exhibition and a Gandhi lecture series that were organised in the garden cabin (Fieldnote P; Fieldnote Q). Interestingly, some of these concepts and perspectives overlapped with the types of knowledge I used as a scholar, the institute I worked at (DRIFT) and associated bodies of knowledge. Multiple references to Professor Rotmans and DRIFT by some Gandhi-gardener made me realise that my knowledge was introduced before my presence. Interestingly, in one instance one of Professor Rotmans' books was experienced as inspiring, but also somewhat expensive. After a discussion on the insights of this book, it was sensible for me to present this book as a gift (Fieldnote R). Conceptual frames like complex systems, evolutionary thought, and forms of critical transition thinking were used by some more reflexive Gandhi-gardeners,[14] but this was often linked to very concrete practices, such as breathing techniques (*Pranayama*), using yoga for children and adults, but also of connecting ideas of the medical effects of some herbs related to the physical design of the Gandhi-garden. Such "pre-modern" (or rather "non-modernist") modes of knowing and inspiration are considered as useful alternatives in our society again. As one per-maculture gardener put it: "Many cultures have been detached from their own past (...) wisdoms from earlier days can be proven scientifically today"[15] (Inter-view TD). This participant also stated that: "Permaculture is just a design system which you can apply on all kinds of things, ranging from a peanut butter sand-wich to a society".[16] Interestingly, in 2012 the municipality of Rotterdam pub-lished an official 'strategic document' for urban farming called *Food and The City* (Municipality of Rotterdam, 2012). The document states that urban farming can also reduce 'food miles' and improve 'social cohesion' among its particip-ants.[17] This suggests that even though local authorities do not explicitly support permaculture as a principle for maintaining public green, urban farming and local food systems are accommodated to some extent.

Forms of 'forgotten knowledge' (e.g. permaculture) and animistic knowledge were presented to me in many ways. One telling experience was that one day we drank tea in the garden. There was a bee flying near us and then landed on the table. One of us tried to direct the bee to somewhere else, when the garden's beekeeper told us to stop and watch the bee (Fieldnote S). The bee seemed to become a symbolic object for an animist and spiritual experience, as bees were crucial and wonderful organisms that enabled plants, fruits and vegetables to breed and provide us with food. Such eco-frames and holistic experiences were not only derived from transcendent notions and spiritual thought. For some, gar-dening was linked to moral activism, namely producing food for the needy (e.g. via food banks). As someone put it: "One can say 100,000 times "allow me to provide service with love", which one can also actually do this in a garden"[18] (Interview TE). One of the most inspirational sources experienced by me (and many other participants), was simply working in the garden and gardening together. This is connecting the soil to the spirit in very satisfying ways. I even started with my own mini vegetable garden of one square metre in my private yard.

Transition scientivism at work: reflecting on Rotterdam's Gandhi-garden

I now return to the notion of transition scientivism as a navigational tool for action researchers to (co-)produce counter-hegemonic knowledge, and zoom in on the four roles of a transition scientivist. A number of issues and examples can be reflected on with regard to my roles as a transition scientivist.

The counter-hegemonic knowledge broker

During my action research work, I tried to make sense of the different forms of knowledge and inspiration that circulated in the Gandhi-garden. Some of these sources were literally similar to the concepts I used in my research, namely academic transition concepts informed by systems theory and governance thinking, even my supervisor was mentioned as an inspiring source. Other sources were linked to this type of 'transition knowledge', including socio-ecological resilience thinking, Gandhian philosophy of non-violence and more spiritual conceptions to understand societal structures and problems. In other instances, more specific and practical know-how was employed, such as permaculture knowledge to design the garden and sharing economy principles to share seeds and other 'goods'. Even though, as a 'broker', I did not facilitate multiple ways of knowing by organising workshops between e.g. Gandhi-gardeners, policy makers and local residents to expand the meaning and impact of the garden. However, my own (academic) knowledge production was limited to understanding specific forms of knowledge (sometimes totally unexpected to me) and reflecting with other participants on the similarities between conceptual, animistic, spiritual and political knowledge (in virtually all instances there were similarities). I considered this to be a network of heterogeneous knowledge sources that co-constituted each other's legitimacy. This local web of different knowledge claims, then, supported a broader epistemic repertoire to counter urban capitalist consumption culture, but also the lack of green spaces, and individualism in Rotterdam.

Significantly, the types of knowledge that were mobilised seem to alleviate the position of precarious human and non-human communities (poor residents, mentally disabled, urban eco-systems). Interestingly, to some extent, the urban gardening efforts of Gandhi-gardeners resonated with official government policy in terms of accommodating such a project to address food miles and social cohesion. I did not try to foreground the need to 'also include and accept' the perspective of hegemonic knowledge about e.g. agricultural farming and economic growth, as this was often discussed by and with different participants and was knowledge to be resisted and dismantled. So, as a transition scientivist, I tried to make sense of and discuss with other participants the diverging knowledge claims associated with a type of 'activist gardening' in Rotterdam.

The radical change agent

In relation to traversing counter-hegemonic knowledge as an action researcher, I played the role of change agent, at least in a minor way. As argued above, for a transition scientivist, this does not mean emancipation through dialogue and trust building, but via practices of systemic challenging and politicised struggle. Being a more 'radical' change agent can be exemplified by my participation in some of the activist practices of Gandhi-gardeners, such as joining the March Against Monsanto as well as my choice to speak to local citizen journalists about my participation. Furthermore, while interviewing policy makers in Rotterdam, I used the Gandhi-garden as an example that urban gardening meant more than sticking to policy objectives, since they aimed at experimenting with alternative economic models, urban farming networks, and forms of citizen-led urbanisation. Even though, I could not assess the extent to which my arguments were taken seriously, I tried to challenge a narrow definition of local urban gardening in policy settings. Despite my uncoordinated and small-scale 'interventions', as a more politicising change agent (Marcuse, 2009), I tried to avoid consensus-building with policy makers and other 'outside actors', but rather sought to frame urban gardening practices in terms of forms of environmental activism and democratic bottom-up urbanisation.

The critical-reflective scientist

Me being supportive of transition research as an inspiring field, while being critical towards some of its normative assumptions (see above), was quite an ambivalent position. My action research actually helped to clarify in what way I was critical. During gardening sessions and the many talks with gardeners it became much clearer why and how they/we pursued social change. As a young academic, I learned that I could not hide behind certain "neutral" scientific concepts and methods, given the stakes. My action research was embedded in the research institute I was working at (DRIFT, at the Erasmus University Rotterdam). DRIFT enjoys a very specific position within the university, as it seeks to explicitly combine practical sustainability-led project work with theoretical reflection and evaluation. However, despite this 'protected' academic space, within the broader social science disciplines related to my research practice (transition studies, sustainability science, governance studies) and their underlying 'quality criteria', I tried to employ concepts, methods and vocabularies that foster critical inquiry (Jhagroe and Loorbach, 2015; Jhagroe, 2016; Pel *et al.*, 2016; Avelino *et al.*, 2016). I would argue that critical analysis is in fact a marginal practice in the domain of sustainability transition research, in academic conferences, discussions and journals. Adopting a 'normal' (i.e. hegemonic) formalist scientific method and writing style often creates an aura of disengagement and neutrality. However, this is exactly the opposite of what I tried to do. As a transition scientivist, I, for instance, joined an activist March, worked with urban gardeners, helped with an exhibition on the legacy of Gandhi, and spoke out publicly against dominant models of economic growth and urban planning. My action research practices have also been translated in my analytical and writing practices. I have been trying to disclose the critical potential of action research in the domain of sustainability transition scholarship. Increasingly, I also consider part of my critical scholarship being outspoken about sustainability, democracy and (in)justice in different media outlets.

The critical self-reflexive scientist

Before stepping into the Gandhi-garden, I did not have the illusion that I was 'neutral' in any way. This became even more apparent when a Gandhi-garden participant told me to "never trust scientists", but that this comment was not a "personal" attack, but related to him being sceptical about dominant scientific knowledge about economic models and managing eco-systems. On a different day, while gardening and talking to other participants, one Gandhi-gardener suggested to me that I bring the deep knowledge of the garden "to the university". As if it was not already clear, my very presence and associated knowledge production was clearly normative. During the March against Monsanto, when I was confronted with being neutral and keeping distant, or being outspokenly critical, being normative or not was not the question, but being normative in what way. Abstaining from speaking out during that Monsanto March was also normative (based on a particular norm), but different than explaining why we were there, as protesting 'bodies on the street'. The boundary between my personal and professional research life, also seemed to blur, when I was given a small vegetable garden on my birthday by my family. They knew I was researching 'sustainability' and was into urban gardening for 'work' (which I experienced as satisfying and inspirational). What other way than putting 'into practice' what I was talking about all the time? Having made my own salads (now using home grown carrots, beets, red lettuce and herbs, as well as produce from the Gandhi-garden), this further inspired me to also discuss homegrown vegetables and gardening with friends and family (e.g. about agricultural systems, growth-based economics, and the politics of soil). My action research practices in the Gandhi-garden, thus, had consequences for my normativity and personal social life. However, at times, I found it difficult to be 'consistent', for instance when I used the car to go the garden instead of more time-consuming public transportation. Using a fossil-fuelled car, and buying groceries from a 'normal supermarket', do not sit well in relation to the socio-political ambitions of the Gandhi-garden (which I agreed with). So, my action research also confronted me with my own normative inconsistencies.

Concluding remarks

The guiding question of this chapter was: *how can action research co-produce counter-hegemonic knowledge in the context of sustainability transitions?* I proposed the notion of transition scientivism as a navigational tool to for action research guided towards counter-hegemonic knowledge (co-)production. This heuristic has been developed in conversation with critical transition research and critical action research. Transition scientivism, as critical action research, slightly reframes and rearticulates action researcher's roles in the domain of transition research (Wittmayer and Schäpke, 2014). An action research account of urban gardening in Rotterdam has been presented and reflected on, using a transition scientivist frame. In this concluding section, I briefly reflect on the question: what are the strengths and weaknesses of transition scientivism? What is the added value if one embarks on a journey as a transition scientivist?

On the one hand, I believe that my action research informed and inspired gardeners, as I perceive(d) it, as it helped them frame their complex position in terms of more 'systemic challenges' and a perspective on sustainable change through a deeper societal critique. In a way, I was (implicitly) supporting the Gandhi-garden by making sense of their activities using concepts of my own sustainability transition research. More specifically, my roles as an action researcher justified and accommodated – in different ways – the social change the community garden sought to achieve: via bodily work (during gardening sessions and demonstrations) and via discursive work (over talks and conversations about sustainable food systems and a more social economy, also during interviews with policy makers and other institutional actors). At the same time, the actual action research also inspired and taught me as an academic to be more outspoken and blunt regarding the critical potential of transition informed action research. The critical work associated with transition scientivism also confront action researchers with their own hegemonic beliefs and routines, e.g. regarding economic systems and urban planning. On the other hand, a transition scientivist clearly has a different value than action researchers that are more open to accommodating 'multiple perspectives' and building trust and coalitions. This pragmatic approach is backgrounded by more politicising practices that call into question hegemonic economic and social knowledge/power regimes. At the outset, the type of knowledge production that is co-produced and mediated by a transition scientivist is different than more pragmatic or dialogical-relational action research. Consequently, a key weakness is the lack of seeking consensus and coalitions among participants and 'outside actors'. However, since more explicit critical inquiry and scholarship is (still) marginal in the field of transition research, I argue that transition scientivism, as a bottom-up research practice of counter-hegemonic knowledge (co-)production, can complement dominant and consensus-oriented transition research. The potential of transition scientivism is its additional value to and critical perspective on emerging action research in the field of sustainability transitions.

Acknowledgements

The author would like to thank all Gandhi-gardeners for their openness, dedication and inspiration

Appendix

Table 4.2 Overview of interviews

Interview TA	Gandhi-gardener	9 July 2013
Interview TB	Politician, local governor	29 January 2014
Interview TC	Gandhi-gardener	16 October 2013
Interview TD	Member of Transition Towns Rotterdam, related to Gandhi-garden	15 January 2014
Interview TE	Gandhi-gardener	27 August 2013
Interview TF	Gandhi-gardener	6 January 2014
Interview TG	Gandhi-gardener	10 January 2014
Interview TH	Gandhi-gardeners	20 December 2013
Interview TI	Active citizen and professional, related to Gandhi-garden	3 January 2014
Interview TJ	Members Transition Town Rotterdam region	7 June 2013
Interview TT	Gandhi-gardener	Different moments during action research

Table 4.3 Overview of field notes

Fieldnote C	Transition Town Rotterdam (Gandhi-garden introduction)	28 May 2013
Fieldnote D	Transition Town Rotterdam (March Against Monstanto)	12 October 2013
Fieldnote E	Transition Town Rotterdam (workshop Facebook)	31 May 2013
Fieldnote F	Transition Town Rotterdam (discussion about Monstanto and activism)	4 June 2013
Fieldnote G	Transition Town Rotterdam (visit of Palestinian children)	4 June 2013
Fieldnote H	Transition Town Rotterdam (discussion about economy, society and politics)	9 June 2013
Fieldnote L	Transition Town Rotterdam (on gardening and health)	14 July 2013
Fieldnote M	Transition Town Rotterdam (on using car and luxury)	25 June 2013
Fieldnote O	Transition Town Rotterdam (discussion about Krishna consciousness)	25 June 2013
Fieldnote P	Transition Town Rotterdam (Gandhi exhibition)	11 September 2013
Fieldnote Q	Transition Town Rotterdam (Gandhi lecture series)	27 November 2013, 8 January 2014
Fieldnote R	Transition Town Rotterdam (on book Jan Rotmans)	14 July 2013
Fieldnote S	Transition Town Rotterdam (bee experience)	25 June 2013

Notes

1 The fifth role, i.e. of a 'process facilitator', is insufficiently meaningful for a counter-hegemonic action research compared to the other four.
2 Source: http://modernfarmer.com/2013/04/map-whos-living-off-the-grid.
3 See: www.transitionnetwork.org/support.
4 See: www.transitiontownrotterdam.nl/over-ons.
5 In Dutch:

> Transition Town Rotterdam is een netwerk van mensen en initiatieven die samen-werken om, hand in hand en wijk voor wijk, de stad te veranderen in een gezonde, veerkrachtige en levendige stad; een stad die, in evenwicht, leeft van lokale natu-urlijke hulpbronnen; een stad die door haar veerkracht economische schokken op kan vangen; een stad waar iedereen zich thuis kan voelen in de lokale gemeensc-hap en lokale natuur; een stad waar kinderen gezonde lucht inademen, leren hoe gezond voedsel verbouwd wordt en beseffen dat zij later met eerzaam en beteken-isvol werk voor hun gemeenschap kunnen voorzien in hun leven; kortom, een stad die een voorbeeld is voor anderen en hoop geeft voor de toekomst.
>
> (See: www.transitiontownrotterdam.nl/over-ons)

6 See: www.transitiontownrotterdam.nl/over-ons.
7 See images: www.youtube.com/watch?v=JDRWAO8IUVk.
8 See: www.transitiontownrotterdam.nl/initiatieven.
9 In Dutch:

> Daarnaast bieden we extra ruimte voor mensen die het land, het werk op het land en haar vruchten het meest nodig hebben. In de toekomst willen we op delen van de tuin ruimte bieden voor reintegratieprojecten, educatieprojecten en de voedselbank.
>
> (Translation SJ, www.gandhituin.nl/mappen/Over%20Ons/Over%20Ons.html)

10 In Dutch: "Alleen in een economie van uitsluiting, hebzucht en overconsumptie ontstaat schaarste, armoede, uitputting van natuurlijke hulpbronnen en klimaatverand-ering". Translation SJ, www.gandhituin.nl/mappen/Over%20Ons/Over%20Ons.html.
11 This is how I refer to *direct* participants of the Gandhi-garden.
12 See: www.march-against-monsanto.com.
13 Many Gandhi-gardeners looked for sources through books, but most used the Internet for self-study and making sense of things as they go.
14 I was struck by the creative ways in which some participants used knowledge and philosophy, such as linking Sufism with eco-systems theory, or linking Deleuze and Foucault to legal thought. Not only that, but these ideas informed some of their very material and physical practices and initiatives. Even though they were not 'official and institutionalised scholars', in practice they were doing engaged scholarship in a way I have rarely seen.
15 In Dutch: "Heel veel culturen zijn van hun verleden losgeraakt, (…) wijsheden van vroeger zijn nu gewoon wetenschappelijk te onderbouwen".
16 In Dutch: "Permacultuur is gewoon een ontwerpsysteem, die kun je alles toepassen dat je kunt ontwerpen, van een broodje pindakaas tot een samenleving".
17 The underlying approach and advice for his urban farming strategy is delivered by a so-called 'think thank urban farming' (Municipality of Rotterdam, 2012: 14). This think thank is comprised of local administrative bodies, programme bureau sustain-ability, agriculture experts, environmental agency and other organisations.
18 In Dutch: "Sta mij toe liefdevolle diensten te doen … dat kun je 100.000 keer roepen, maar je kunt het ook doen in een tuin".

References

Audet R (2014) The double hermeneutic of sustainability transitions. *Environmental Innovation and Societal Transitions* 11: 46–49.

Avelino F, Grin J, Pel B and Jhagroe SS (2016) The politics of sustainability transitions. *Journal of Environmental Policy and Planning* 18(5): 557–567.

Barr S and Pollard J (2017) Geographies of transition: narrating environmental activism in an age of climate change and 'Peak Oil'. *Environment and Planning A* 49(1): 47–64.

Burns D (2007) *Systemic action research: a strategy for whole system change*, Bristol: Policy Press.

Demaria F, Schneider F, Sekulova F and Martinez-Alier J (2013) What is degrowth? From an activist slogan to a social movement. *Environmental Values* 22(2): 191–215.

Foucault M (1980) *Power/knowledge: selected interviews and other writings, 1972–1977*, New York: Pantheon.

Geels FW (2010) Ontologies, socio-technical transitions (to sustainability), and the multi-level perspective. *Research Policy* 39(4): 495–510.

Geels FW, Berkhout F and van Vuuren DP (2016) Bridging analytical approaches for low- carbon transitions. *Nature Climate Change* 6: 576–583.

Howarth D (2010) Power, discourse, and policy: articulating a hegemony approach to critical policy studies. *Critical Policy Studies* 3(3–4): 309–335.

Ison R (2017) Systemic action research. In: *Systems practice: how to act*, London: Springer, 275–291.

Jhagroe SS (2016) *Urban transition politics: how struggles for sustainability are (re)making urban spaces*. Doctoral dissertation, Dutch Research Institute for Transitions (DRIFT).

Jhagroe SS and Loorbach D (2015) See no evil, hear no evil: the democratic potential of transition management. *Environmental Innovation and Societal Transitions* 15: 65–83.

Kemmis S, McTaggart R and Nixon R (2013) *The action research planner: doing critical participatory action research*, Springer Science and Business Media.

Kemp R and Rotmans J (2009) Transitioning policy: co-production of a new strategic framework for energy innovation policy in the Netherlands. *Policy Sciences* 42(4): 303–322.

Kenis A, Bono F and Mathijs E (2016) Unravelling the (post-)political in transition management: interrogating pathways towards sustainable change. *Journal of Environmental Policy and Planning* 18(5): 568–584.

Kern F (2009) *The politics of governing 'system innovations' towards sustainable electricity systems*. Doctoral thesis, Science and Technology Policy Research Department. Sussex: University of Sussex.

Marcuse P (2009) From critical urban theory to the right to the city. *City* 13(2–3): 185–197.

Markard J, Raven R. and Truffer B (2012) Sustainability transitions: an emerging field of research and its prospects. *Research Policy* 41(6): 955–967.

Municipality of Rotterdam, district North (2014) *Noord is Noord. Een Boekje Vol Inspiratie*, Rotterdam: Municipality of Rotterdam, district North.

Pel B, Avelino FR and Jhagroe SS (2016) Critical approaches to transitions theory. In: Brauch HG, Oswald Spring U, Grin J and Scheffran J (eds.) *Handbook on sustainability transition and sustainable peace*, Springer International Publishing, 451–463.

Rauschmayer F, Muenzing T, Frühmann J (2011) A plea for the selfaware researcher: learning from business transformation processes for transitions to sustainable development.

In: Rauschmayer F, Omann I, Frühmann J (eds.) *Sustainable development: capabilities, needs, and well-being*. London: Routledge, 121–143.

Ravetz JR (2006) Post-normal science and the complexity of transitions towards sustainability. *Ecological Complexity* 3(4): 275–284.

Schostak J and Schostak J (2008) *Radical research. Designing, developing and writing*, London: Routledge.

Scott-Cato M and Hillier J (2010) How could we study climate-related social innovation? Applying Deleuzean philosophy to transition towns. *Environmental Politics* 19(6): 869–887.

Shove E and Walker G (2008) Transition management and the politics of shape shifting. *Environment and Planning A* 40(4), 1012–1014.

Von Eggers MN (2013) Governmentality, police, politics: Foucault with Rancière. *Kulturrevolution* 64: 45–50.

Wiek A (2007) Challenges of transdisciplinary research as interactive knowledge generation. *Gaia* 16(1): 52–57.

Wittmayer JM and Schäpke N (2014) Action, research and participation: roles of researchers in sustainability transitions. *Sustainability Science* 9(4): 483–496.

Wittmayer JM, Schäpke N, van Steenbergen F and Omann I (2014). Making sense of sustainability transitions locally: how action research contributes to addressing societal challenges. *Critical Policy Studies* 8(4): 465–485.

Wyly E (2010). City. In: Davies JS (ed.). *Critical urban studies: new directions*, New York: SUNY Press.

Co-inquirer reflection

Rutger Henneman, Transition Towns Rotterdam

I considered the Gandhi garden as an intervention in Rotterdam's political economic reality. Its current dominant economic system is damaging for its people and environment, it is violent. In the Gandhi garden, on that particular piece of ground, with that particular group of people, we realised a non-violent economy. This intervention was supposed to contribute to a collective quest for truth: truth about how best to life and co-exist. By changing reality in a specific way, we contributed to the discussion about how to organise society and the foundations of our modern culture. Personally, I understood the establishment of the Gandhi garden as an advanced form of action research. Seeking truth by doing.

When you are preoccupied with 'doing' all the time, it is wonderful that suddenly a scholar shows up who wants to examine the meaning of the Gandhi garden with an action research mentality. And at that time, most people participating in the Gandhi garden were hands-on 'doers' with little scientific, philosophical and ethical background. It was really refreshing to meet Shivant, who focused on the Gandhi garden in the context of his dissertation. I hoped and still hope to witness the development of a truly engaged science; a science that addresses questions about how to fundamentally organise society, and what societal structure results from living a fulfilled life and a fulfilled co-existence.

I did not know Shivant before. But, during Shivant's first interview, I felt that our relationship was good right away. I recognised Shivant's genuine research into how to reconcile a desire to contribute to a better world with a scientific vocation. Shivant also blended in smoothly with the Gandhi garden group. I noticed he gave people the feeling he had a connection to their lifeworld, which led people to respond enthusiastically and to be willing talk to him. I felt the same. I really felt we were talking and thinking together, instead of him interviewing me. It did not feel as being an object of study, but as a partner in a common exploration. Soon, I also started seeing Shivant as a friend.

Often, during interviews, I do not like to talk about my criticism of other people in the garden. I think their ideas are often ill-supported, or not politically informed, and too woolly. In my experience, the Gandhi garden is actually also a political experiment: an experiment with a fundamentally different sense of societal organisation, which really conflicts with the current dominant neoliberal ideology. Many fellow gardeners do not want to engage with the 'politics of it'.

I find the a-political attitude of many 'new' forms of spirituality problematic. But, very soon I noticed I could easily talk to Shivant about this.

I like to see that the Gandhi garden leaves its marks in the academic world as well. The Gandhi garden experiment also contributes to how a small number of scientists think about challenges and theoretical explorations about fundamental social theory. This is especially interesting, since it adds to our understanding of action research questions and the overlap of engagement and science. It has contributed to my experience that the projects I am engaged in are important and worthwhile.

The conclusions of Shivant also provide me with more insights into the potential but also the limits of the social meaning and effect of the Gandhi garden as a utopian project. Especially with regard to the question of its political value, Shivant's research gave me a helpful perspective. It allowed me to better see what a project like this can do (and what it cannot). Consequently, this contributed to my appreciation of the role of gardens in my own personal strategy to make Rotterdam a sustainable, social and non-violent city.

On that account my conversations with Shivant and his research has added to the stream of considerations which led me to become more politically involved. They have been part of an ongoing stream of inspiration which strengthened my determination to take next steps (after starting gardens). Shivant has been actively involved in an important next step. We have developed together the online magazine 'Het Potentieel'. We are still part of the four main editors. This magazine has the purpose to instigate a practically oriented debate about the fundamental social structures of society. Especially focusing on practical experiments with alternatives. Now I have taken a next step, which is to unite the many 'green' initiatives in Rotterdam to become more politically active. We founded an association of green initiatives. I am on the board. And we just had our first political success by lobbying and preparing a motion (Dutch: motie) in the city council of Rotterdam for a 'Green Front Office' Dutch: 'groenloket'). The city council has voted in favour. This is the first cooperative political involvement of the green movement in Rotterdam. We intend to become a political force to stay: to help the city to take big steps towards a green and sustainable future. You can say that, among many other sources of inspiration and conversation partners, Shivant (my conversations with him, and his research) has been part of the stream of inspiration for me to take these steps.

Part II

Critical-relational heuristics for action research

5 Cultivating 'sanction and sanctuary' in Scottish collaborative governance

Doing relational work to support communicative spaces

James Henderson and Claire Bynner

Introduction

In this chapter, we consider our learning on action research theory and practice as part of What Works Scotland's (WWS) research on public service reform in Scotland. The WWS programme is a collaboration between the Universities of Edinburgh and Glasgow and jointly funded by the UK Economic and Social Research Council and the Scottish Government. It aims to deepen the impact of reform through research, evidence-use and the development of collaborative approaches to policymaking and delivery. From Spring 2015 to the end of 2016, WWS researchers facilitated collaborative action research (CAR) with four local Community Planning Partnerships (CPPs). Staff and professionals from across public and third sectors within these multi-agency public service partnerships have been working together to undertake local projects, and applying action research methods across diverse topics including: community-led action planning; service evaluation; participatory budgeting; welfare reform; and community capacity-building.

Scottish public service reform puts emphasis on a collaborative governance of 'partnership and participation' (Escobar, 2017). CPPs are statutory partnerships covering 32 local authorities mandated through legislation – the Local Government in Scotland Act 2003 and the Community Empowerment (Scotland) Act 2015. These partnerships are coordinated by the local authority and bring together multiple agencies and sectors to collaborate and develop public participation to design local services. WWS has worked to explore, support, and reflect critically on the potential of action research as a methodology for working with these local partnerships to support a shift towards collaborative governance. This research has, however, been undertaken in the context of public spending constraint, stubborn inequalities and long-term questions over the effectiveness of local partnership working (Headlam and Rowe, 2014; Matthews, 2014; Schmachtel, 2016).

In the first half of this chapter, we describe aspirations for a 'Scottish approach' (Cairney *et al.*, 2016) to public service reform as part of broader international trends for collaborative governance (Bryson *et al.*, 2014). We highlight on-going critiques of statutory, strategic and local partnership working, and so the challenges for aspirations for collaborative governance. Our action research methodology is positioned within a 'participatory worldview' as understood by Reason and Bradbury (2006). It seeks to integrate collaboration, action, and research in pursuit of democratic social change (Greenwood and Levin, 2007), drawing from Bartels and Wittmayer's (2014) articulation of a relational and critical action research concerned to impact on wider social, political, economic, and ecological crises.

In the second half of the chapter, we turn to consider our developing theory and practice in two of the CPP case sites. We provide descriptions of the action research in both sites and discuss emerging themes in more depth. We focus on the challenge in these multi-agency collaborative governance settings of negotiating what Dickens and Watkins (1999) term 'sanction and sanctuary': the need to sustain management commitment (sanction) to the action research process and for this to include protecting space for staff to engage in more critical, reflexive work (sanctuary). In so doing, we illustrate the value of 'inflight approaches' that adapt pragmatically to existing opportunities and context. Yet, such flexibility is uncomfortable and requires the action researcher to also 'hold steady' to an accountable action research process (Bruce *et al.*, 2011). These discussions of our practice allow us to return and reflect in more depth on the relational and critical dynamics addressed in this book – in particular 'starting up' and 'reflexivity and impact'.

The Scottish policy context: shifting to collaborative governance

Over recent decades, transformations in economies, technologies, and societies have created a range of complex, interrelating problems for developed states. There is a growing urgency to address seemingly intractable challenges of inequality, climate change, and global insecurity; and increasing demand on public services while political processes constrain public spending. In seeking to respond to this context, current discussions of public service reform are shifting from a focus solely on new public management, with its emphasis on business-type practices and efficiency, to include more collaborative forms of governance (Osborne, 2013). Such collaborative governance aspires to a democratic engagement in which government seeks to lead and address 'wicked' social problems through partnership and participation with the third sector, communities, service-users, and citizens (Bryson *et al.*, 2014; Escobar 2017).

In the UK, long-standing shifts towards corporate management since the 1960s and 1970s have seen new public management and multi-agency partnerships alongside an increasing emphasis on community participation, deployed in the search for efficiencies and to mitigate the impact of growing inequalities (Atkinson and Moon, 1994; Cochrane, 2007; Matthews, 2014). The growing influence of collaborative governance in Scotland, is now being articulated as a 'Scottish Approach' following the recommendations of the 2011 Commission on the Future Delivery of Public Services or 'Christie Commission' (Cairney *et al.*, 2016; Christie Commission, 2011). The Commission's meta-narrative promotes a public service ethos committed to collaborative governance to 'prevent inequalities' as seemingly intractable wicked issues, and positions this as aspirations for a more equitable society and economy. The Christie Commission attempts to 'square the circle' as to how to achieve a fairer society in the context of a UK Government 'austerity' programme that severely constrains public spending through emphasis on efficiency, improving performance, and reducing demand on services by reducing inequality (Christie Com 2011; Matthews, 2014; Cairney *et al.*, 2016; Escobar, 2017).

In broadly accepting these recommendations, the Scottish Government (2011) has continued to promote Community Planning Partnerships (CPPs) as central to this ambitious agenda (Matthews, 2014; Escobar, 2017). The Community Empowerment (Scotland) Act 2015 has brought further reform of CPPs through widening statutory responsibilities for collaborative leadership beyond local authorities to other public agencies including Police, Fire and Rescue, and Health Boards. The Act also seeks to create new spaces for the third sector and communities to be further involved in service design and delivery.

However, the considerable challenges for collaborative governance are highlighted through the literature on the realities of partnership working. Headlam and Rowe (2014) examine the power dynamics that have characterised previous partnership initiatives in the UK. They argue that partnerships are vulnerable to shifting policy dynamics with new funding and larger services and organisations well-versed in how to 'follow the money', leaving behind communities and committed local bodies. Further, such partnership might be better understood as incorporation into top-down policy agendas and the priorities of the larger public institutions. It is focused on building consensus rather than recognising and working with conflicting political priorities; preferring to work with existing budget allocations rather than asking challenging questions and seeking strategic solutions.

Matthews (2014), focusing on the Scottish experience, observes that whilst partnership may seem common sense (a 'no-brainer'), the reality is one of shifting policy initiatives and an alien language of 'strategic partnership' that creates barriers to community participation. Similarly, Schmachtel (2016), in relation to German public education partnerships, points to local partnerships as 'rationalising myths' used to control local dialogue and maintain the 'structural (neo-liberal) status quo'. Finally, Cook's (2015) review of evidence on public service partnerships adds a further note of caution as to expectations around partnership-working, suggesting that it tends to incremental change rather than the radical transformation anticipated in a Scottish Approach.

Recognising the contradictions of local partnership, Bartels (2015) generates theory and practice on the development of 'communicative capacity' between public services, citizens, and policymakers. He focuses on the need for *all* to seek to deepen understanding of the situation (the context); work with the substantive issues involved; and sustain productive working relationships. In facilitating communicative capacity, Escobar (2017) highlights the complex participatory and political roles of public participation professionals as they network across organisational cultures and boundaries as 'boundary spanners' (Williams, 2013).

This growing body of theory, policy and practice points to the ambiguities, yet arguably, the potential of multi-agency collaborative governance in creating democratic social change. The imbalances of power within local partnerships are seemingly inherent, and yet the opportunity to embed genuinely critical, reflexive spaces within them sustains aspirations for engaging with the considerable social and global challenges we now face.

Our developing approach to collaborative action research

It is within this ambiguous, ambitious and shifting policy context that WWS is undertaking an extensive research programme. We are seeking to use action research, evidence-use and other social research to support and inform the development of partnership-working and community participation within CPPs, whilst also reflecting critically on the realities of public service reform through multi-agency collaborative governance.

Our collaborative action research (CAR) has been informed by Reason and Bradbury's (2006) understanding of the action research tradition as a 'family of approaches' working within a 'participatory worldview'. It is eclectic, aspirational, and adaptive, drawing from various methods, and open to multiple perspectives, understandings and varieties of action and change (Reason and Bradbury, 2006; Kindon *et al.*, 2007). Broadly speaking, we understand CAR to involve elements of (1) collaboration and participation; (2) research and inquiry; and (3) action and change. These can be integrated in varied forms but will be committed to democratic and dialogical practice (Greenwood and Levin, 2007; Wagenaar, 2007; Bartels and Wittmayer, 2014).

Drawing on CAR models already used in public service improvement (Chapman and Hadfield, 2015; Miller and Barrie, 2016) we sought initially to apply a 'group-based inquiry' approach. By group-based inquiry we refer to a process involving a group of co-researchers with different professional identities, knowledges, and backgrounds working in the same geographical area and exploring a co-produced topic with the aim of seeking deeper insight and understanding to inform future policy and practice. The process combines participatory approaches with critical thinking, reflexivity, and aspirations for pragmatic change. However, as we discuss below, our approach to action research has continued to develop in the field.

To develop group-based inquiries, WWS invited Scotland's 32 CPPs to apply in Autumn 2014 to participate in the WWS CAR process. Four were selected showing the spatial and social diversity of Scotland – urban, rural and varying concentrations of inequality and uneven development. In this chapter, we bring insights from two of these four case-sites; those in which we, the authors, were the core action researchers. During the start-up phase, we focused on establishing one or more inquiry teams in each case-site and using a three-phase cyclical model of inquiry: scoping, exploring evidence, testing change (Chapman and Hadfield, 2015). National retreats (two-day workshops) provided opportunities for peer networking across the case-sites.

Within the WWS research team, layers of collaborative working were also developed. The four core researchers, one per site, and an action researcher with related experience, met regularly as a peer learning and support group to discuss action research theory and practice. There has been varied co-working in these two case-sites involving other members of the WWS team. We, the authors, have also met regularly to generate discussions that informed an earlier conference paper and now this chapter. Both of us have been able to draw on previous experience to inform our action research and discussions. Claire has direct experience of working as a participation professional within a Scottish local authority and undertaken research into the emergence of 'super-diverse' neighbourhoods. James has worked on community-based and service-based research using action and case-study research methodologies. We approached our case sites with pre-existing commitments to public participation, social justice, and strengthening the influence on policymaking of marginalised communities.

The data that inform the illustrations, discussions, and analysis presented here, were collected during our action research in differing ways and varied across the two case-sites, including: desk research using CPP documents and public records; our formal recordings of meetings, discussions, and events; and co-produced reports, consultations, and reflective writing. The, at times, embedded nature of our work supported access to meetings and promoted informal discussions, generating informal notes and related reflections that gave further direction to our research and formal data collection. Participatory analysis of elements of the data included discussions between the two authors, with our WWS colleagues, and with CPP participants.

Developing our theory and practice through experience in the field

Given the aspirations of action research to support partnerships in shifting towards collaborative governance, we recognised the need to build CPP management support for the inquiry teams, and looked to develop wider networks within the partnerships of those seeking to support such change (Chapman and Hadfield, 2010, 2015). Initially, as outlined above, we sought to apply a group-based action inquiry CAR approach. However, this approach was to be challenged, as is explored later, in these two case-sites by the demands of policy and institutional contexts. We, therefore, increasingly drew on relational and critical thinking on action research (Bartels and Wittmayer, 2014) and related theory and practice. Here, we outline our changing approach to action research in this context and the developing influences on our theory and practice.

We understand this relational work as concerned for both people and systems: our co-researchers, other local advocates, and key decision-makers; and the institutional systems and policy context in which they are embedded. Such relational work seeks to build and facilitate *communicative spaces* that can engage with complex issues and dilemmas (Eady *et al.*, 2015; Escobar, 2011; Wittmayer *et al.*, 2014). Crucially, this requires both backstage (more private) and frontstage (more public) working (Escobar, 2017) that can create and sustain spaces to work on substantive issues, build productive relationships and understand each in context – so seeking to generate communicative capacity (Bartels, 2015).

In seeking a critical approach, our concern has been to avoid an *institutional instrumentalisation* that simply absorbs action research into institutional and policy objectives (Boezmann *et al.*, 2014). Our aim has been to support a 'culture of inquiry' open to questioning, reflection, and consideration of alternatives (Argyris, 2003; Hadfield, 2012). We have sought communicative spaces that can begin to engage with substantive issues, rather than only institutional objectives, and within the wider context of seeking democratic social change for a 'better society and future' (Sayer, 2009; Bartels and Wittmayer, 2014). Our research has then looked towards an *actionable knowledge* that integrates *workability* – knowledge relevant to exploring the initial problem; *credibility* – socially applied and scholarly knowledge; and *reflexivity* – a critical, self-positioning knowledge (Bartels and Wittmayer, 2014).

In seeking such critical spaces, we have therefore needed to deepen our understanding of relational and pragmatic strategies. Dickens and Watkins (1999) use the evocative heuristic of *sanction and sanctuary* as a focus for gaining and sustaining support (sanction) from management (leadership) and to involve them in understanding and protecting that process (sanctuary); and, to build understanding and commitment more widely across the organisation – its culture, networks, and wider stakeholders. They developed their thinking through action research in a private sector organisation, a context distant from multi-agency collaborative governance. Yet, this experience of a corporate environment resonated with our need to win and sustain wide-ranging support for our research, and offered core thinking from which we began to integrate two further practices.

First, as we illustrate later, the need for *inflight approaches*. The term arose in a peer mentoring conversation[1] when Claire was discussing the setting-up phase and the challenges of gaining sanctuary and sanction from management and staff for a group-based-inquiry. She needed a more flexible approach to work within the action-present of programmes and projects that were already under development ('in-flight') while at the same time providing opportunities to challenge and 'disrupt' institutional norms and assumptions. Here, we use 'inflight' as a metaphor, somewhat akin to Herr and Anderson's (2005: 69) description of action research as "*designing the plane whilst flying it*" where research design will inevitably be subject to change as the project progresses. However, we use the term to highlight the need to build on and work with initiatives and activities that are already happening or are required given current policy objectives. The destination is (seemingly) clear but the action research process needs further crafting as the journey continues so as to increase the range of safe communicative spaces (sanctuary) and therefore the potential for moments of critical reflection.

Second, in working with such inflight flexibility and the benefit it brings of being embedded in day-to-day practice, we were also concerned for sustaining an accountable, trusted research process – *holding steady, whilst changing tack.* Bruce *et al.* (2011; citing Anderson and Herr, 1999) highlight the need for a complex research validity – a trusted research – focused on process and outcome, but also commitment to inclusiveness, catalysing change, and accountability to a wider research community.

In the discussions of our action research that follow we illustrate the integration of these developing elements of critical and relational practice, sanction and sanctuary, inflight approaches, and holding steady. These are presented initially through individual case-site descriptions, and then in discussion of practice and emerging issues relevant to the critical and relational themes at the heart of this book.

Working in the case-sites

Westdale Community Planning Partnership: Westdale[2] is a local authority area struggling to manage the post-industrial economic context. It has relatively high levels of welfare claimants and employment or income-based deprivation. At the time of this research, as more generally across Scotland, the CPP was in the process of establishing a new, localised approach to governance whilst under significant budgetary pressure. Implementation of this approach was being led by community planning (CP) staff and involved a range of CP partners including police, community safety, housing, waste management, neighbourhood services, culture and libraries, and voluntary sector.

Initial discussions with the CP team led to a group-based inquiry on how to design a meaningful process of dialogue and participation in the development of *community action plans.* Five local authority officers with professional backgrounds in policy, performance, and community development were involved in the process, with intermittent involvement from CP management and other CP staff team members. Early discussions highlighted the challenges for the programme, including: resistance to change at the level of middle management; poor inter-departmental cooperation; failure to resolve persistent complaints over relatively small issues; and the public showing 'engagement fatigue'.

In addition, CP officers were often responding to new policy agendas and implementing policy decisions taken at a strategic level within the CPP. The institutional culture was to 'act first, then rationalise': "We are required to do things first and then provide a rationale for what we have just done ..." (CP Officer). Working with university researchers was therefore uncomfortable since it exposed the extent to which practice differed from an idealised view of evidence-based policy making: "The difficulty of working with What Works is that we should be able to hand you over something that has got a nice set of processes, practices, worked out policies and thinking, papers and reports, and we can't" (CP Officer). Whilst WWS' group-based inquiry model, described earlier, envisaged setting up a collaborative inquiry team, it quickly become clear that this was not a priority for CP management or staff. They were under pressure to build commitment to the neighbourhood programme across public service partners, and CP management preferred to use WWS resources to organise a Development Day to encourage support for the programme. Given our aspirations for relational work, we decided to shift away from the group-based inquiry to an 'inflight approach'. This entailed working within existing collaborative spaces and activities and seeking opportunities for integrating action research within planned and developing community planning activity. In adopting this approach, we recognised that there was a risk that action research would be subsumed into instrumental goals and needs: balanced against this were the immediate demands of policy implementation and our need to build credibility and prove useful.

Working with the CP staff team, we planned and delivered a participative approach to the Development Day. Staff were trained to conduct interviews with peers in other local authority areas and produced a video. The Day was facilitated by WWS, and over 30 local employees from mainly public sector organisations participated and discussed barriers and enablers to community empowerment. Participants highlighted their concern to shift to a new institutional approach underpinned by values of: "openness to change; willingness to learn; inclusion and diversity; trust, honesty and genuine commitment" (from record of the Day). Despite the success of the Day, maintaining a consistent level of involvement from across the staff team to the group-based inquiry process proved difficult. As quickly as the research began to gain momentum, a new external political priority arose – the resettlement of Syrian refugees. This pattern of management diverting staff resources at short notice repeated itself. At a later stage, further group-based inquiry work stalled as the focus shifted to another national policy priority, 'participatory budgeting'.

We sought to respond to this institutional context by organising learning and development events that could engage the wider network of community planning partners. These events included a seminar on 'community-led approaches to poverty'; and training on 'community conversations that matter'. Our aim was to increase the capacity of CP staff and partners to adapt to the changing institutional context. While levels of participation in the learning and development work were encouraging, commitment to group-based work remained intermittent and sporadic.

We also provided more traditional research inputs to meet the needs of CP management: external research support for the analysis and publication of neighbourhood data profiles; research on evidence use within the CPP; and research into the resettlement experience of Syrian refugees. In this way, we found opportunities to engage creatively with the CPP, meeting the emerging need for skills in participatory practices; and addressing limited capacity by undertaking a greater proportion of the research work ourselves or bringing in specialist research resources as required.

Kirkthistle Community Planning Partnership: covers a mixed social geography of rural towns and communities, and 'urban' towns – some bordering a larger urban area. Levels of inequalities for the CPP are lower than the Scottish average. Nevertheless, there are significant numbers of people living in or at the margins of poverty, particularly given the higher costs of living in rural areas (Hirsch *et al.*, 2013); some in deprived neighbourhoods, others spread more thinly across the whole. The CPP is structured centrally as a Board of senior management and elected councillors, Executive Group of strategic managers, central policy and strategy team (central team) employed by the local authority, and thematic (central) and local community planning (multi-agency) working groups.

Early conversations with the CPP's central team and the Health and Social Care Partnership (HSCP[3]) led to the development (March – June 2015) of two broad tranches of inquiry, pursued initially as group-based inquiries, and described below. These continued in various guises through to December 2016, with some limited activity in 2017.

1 Community-capacity building inquiry work

The broad focus of this inquiry was on developing community capacity-building strategies for health and well-being across public service partners to reduce pressure on services.[4] It continued to be led by the HSCP but always involved wider CPP partners too. A group-based inquiry took root as a multi-agency team – the Inquiry Team – involving staff from service improvement, policy, third/community sector, public health and ourselves (nine in total).

The initial inquiry focus was on learning from a pilot community development (Community Links) worker project aiming to improve community health and well-being and so reducing demands on local health and social care services. The inquiry pursued a range of activities over 15 months: desk research; study visit and interviewing; data analysis, participatory discussion and reflective writing; report writing and related consultation work. A report on 'good practice and what supports it' was co-produced, which highlighted, too, the potential for further inquiring into community development and its role in mitigating the impact of inequalities locally.

The inquiry was demanding of time and commitment from the core members although the collaborative nature of the project was also valued: "… it was a truly collaborative process. In other pieces of work, we speak about working with collaboration, but, now I've done this, what we did before wasn't that" (team member). Changing priorities and staffing within the HSCP, CPP, and third sector, however, impacted on the core team and it became more difficult to maintain momentum and use the report directly to support discussions across the CPP beyond consultation work on the report itself:

> … for me, it is what happens now, and the influence it [the research] can have. So, in a way, it almost doesn't feel finished, for me. I would like something, either for it to have influence over something still to happen, or to know that folk have given it consideration, the reports we've done, when they're looking at something new.…

> (Team member)

However, this consultation work supported further dialogue with HSCP strategic management as to what was next for their strategic approach on community capacity-building more broadly and generated commitment (sanction) to further action research and spaces for discussion and reflection (sanctuary) within the CPP, as highlighted below.

2 Collaborative partnership-working inquiry work

The other tranche of action research was focused on supporting partnership-working through the role of collaborative working and evidence across central and local partners, and coordinated through the CPP central policy and strategy team. It was initially focused on establishing a group-based inquiry. Early scoping discussions highlighted tensions between the central and local community planning teams as to the focus of an inquiry, and the CPP central team shifted to prioritising working with us to explore how best to meet elements of the Community Empowerment (Scotland) Act 2015. Sanction for our work together was revived through adoption of this inflight approach and development of a series of one-off collaborative research activities which WWS facilitated and provided input as speakers or evidence to support discussions. These included:

- *Two development workshops:* with the CPP Board and Executive Group as these bodies worked towards the statutory requirements generated by the Community Empowerment (Scotland) Act 2015.
- *Two learning days with a range of practitioners:* to bring together public and third sector staff (35+ participants each time), including those working in operations and in strategy, from across the CPP partners to explore the Christie Commission agenda of partnership-working, participation and preventing inequality – with presentations offering both research evidence and local practice experience to inform discussions.
- *Two collaborative workshops:* one for CPP partners in relation to beginning to develop a strategic action plan, as part of a CPP statutory duty, in this case coordinated by the Alcohol and Drugs Partnership. The other on scoping issues for a community capacity-building strategy across CPP partners and coordinated by the HSCP. In both cases, local practitioners discussed developing policy and practice and, again, drawing from other sources of evidence.

These research activities provided space (sanctuary) to support questioning discussions, including in relation to preventing inequalities. Further, they, and the activity described in (1), generated five inquiry reports involving various degrees of co-production, consultation and space for reflective writing with co-researchers and other stakeholders. These reports extended the communicative spaces generated (sanction and sanctuary) and provided continuity across the different action research activities arising from our now inflight approach. They, alongside use of the meta-narrative on collaborative governance (Christie Commission, 2011) and focus on inequality, allowed the researchers to 'hold steady' to an accountable research process across the whole of our work within the CPP.

Reflecting on the challenges of relational and critical action research

Experiences of undertaking action research in each of the four WWS CPP case-sites have been distinctive, suggesting the need for diverse, context-relevant approaches to action research. Discussions of these two case-sites will not provide easy generalisations but contribute to emerging understanding of relational and critical working in multi-agency collaborative governance settings. Here we explore our learning through two broad discussions: the first, as to our experiences of pursuing relational and pragmatic strategies to sustain critical, communicative spaces; the second, on the implications of this learning for this book's focus on critical and relational theory and practice.

Exploring relational and pragmatic action research strategies

Seeking sanction and sanctuary in multi-agency partnership settings

As outlined in our earlier methodological discussions, central elements in building sanction and sanctuary (Dickens and Watkins, 1999) include: relational work with management and leadership to build understanding and commitment and help unblock processes when needed; and wider engagement with staff teams and other stakeholders.

In Westdale, we developed and maintained sanction for the action research through on-going discussion with CP management. They, in turn, engaged with senior management in the local authority and CPP partners and local elected representatives to seek multi-level approval. In presenting to the CPP Board, CP management highlighted three key benefits of CAR and working with WWS:

> Collaborative action research enables free and open discussion about what works, doesn't work and needs to be improved. It is a highly effective form of professional development for staff. It allows meaningful use of data and access to wider advice and support.

Despite such high-level discussions and management sanction for 'free and open discussion', CP officers were wary and found this new openness uncomfortable. On writing about the background to the neighbourhood programme as part of the action research process, one CP officer reflected:

> ... for me I feel quite exposed writing this down explicitly. I think that management will have a fit ... I would normally draft it up in a way that would be less explicit or contentious. The process is that nothing leaves this office that hasn't been sanitised.

Further, despite the sanction of management to participate, staff seemed to lack the necessary sanctuary – institutional support and safety – to pursue open dialogue in which complex policy problems could be unpacked and examined in more depth. It became increasingly clear that in a context of high policy demand and low staff resource, management can give sanction with genuine intent yet the time and space (sanctuary) for action research will not necessarily follow. Shifting policy priorities militated against an action research process that requires commitment over time. As new political imperatives and policy initiatives arrived, we struggled to protect the research process from external pressures. Early group-based inquiry quickly became constrained by waves of new policy initiatives and institutional change. Sanction had to be re-negotiated, re-booted even, as a series of one-off activities and the brokering of relevant resources.

In Kirkthistle, for the HSCP-focused research on community capacity-building, early sanction with management was developed by key members of the Inquiry Team who worked at the interface between operational and strategic management (development and policy): "… there was enough trust from the HSCP, that if I was involved and thought it was a good idea, then they would run with it" (team member). Broadly, this sustained sufficient sanction and sanctuary for 15 months of action research to complete a report. This example, alongside another co-produced report on previous experience of collaborative learning, suggests the HSCP is exploring the development of a culture that is looking to the potential of staff-led initiatives – a loosening of command and control. The Inquiry Team also supported the development of the two CPP-wide learning days organised with the CPP central team, and this process deepened our discussions with both CPP and HSCP management. Whilst the Inquiry Team's work lost momentum, as described in the case-site description, the relationship with HSCP management now supported the emergence of further research on a strategy for community capacity-building including: ongoing discussions, a collaborative workshop, and co-produced case-study material for a report. Given further time, this second wave of sanction and sanctuary *may* have supported yet further action research developments.

For the CPP-focused research in Kirkthistle, sanction from senior and strategic management remained more limited and focused on individual research activities, largely coordinated with the CPP central team. These had a certain influence on the CPP's own thinking, for instance, in establishing its own internal review process:

> … a really good example is the CPP project review group … looking at (and building) on the back of the work you guys (WWS) did initially … in terms of kicking this off, that was a real catalyst for us looking at how the CPP functions and recognising that probably it wasn't fit for purpose, particularly if we were focusing on the new line of priorities.
>
> (CPP Partner)

Such work also began to widened relationships with CPP strategic partners, including a closer working relationship with the Alcohol and Drugs Partnership whilst, as highlighted in the case-site description, the research activities and report-writing could offer spaces for more questioning discussions with CPP partners.

Looking across the two case-sites the following patterns are suggested:

1 Sanction for smaller 'one-off' pieces of action research activity were gained from strategic management within CPPs as they sought to explore the potential of action research to support institutional priorities.
2 Sanction for sustained group-based inquiries proved difficult to maintain. There were early examples in both CPPs, but limited appetite from management in either case for further such work; although, further opportunities may have emerged for longer projects.
3 In both CPPs, there was some engagement with wider partners and staff teams including the third/community sector, for example: Westdale CPP's Development Day; Kirkthistle CPP's learning days. This did not, however, build towards wider stakeholder engagement, e.g. community organisations and service-users, despite current policy emphasis on multi-agency collaborative governance. Both CPPs, and the HSCP, were needing to focus their resources on coping with high policy demand in a resource-constrained context.

Inflight approaches that seek to 'hold steady'

In illustrating the complexities of the relational work with management for sustaining sanction and sanctuary for CAR, it is important to recognise our shift from group-based inquiries, as separate spaces with related sanctuary, to a more flexible inflight approach being designed activity by activity, as the CPPs sought to implement public service reform.

In Westdale, the focus on group-based inquiry work, although continuing intermittently, shifted towards activity-by-activity collaborative learning through a Development Day, a seminar on poverty, and staff training on community dialogue, supported by more traditional social research inputs. In Kirkthistle, in seeking to maintain our relevance, and sustain management sanction for ongoing action research, we were focused on CPP and HSCP institutional objectives of organisational capacity-building, evidence-use and implementing the Community Empowerment (Scotland) Act 2015 and related legislation.

A *mutual instrumentalism* evolved here between the CPPs and ourselves, given both public sector and academic institutions had good reasons to build mutually beneficial CAR programmes. For ourselves, for instance, the action research provided access to crucial on-going learning opportunities on collaborative governance and the potential to carve out small *critical, reflexive spaces*. Our funders, the Economic and Social Research Council and Scottish Government, were also expecting insights from this action research.

The risk, however, was that such a pragmatic, relational approach would then 'collapse' into a purely institutional instrumentalism, on both sides, pursuing institutional objectives alone, rather than communicative spaces for reframing alternatives (Argyris, 2003), and so generating actionable knowledge relevant to immediate problems only (Bartels and Wittmayer, 2014). 'Holding steady, whilst changing tack' to an accountable, valid and trusted research process (Bruce *et al.*, 2011), concerned to be critically reflexive and credible, was therefore crucial to our approach.

Full discussion of a trusted process is not possible here, but we illustrate our commitment to exploring critical, communicative spaces. For instance: in Westdale, the focus on collaborative learning through the Development Day supported wider staff teams in demonstrating their desire for more accountable, collaborative governance. The seminar on 'community-led approaches to tackling poverty' promoted dialogue on the significant challenges of preventing inequality.

In Kirkthistle, we drew sanction and built sanctuary via the Christie Commission (2011) meta-narrative to sustain dialogue across the action research activities and reports on more challenging issues. For example, accumulating knowledge and deepened discussion of 'preventing inequality' and the role of community capacity-building in relation to this, as illustrated by inputs from three different CPP partner staff:

> emphasis on communities, is it always a 'good thing' or might it help sustain inequality?
>
> (Learning day, December 2015)

> researchers … continue to point towards 'whole population' and economic approaches to preventing health inequalities…. How can communities and the community sector realistically seek to impact on inequalities in such a context….
>
> (Collaborative workshop, December 2016)

> … the need for upstream action to address inequality, much of this action is outwith the preserve of CPPs, lying with Scottish and Westminster Governments….
>
> (Consultation response, Summer 2017)

Across both case-sites, and through integrating an inflight approach with a commitment to holding steady to critical reflexivity, we have pursued a *mutual instrumentalism* in order avoid a purely institutional instrumentalisation of the research.

Considering the core challenges for relational and critical theory and practice

Starting, re-starting and re-booting: policy and institutional shaping of the research agenda

Both case-sites illustrate the role of the national policy context in shaping our action research work: the public service reform agenda as meta-narrative

(Christie Commission, 2011) and related legislation and policy; and, other policy, for example, health and social care integration, participatory budgeting, Syrian refugee re-settlement; and public spending constraints.

In Westdale, despite good intentions for greater management openness, staff were concerned that the expectations of managers and elected officials were unrealistic; seeking "neat solutions" rather than exploring complexity "they like a big hole and a big shovel" (CP officer). Further, management was shifting priorities as it juggled the challenges of reform, other initiatives, and constrained resources. These priorities continued to shape and re-shape the action research agenda.

In Kirkthistle, the scale of policy and institutional challenge was likewise apparent. For instance, one local partner spoke of the challenges for the HSCP in taking forward health and social care integration:

… what they've got is some massive, massive problems of their own: shortage of doctors, shortage of money, shortage of virtually everything; transport to and from hospital. It appears they have got some massive issues that they're working on and that's occupying all of their time at the moment, and I can understand that.

Our aspirations for action research with the CPP and HSCP continued to be re-shaped to meet institutional needs in the context of resource constraints and other national policy demands.

We thus changed strategy to inflight approaches to work with these policy and institutional dynamics and sustain the action research processes. A more ambitious action research agenda, for instance aiming to widen the circle of co-researchers into multiple layers of partnership and community stakeholders, and to deepen engagement to generate more reflexive inquiry, was beyond the scope of current CPP aspiration and capacity. Senior and strategic management across CPP partners was focused on implementing the policy agenda; wider, more autonomous group-based inquiry was not relevant to their immediate concerns.

The Scottish policy narrative (Christie Commission, 2011) aspires to a multi-agency collaborative governance, yet the current realities for these CPPs point rather to a collaboratively inspired approach that tends to top-down implementation of mandated partnership. Over time, where more localised structures – local teams and participatory structures – 'bed in', and where CPPs extend their resourcing for local 'horizontal' collaborations with the third sector, communities and service-users, then wider local democratic working can sound more plausible.

Reflexivity, impact and systems change

This has been far from any idealised action research process built around group-based inquiries and formal dissemination strategies and workshops. Spaces for staff for more critical reflection have left some feeling exposed or been approached with caution, as illustrated in Westdale. Both top-down working cultures and job insecurity in the current policy context, alongside high policy demand and resource constraint, likely contribute to such tensions. Institutional compromise and mutual instrumentalism have remained central to the action research, and wider stakeholder engagement limited. Yet, we have continued to seek to focus on sanctuary for such critical reflexivity with CPP practitioners as a commitment to a trusted and accountable research process concerned to engage with the realities of current policy and practice; and so that the WWS programme can work with these challenges in its learning exchange year in 2018.

Generating suitable sanctuary in relation to such thinking is a key area for further practice development. In both CPPs, the use of the Christie Commission's (2011) meta-narrative has continued to provide the permission (sanction) to recognise past failures and current complexities in seeking to reduce inequalities (Gibb, 2015). However, given the ambiguous policy context described earlier in relation to mandated multi-agency collaborative governance, it may be challenging to create further sanction to deepen such reflection. Communicative spaces will generate uncomfortable questions as the tensions across policy and practice surface, whilst CPPs are seeking to hold the central policy tension between seeking cost efficiencies to manage resource constraints, on the one hand, and reducing inequalities and creating a fairer society, on the other.

Concluding thoughts

Sustaining sanction and sanctuary, in-flight approaches and holding steady to a trusted process

We have worked to build and sustain sanction and sanctuary (Dickens and Watkins, 1999) with strategic and senior management within these two CPP case-sites to support critical and relational CAR. In both sites, early group-based inquiry work was agreed but then did not prove sufficiently relevant to sustain continued sanction in these high policy ambition and demand, yet resource constrained times. We, therefore, changed tack to pursue inflight approaches that gained further sanction, and a focus on creating or adapting existing collaborative spaces, planned activity-by-activity. In the process, we have sought to generate sanctuary for communicative spaces in which more critical questioning can be facilitated.

The Scottish policy context, including the Community Empowerment (Scotland) Act 2015, has supported the achievement of sanction with CPP management for 'free and open discussion' when seeking to deliver activity relevant to that policy agenda. This has had benefits for CPPs and ourselves in terms of sustaining and resourcing action research concerned for more immediate, workable knowledge (Bartels and Wittmayer, 2014), resulting in a mutual instrumentalism between academic and governance institutions. As the policy context shifted, with new initiatives emerging, the CAR process likewise shifted and needed to re-start and, even, re-boot. This continual re-shaping via the policy context has presented barriers to wider staff and stakeholder inclusion in shaping the research agenda, thus far.

However, this same reform agenda and the Christie Commission (2011) meta-narrative have also sustained opportunities (sanctuary) for communicative spaces, and related reflexivity, in both case-sites. For instance, legitimising dialogue on the value and challenges of collaborative working, and on the aspirations and realities for these CPPs of focusing on preventing inequalities. By bringing together strategies of sanction and sanctuary and inflight approaches, whilst seeking to maintain focus (hold steady) to an accountable, trusted research process (Bruce *et al.*, 2011), we have continued to aspire to relational and critical working that aims to integrate workable, credible and reflexive knowledge (Bartels and Wittmayer, 2014).

The realities of communicative spaces in a demanding policy landscape

This emerging approach to CAR in this Scottish policy context has necessarily been action-focused and practical. In this environment, carving out space (sanctuary and sanction) for reflection, reflexivity, and discussion of longer-term visions and context has been an on-going challenge. This raises questions for theory and practice as to how to deepen sanctuary for action research concerned for communicative spaces in such a context, so that it can maintain focus on aspirations for democratic social change towards a better society and future (Bartels and Wittmayer, 2014; Sayer, 2009) – with implications for action research as a trusted, accountable process.

The scale of policy change, challenge, and related turbulence currently in Scotland is visible through our work. This leaves us reflecting as to whether such change is now endemic and, if so, how action researchers might work with the pace of such change to build sanctuary. Or if, alternatively, these changes will 'bed-in' and provide opportunities for more settled, deepening communicative spaces. Our concern here is that action research might simply become the latest managerial trend, offering a low-cost resource for training, consultancy, and professional development to support CPPs in keeping up with the pace of change.

Our experiences in these two CPPs suggest that the *strength* of action research should be better understood as working alongside practitioners and stakeholders within multi-agency collaborative governance to provide safe spaces and resources to support reflexivity and critical dialogue on the substantive wicked issues and challenges they face. Handling this turbulent political and institutional context is a challenge for action research theory and practice, one that requires commitment and creativity. The key to success will be the skilled work involved in developing communicative spaces, that support critical reflexivity and longer-term change, through the ongoing negotiation of sanction and sanctuary.

Acknowledgements

Many, many thanks to our What Works Scotland colleagues for their support, including: in particular, Hayley Bennett and Richard Brunner – for ongoing discussions and support over the last three years as fellow Research Associates; Nick Bland and Oliver Escobar – for feedback on drafts and ongoing encouragement; Chris Chapman, Kevin Lowden and Nick Watson for support to develop the conference discussion paper from which this chapter has evolved; and Nick Bland and Ken Gibb who co-worked the two case-sites in this chapter with ourselves. Likewise, to the internal reviewer, external reviewer, and the editors for their valuable feedback on drafts of the chapter. The final responsibility remains with us, the authors. Our very sincere thanks, too, to the many local CPP practitioners who worked with us or supported the action research process in many and varied ways in both case-sites explored here. Particular thanks to Alison McPherson from 'Kirkthistle' Community Planning Partnership who has contributed 'practitioner reflections' to this chapter, so deepening the layers of understanding presented here.

This work was supported by the Economic and Social Research Council, grant number ES/M003922/1.

Notes

1 Mark Hadfield, co-author of Chapman C and Hadfield M (2015), suggested that it is possible and sometimes desirable to 'disrupt' existing projects by introducing an action research approach 'inflight'.
2 The names of both CPPs, Westdale and Kirkthistle, have been changed to support anonymity.
3 The Public Bodies (Joint Working) (Scotland) Act 2014 integrates adult primary health and social care services (in almost all cases) as Health and Social Care Partnerships, reporting to an Integrated Joint Board (IJB). The legislation focuses on localised partnership-working and plans; the increasing role of the third sector, communities and service-users; and seeking both to reduce health inequalities and improve the effective and efficient use of resources.
4 Community capacity-building is a broad term that points to activities, resources and support that strengthen community groups and individuals, but potentially community organisations too, in taking forward actions and playing leadership roles.

References

Anderson GL and Herr K (1999) The new paradigm wars: is there room for rigorous practitioner knowledge in schools and universities? *Educational Researcher* 28(5): 12–21.
Argyris C (2003) A life full of learning. *Organization Studies* 24(7): 1178–1193.
Atkinson R and Moon G (1994) *Urban policy in Britain: the city, the state and the market*, Basingstoke and London: The Macmillan Press Ltd.
Bartels KPR (2015) *Communicative capacity: public encounters in participatory theory and practice*, Bristol: Policy Press.
Bartels KPR and Wittmayer JM (2014) Symposium introduction: usable knowledge in practice. What action research has to offer to critical policy studies. *Critical Policy Studies* 8(4): 397–406.

Boezeman D, Vink M, Leroy P and Halffman W (2014) Participation under a spell of instrumentalization? Reflections on action research in an entrenched climate adaptation policy process. *Critical Policy Studies* 8(4): 407–426.

Bruce C, Flynn T and Stagg-Peterson S (2011) Examining what we mean by collaboration in collaborative action research: a cross-case analysis. *Educational Action Research* 19(4): 433–452.

Bryson JM, Crosby BC and Bloomberg L (2014) Public value governance: moving beyond traditional public administration and the new public management. *Public Administration Review* 74(4): 445–456.

Cairney P, Russell S and St Denny E (2016) The 'Scottish approach' to policy and policymaking: what issues are territorial and what are universal? *Policy and Politics* 44(3): 333–350.

Chapman C and Hadfield M (2010) Supporting the middle tier to engage with school-based networks: change strategies for influencing and cohering. *Journal of Educational Change* 11: 221–240.

Chapman C and Hadfield M (2015) *Supporting collaborative action research: developing a more systematic approach.* Report, What Works Scotland.

Christie Commission (2011) *Commission on the future delivery of public services.* Report: Scottish Government.

Cochrane A (2007) *Understanding urban policy: a critical approach,* Oxford: Blackwell Publishing.

Cook A (2015) *Partnership working across UK public services.* Report: What Works Scotland.

Dickens L and Watkins K (1999) Action research: rethinking Lewin. *Management Learning* 30(2): 127–140.

Eady S, Drew V and Smith A (2015) Doing action research in organizations: using communicative spaces to facilitate (transformative) professional learning. *Action Research* 13(2): 105–122.

Escobar O (2011) *Public dialogue and deliberation: a communication perspective for public engagement practitioners.* Report: Edinburgh Beltane.

Escobar O (2017) Making it official: participation professionals and the challenge of institutionalizing deliberative democracy. In: Bherer L, Gauthier M and Simard L (eds.) *The professionalisation of public participation,* London: Routledge, 141–164.

Gibb K (2015) *What works and learning from failure.* Report: What Works Scotland.

Greenwood DJ and Levin M (2007) *Introduction to action research: social research for social change* (2nd edn), Thousand Oaks, CA: Sage.

Hadfield M (2012) Becoming critical again: reconnecting critical social theory with the practice of action research. *Educational Action Research* 20(4): 571–585.

Headlam N and Rowe M (2014) The end of the affair: abusive partnerships in austerity. *Journal of Urban Regeneration and Renewal* 7(2): 111–121.

Herr K and Anderson GL (2005). *The action research dissertation: a guide to faculty and students,* London: SAGE Publications Ltd.

Hirsch D, Bryan A, Davis A and Smith N (2013) *A minimum income standard: for remote rural Scotland.* Report: Highlands and Islands Enterprise.

Kindon S, Pain R and Kesby M (2007) Participatory action research: origins, approaches, methods. In: Kindon S, Pain R and Kesby M (eds.) *Participatory action research approaches and methods: connecting people, participation and place,* London: Routledge, 9–18.

Matthews P (2014) Being strategic in partnership–interpreting local knowledge of modern local government. *Local Government Studies* 40(3): 451–472.

Miller E and Barrie K (2016) *Learning from the meaningful and measurable project: strengthening links between identity, action and decision-making*. Report, Health Improvement Scotland.

Osborne SP (2013) A services-influenced approach to public service innovation. In: Osborne SP and Brown L (eds.) *Handbook of innovation in public services*, Cheltenham: Edward Elgar Publishing Ltd, 60–71.

Reason P and Bradbury H (2006) 'Preface', In: Reason P and Bradbury H *The Handbook of action research: concise paperback edition*, London: SAGE Publications Ltd, xxi–xxxii.

Sayer A (2009) Who's afraid of critical social science? *Current Sociology* 2009 (57): 767–786.

Schmachtel S (2016) Local partnerships as 'rationalized myths': a critical examination of the micro-discourse in educational partnership working. *Critical Policy Studies* 10(4): 448–467.

Scottish Government (2011) *Renewing Scotland's public services: priorities for reform in response to the Christie Commission*, Edinburgh: Scottish Government.

Wagenaar H (2007) Philosophical hermeneutics and policy analysis: theory and effectuations. *Critical Policy Studies* 1(4): 311–341.

Williams P (2013) We are all boundary spanners now? *International Journal of Public Sector Management* 26(1): 17–32.

Wittmayer JM, Schäpke N, van Steenbergen F and Omann I (2014) Making sense of sustainability transitions locally: how action research contributes to addressing societal challenges, *Critical Policy Studies* 8(4): 465–485.

Co-inquirer reflection

Alison McPherson

When the Inquiry Team was starting up, my manager invited me to get involved as it could study the learning from my previous job as 'Community Links' worker. Participating in the Inquiry Team and undertaking Collaborative Action Research was entirely voluntary and I welcomed the opportunity to have my conclusions, thinking, and learning, challenged on the three years I had been involved in this community development approach to improving community health and well-being.

The Inquiry Team brought together people from different backgrounds and sectors. This often brought a whole new, more rounded perspective as they would be able to relate my way of working to their own fields. I did not know anyone else on the Inquiry Team apart from my manager. I brought hands-on experience of developing it in a direct service delivery role as opposed to a strategic or managerial role. I felt that my contributions were welcomed and valued even though most other members held more senior positions. They said having someone who had been involved directly in delivering the service added depth of understanding.

Before the Inquiry Team I had already formed my own thoughts and conclusions on why some things had succeeded whilst others had been less successful. This was mainly based on project evaluations we had conducted for funders as well as feedback from individuals who had taken part in activities. Some of the early work of the Inquiry Team involved reading about other Community Links projects across Scotland to broaden our learning and understanding. This was a familiar step for me.

However, I had never been involved in this type of research before. The process and language were new to me. From the attention to detail in complying with good practice in research to having discussions recorded during our meetings, it was all very different. Initially it took time to become familiar with the acronyms and terminology. As the researchers were based at some distance from our area, a considerable amount of contact and correspondence was done electronically or by phone. Inquiry Team meetings were lengthy at four hours, and so demanded a considerable time commitment from all involved and the ability to balance it with the day job.

Normally you work in a team and you know each other's backgrounds and what their priorities are, so you agree a way forward quicker. The Inquiry Team did not have the pressure of direct service delivery, so the pace of work could be frustrating. In our day jobs, we are conditioned to show immediate results. We are normally under pressure to produce results in a much shorter timescale. Having the time to see the bigger picture was quite a luxury. We tend to do a bit of work and not understand fully what has happened. The project or funding comes to an end and then people start pitching in their ideas for the next project, forgetting to think about what happened with the last one. We never join it up as a way of working because we do not have time. We just react to the new money that becomes available. All the time and effort to set things up, whether they are successful or not, disappear when the funding disappears.

By the end of our first research cycle several members of the original Inquiry team had moved on to new jobs or were unable to attend for various reasons. It was difficult to encourage others to take their place because of the time commitment and because we did not have a clear idea of the focus of the next cycle of inquiry. One of the biggest challenges for us was the question: where does this information go to influence and make an impact? You can put your conclusions into a report and put it out there, but you do not know whether people will read it or not.

I did not have a clear vision of how the process would come to an end. Once we produced a report, that was an ending for me. Thinking back, I think the process itself was just as important. Maybe I did not fully appreciate that at the time. The experience of bringing people together was interesting and useful in itself. In my current job, new ways of working are emerging, with an expectation that local communities will play a more active role in defining their needs and seeking solutions. The learning and process of the Inquiry Team continue to be useful. In one area, we have now held a public deliberation exercise and that process had in it some elements that were similar to collaborative action research – gathering information, training, time and space to have discussions, full dialogue and deliberation on the project and decision making. I think this is becoming a way of working.

It has also been a valuable experience as links between different sectors and partnership working becomes the norm. It has given me confidence that you can work well together. It can work if you get people to listen and understand each other. The basis for this has been to allow the time to get to know each other's roles and strengths.

In some ways our action research process was overtaken by the speed of all the changes taking place around and about us. New health and social care teams are being formed and new structures and links to community planning and the third sector are being put in place. Relationships across sectors and ways of working are moving on. All these things are happening at high speed. It is quite unsettling for a lot of people. There is job insecurity and a lot of movement between jobs.

But you cannot rush this. You need to take the time to build relationships and get to know people and find areas of common interest. You cannot side-step that part. The Inquiry Team was a small element of that process.

6 Negotiating space for mild interventions

Action research on the brink between social movements and government policy in Flanders

Erik Paredis and Thomas Block

Introduction

Over the last three decades, sustainable development has grown into one of the main policy concepts to deal with the combination of social and environmental crises that we are dealing with globally. The role and importance of sustainable development is, however, contested. While in the 1990s sustainable development still held some promise of fundamental change, over the last years, a lot of analysts have observed that the mainstreaming of sustainable development has not been able to produce any significant changes in policies, practices or institutions (Dryzek, 2005; Leach *et al.*, 2007; Martinez-Alier *et al.*, 2010). On the other hand, the 2015 climate agreement in Paris and the approval of the 2030 Agenda of the UN with the adoption of Sustainable Development Goals (SDG's) has been reason for some optimism (Sachs, 2015; Nilsson *et al.*, 2016). The challenge of developing more sustainable societies is often framed as one of 'transitions' (Grin *et al.*, 2010) or 'transformations' (Scoones *et al.*, 2015). Transitions are radical changes in societal systems, such as the energy system, the mobility system or the agro-foodsystem. Such transitions are long-term processes that change structures, practices and cultures that are deeply anchored in society, and that will consequently be a site of contestation, power and politics (Avelino *et al.*, 2016).

The growing realisation that challenges such as climate change, food security, mass migration or worldwide inequality will remain on the agenda for decades to come, poses important questions for social movements and civil society organisations. As Johnston (2014: 1) observes: "Social movements are key forces of change in the modern world (…) they move history along, sometimes in significant ways". Well-known historical examples are the struggle for voting rights, labour rights or women's rights. If the role of social movements has been so important in the past, it will probably also be crucial in pushing for the deep changes that are needed to bring about more sustainable societies.

This chapter analyses and reflects on action research developed with a network of civil society organisations in Flanders, Belgium's northern Dutch-speaking region. This Transition Network Civil Society (in Dutch *Transitienetwerk*

Middenveld, TNM) was formed in 2010 by civil society organisations and activists out of a concern to promote just and more radical forms of sustainability transitions than the Flemish government was doing at the time. TNM developed its own vision of a sustainable and just transition, set up activities to invigorate its network, organised lobbying activities, and tried to inspire its member organisations with transition thinking. Although TNM is critical of government policies, the funding to set up the action research was provided by a policy research program from the Flemish government that was aimed at fostering transitions in Flanders and strengthening transition policy. This situates the research in one of the main themes of this book, namely the tension between 'relationality' (building relations with the government and the civil society organisations) and 'criticality' (critical towards government policy, but also towards long-established positions and strategies of social movements).

The research question we try to answer in this chapter is: how can action research play a role in a network of civil society organisations that aim to influence sustainability transitions, and this in a context of contested government policy? While answering this question, we weave the four-tier framework that Bartels and Wittmayer (see Chapter 1) suggest for a critical and relational form of action research in policy analysis into the text. The framework proposes paying attention to (1) negotiation of the starting point of the research process; (2) enacting multiple roles and relationships; (3) addressing hegemonic structures, cultures and practices; and (4) evaluating reflexivity, impact and change. Our focus is mainly on starting points and roles.

The chapter analyses how important context and starting points are to understand what may seem paradoxical, namely that a network that is critical of government policy and wants to develop more radical ideas and practices of transition, is supported by action research funded through a policy programme. It also shows how action research for sustainability transition can follow, what we term, a 'mildly interventionist' mode: the TNM members organised the process themselves and decided which steps to take, with the researcher following the rhythm of the process and looking for opportunities where an intervention could move the process forward, keeping in mind the insights from transition theory and action research.

In the next part, we explain our approach to action research, which is based on sustainability transitions theory and strands of action research that stress leaning and collaboration in joint knowledge-building. The third part focuses on the context in which the action research project was developed and how this shaped the research. It thus mainly relates to the 'starting point' element of the four-tier framework. Part four discusses two episodes of the practice of action research with TNM that influenced visioning and learning. It stresses researcher roles, but also contains elements of impact and addressing hegemony. We end with a discussion and conclusions, structured by the four-tier framework.

Research approach: transitions, action research, sustainability science

The approach to action research developed in the TNM case is guided by sustainability transitions theory, and more in particular by research about transition governance. As said above, transitions are usually defined as radical changes in societal systems. During a transition, a system changes in multiple dimensions: technologies, the actors in the system, the rules and institutions, infrastructures, market circumstances, ways of defining and solving problems, behaviour and practices of citizens, cultural meanings of the system (Geels, 2005). Transitions are long-term processes that go through different stages and that involve a lot of actors. They are complex processes, full of uncertainties about where evolutions are going and about who will win and who will lose (Meadowcroft, 2009, 2011; Grin *et al.*, 2010). There are different opinions about whether and how transitions and socio-technical systems can be influenced. Some authors stress the importance of technological change, in particular through nurturing radical innovations in technological niches and through improving the functioning of niches (Kemp *et al.*, 1998; Schot and Geels, 2008; Hekkert *et al.*, 2007). Others advocate addressing daily practices and routines to shape transitions (Shove, 2003, 2004). The best-known approach, transition management (Loorbach, 2007; Rotmans *et al.*, 2001), suggests creating forums of frontrunners that develop future visions and set up transition experiments.

In spite of their differences, these approaches have several features in common that have inspired the action research with TNM. First, since the trajectories of transitions are full of uncertainties and can impossibly be determined beforehand, actors that have the ambition to influence transitions will constantly be obliged to learn from experiences and adapt to new circumstances. Most authors describe processes of searching, learning and experimenting as a crucial element of transition governance. Second, while government interventions and market mechanisms will be part of the tools to induce and influence transitions, a lot of attention is given to the role that can be played by new policy networks where a plurality of actors – the government being only one of them – interact to understand and tackle problems. Innovators and frontrunners play important roles in these networks. Third, although straightforward steering is not possible, the different approaches assume that smart interventions can influence the direction and speed of a transition. In particular the role of expectations, of future visions and of experiments is stressed. In line with these insights from transition theory, our approach to action research for TNM paid attention to the importance of among other things learning, network formation, visioning and experimenting. In practice, this implied e.g. collaboration in problem structuring and vision development, discussion sessions about roles and strategies for social movements, or preparation and facilitation of working groups on circular economy or SDGs.

The particular form the action research took, was however only partially based on transition approaches. It was also influenced by strands of action research that stress leaning and collaboration in joint knowledge-building, such as action science and community action research. Action science gives attention to discovering together with practitioners 'the tacit choices they have made about their perceptions of reality, about their goals and about strategies for achieving them' (Friedman, 2011: 133). Community action research focuses on collaboration among diverse organisations, creating settings for collective reflection amongst organisations, and leveraging progress in individual organisations (Senge and Scharmer, 2011). In the action research with TNM, this translated in the writing of a so-called learning history (Bradbury, 2006; Gearty, 2008; Roth and Bradbury, 2010). The goal of a learning history is to capture what people have learned during a process of change. The story is intended as a jointly told tale of participants and researchers, providing an opportunity to share experiences and insights. Roth and Bradbury (2010) define it as simultaneously a product and a process: the process focuses on common reflection and learning about the initiative, in that way strengthening the initiative and the cooperation between participants. The hope is that individuals learn, but that there is also organisational learning. It fosters sustainable development 'by facilitating dialogue spaces that allow a multiplicity of voices' (Bradbury, 2006: 241). The product is a written document, a history of the initiative based on document study, interviews and common reflection. The text has three layers: the factual story as shared by the participants, a layer with interpretations and comments of participants about how they experienced particular episodes, and a layer with reflections by the researcher about the other two layers. Typographically, this is made visible in the layout of the text.

Apart from being influenced by transition research and certain traditions in action research, our approach more in general fits in an interpretive or constructivist tradition (Furlong and Marsh, 2010). In ontological terms, this position rejects the idea that value-free science with an independent outsider-researcher is possible. Reality is not discovered, but gets meaning through the interpretation of actors. In a context of controversial and political issues such as sustainability and transitions, this implies that science cannot provide methodologies that simply have to be followed to arrive at unequivocal problem definitions and clear-cut solutions. In particular, in relation to sustainability, numerous authors have stressed that a new approach to science is needed (variously called Mode 2 science, sustainability science, post-normal science) (Nowotny *et al.*, 2003). Some characteristics of this 'science for sustainability' include inter- and transdisciplinary research, co-production of knowledge, systemic integration, contextual knowledge, learning-oriented perspective, production of socially robust knowledge, attention to system innovation and transition (Hugé *et al.*, 2016). Action research fits in well with such an approach to knowledge and science since it aims at collaborative knowledge production and mutual learning between scientists and involved stakeholders (Greenwood and Levin, 2007).

As said above, we are interested in understanding how action research played a role in a network of civil society organisations and activists that aim to influence sustainability transitions. As a first step, we analyse the context in which the research could emerge and its implications. This is immediately related to one of the elements of the four-tier framework for this book, namely the negotiation of starting points for the research.

Box 6.1 A brief timeline of the main events that appear in the analysis in this chapter

- 2004/2006: start of the first two transition management processes in Flanders (for housing and building, and for waste and material policy).
- 2007: start of the Policy Research Centre on Sustainable Development, with two research projects about transition dynamics and transition management.
- 2010: start of the Transition Network Civil Society (TNM), with an invitation to one of the authors to join the network as an engaged researcher. Between July 2010 and January 2012, a lot of the activities of TNM focus on problem structuring and future visioning.
- April 2011: approval of the second Flemish Strategy for Sustainable Development, with transitions at its core.
- July 2011: the Flemish government decides to renew the socio-economic innovation programme Flanders in Action (ViA) by introducing 13 transition management processes.
- 2012: start of the Policy Research Centre TRADO, with a focus on transition research and with action research as a central methodology. One of the research projects provides an opportunity to start action research with TNM.
- 2012: drawing of a mindmap to present the TNM vision.
- 2015: the new Flemish government decides to end the TRADO programme.
- 2015–2016: writing of a learning history with TNM.

Action research for TNM: starting points and context

It holds true for any type of research, that it does not 'just happen'. Research is always shaped by questions of funding, time, access, actors involved and so on. To analyse the starting points and context of our action research in TNM, we have to make a distinction between four logics that together shaped the research. The first is the logic of policy development by the Flemish government in the fields of socio-economic innovation policy, sustainable development and transitions. Second is the development of science policy, and in particular the evolutions in policy research for sustainable development. Third are the interests of policymakers and of us as researchers, in particular of one of us (Paredis) who was the active researcher with TNM. And finally, of course related to the objectives of TNM itself and the composition of its membership. In the relationship between these logics, a space had to be negotiated for action research which would influence its ambitions, practices and outcomes.

The policy context

In a period of around ten years, between 2004 and 2014, a policy context developed in Flanders that was relatively favourable for research about sustainability transitions (Paredis, 2013). The first step in this evolution was the introduction in 2004 and 2006 of two transition management processes in environmental policy (namely in sustainable housing and building, and in waste and materials policy). With these, Flanders became the first region outside the Netherlands to start experimenting with transition management in its government policy. In a next important step in 2011, transitions and transition management became the central element of the Flemish sustainable development strategy. This strategy contained a long-term vision for 2050 and recognised a need for transition in seven systems: housing and building, materials, energy, mobility, food, health, and the knowledge system. The third step followed in the same period when the Flemish government was discussing a renewal of its main socio-economic innovation plan, called 'Flanders in Action' (ViA, *Vlaanderen in Actie*). From 2006 onwards, the Flemish government had through ViA mobilised more than 2000 'captains of society' to develop ambitious plans for the Flemish economy and society. ViA's aim was to make Flanders more competitive, growth-oriented, technologically at the forefront of Europe, and simultaneously greener and more social. The program became one of the cornerstones of the Flemish governmental declaration 2009–2014. However, by mid-2010 it was obvious in government circles that the ViA process had trouble finding a suited policy approach that fitted the high ambitions. That approach was finally found in the sustainability domain, from which the concepts of 'transition' and 'transition management' were imported in socio-economic innovation policy (for a detailed analysis, see Paredis, 2013). Consequently, in July 2011 the government decided to start transition management projects in 13 policy domains.

Because of these developments, by 2012 it had become almost impossible in Flanders to discuss innovation and sustainable development without using the word 'transitions'. There is of course ample room for discussing how far all this transition talk is still true to the original meanings of sustainability transitions (Debruyne and De Bisschop, 2013; Paredis and Block, 2015), but this is not our main point here. These evolutions created a need to strengthen knowledge and experience about transitions and transition management, and thus a relatively favourable context for research. There was in particular an interest in action research, even though this was with the rather utilitarian motivation that such an approach would accelerate the implementation of transition policies in Flanders.

The research context

By 2012, there was also a vehicle available for developing such research, namely the Policy Research Centre TRADO (TRADO is an acronym for *Transities voor Duurzame Ontwikkeling*, Transitions for Sustainable Development). Again, TRADO was the result of a longer evolution. Already in 2002, the Flemish government had created a programme of Centres for Policy Relevant Research (*Steunpunten voor Beleidsrelevant Onderzoek*) for a broad range of policy domains. Between 2007 and 2011, the government funded for the first time such a Centre to support sustainable development policy in Flanders. Four research groups – including our own – from three universities cooperated in the new Policy Centre. In the call for this Policy Centre for Sustainable Development, transitions and transition management were mentioned as research themes and that is how one of us (Paredis) began working on two half-time projects – on transition dynamics and on transition management – in early 2007. Because of the evolutions in the policy domain described above, the round of calls for a new Policy Research Centre 2012–2015 centred fully around transition research. Importantly, the call explicitly mentioned that part of the research had to be action research, as a complement to more conventional forms of research. The main hope was that this would create more impact and thus be a better support for the implementation of sustainability policy and ViA. The new Policy Research Centre TRADO explicitly incorporated methods of action research in its different research streams. It is within one of these – with the title *Structure and agency dynamics in transition governance processes and transition experiments* – that the action research with TNM would be developed.

TRADO thus provided funding and created time and space to develop action research. The particular structure of the Policy Centres – with a Board and project groups with representatives from the minister, civil servants and stakeholders – also provided an environment where the research could be discussed and knowledge and experiences exchanged. This also influenced the choice of TNM as a case study, as will be discussed next.

Converging research interests

The Board of a Policy Research Centre, in a close dialogue between researchers, civil servants and representatives from the minister, decides on case studies. Paredis was appointed as researcher for the project *Structure and agency dynamics in transition governance processes and transition experiments*. The general aim of this project was to understand what hinders or stimulates the involvement of actors in transition processes and experiments and to find ways to deal with obstacles and expand the manoeuvring space of actors. Paredis proposed two case studies for the project, one of which was TNM.[1] TNM seemed an interesting case because until 2010, almost all transition processes in Flanders had been initiated by the Flemish government, while TNM had grown bottom-up. Furthermore, it did not take the typical socio-technical systems perspective of transition management as a starting point but opted for a broad societal approach. These arguments appealed to the minister and civil servants. Partly because the government hoped to increase the interest of civil society organisations in its transition policy, since the objectives seemed unattainable without participation from a broad range of stakeholders (civil society, industry, knowledge actors). But there was more to it. Several of the policymakers had been active in social movements themselves and they valued the role of civil society organisations. Also, on the side of the researcher, the proposal to engage in action research with TNM stemmed from a personal history and interest in the role of social movements, and from a personal conviction that social movements will be crucial in bringing about sustainable change. From 1993 till 2001, Paredis worked for an NGO-network in Flanders (called VODO) as a campaigner, lobbyist and later coordinator. Once he became a researcher at Ghent

University, he regularly remained involved in NGO-activities or tried to involve NGO's in research.[2] Early 2010, he was contacted by the then coordinator of VODO, who was one of the initiators of TNM, with the question to join the starting TNM network. So, the proposal to develop action research also provided an opportunity to spend research time in an engagement that was already existing.

Research projects often leave some room for choosing case studies. Although TNM was partly initiated in reaction against Flemish government policies – as we will see next – this did not hinder the choice in TRADO for TNM as a case for action research. A convergence of interests from the researcher and from policy makers provided this room.

Logics in TNM

Of course, also the objectives and concerns of TNM shaped the research. TNM was formed in 2010 and is still active.[3] The network consists of a mix of around 20 organisations from the 'old' social movements (the two main unions), the 'new' social movements (such as the environmental and third world movement), arts and socio-cultural organisations, an ethical bank and individual members from new media and academia. The direct source of inspiration for TNM, was the book Terra *Reversa. De transitie naar rechtvaardige duurzaamheid* ('Terra Reversa, the transition to just sustainability') (Jones and De Meyere, 2009). The book makes a case for transitions in food, mobility, housing and living, and tourism, but adds that existing transition processes, such as those set up by the Flemish government, disregard social aspects of transition. According to Jones and De Meyere, social movements are the main actors for initiating a radical transition, but only when they can build enough countervailing power and act from a common vision. During a tour of Flanders to promote the book, this idea gained ground with leaders from the unions, NGO's and socio-cultural organisations. Most of these organisations where of course already involved in a broad range of activities around ecology and social justice, but the theme of transitions was new to them. While it seemed to promise a new and dynamic approach to existing concerns, most organisations realised that they could not tackle the theme on their own and that collaboration was necessary to make progress. It took some time to attune expectations between organisations and to assemble a group, but on 1 July 2010, the new network started officially. The network decided to take 'just sustainability' and 'just transition' as its central themes, in that way integrating ecological and social concerns. Its goal was to develop a common vision, position and strategy vis-à-vis Flemish government views and initiatives around transition. Working groups developed specific visions, lobbying and projects for themes such as energy, food and agriculture, mobility, housing and living, work, care, and taxation.

Paredis was invited by the organisers to join TNM, not because he could develop research with or about TNM, but because they sought a mix of voices that could bring TNM into being as a network with a vision of just and ecological transitions and with strategies that could push forward a civil society agenda. Paredis had experience with social movements, awareness of their sensitivities and a network with a diversity of organisations. Furthermore, as a researcher, he had developed a sympathising but critical stance towards transitions and transition management, and this found an ear with the founders of TNM.

An important characteristic of the action research with TMN was that it did not follow a strong interventionist logic with a predetermined set of stages, such as is for example the case in typical transition management projects (Loorbach, 2007; Nevens *et al.*, 2012; Wittmayer, 2016). In transition management, the researchers play a central role in initiating the project, setting up the methodology, guiding the participants through the different stages and providing substantive inputs. The action research for TNM on the other hand, could be characterised as 'mildly interventionist': the TNM members organised the process themselves and decided which steps to take, with the researcher following the rhythm of the process and looking for opportunities where an intervention could move the process forward, keeping in mind the insights from transition theory and action research discussed above (see 'Research approach'). For example, after several meetings with strategy discussions, the researcher and participants concluded that it would be useful to deepen insights in the practicability of social movement theory and transition theory. This led to a presentation and discussion session, a strategy note co-authored with a member of the socialist union and a background paper on the theme. In the next part of this chapter, we focus in detail on two other episodes of our action research approach in practice. Such an approach comes of course with its own challenges, to which we return in the discussion.

The practice of action research with TNM

The preceding paragraphs analysed in detail how the action research with TNM was shaped by its context and starting points. Of course, also other elements of the four-tier framework can be recognised in that discussion, such as the role of a researcher (e.g. in proposing case studies) and of addressing hegemonic structures (e.g. in balancing the rather instrumental view on action research from the government with the goals of TNM). In this section, we focus on our practices of action research with TNM, in particular the element of 'role' will be central, but it also contains elements of 'addressing hegemonic structures' and 'impact and change'. We focus on two episodes during the TNM process, namely the problem structuring and the formulation of a common vision for TNM, and the development of a learning history with TNM.

Finding common ground: a vision in a mindmap

During the first months that TNM came together, starting in July 2010, the process followed a structure that was inspired by transition management: first the TNM steering group tried to formulate a common problem analysis, next to developing a vision for the future. As said above, the role of the researcher was 'mildly' interventionist: he did not play a leading role but participated in the discussions, brought in ideas, and during the problem structuring functioned as kind of knowledge broker by integrating the arguments and preparing several versions of summary documents. Finding common ground over the problem analysis did not pose a major problem for the TNM participants, but next, from late 2010 until the summer of 2011, the steering group tried to develop a common vision on 'just transition'. Almost immediately the broadness of the theme in combination with the diversity of organisations around the table raised a difficult question: what should we focus on? In how much detail should we go? Is it possible to combine all different viewpoints in one vision? The differences in view were deeper than expected. Whereas some of the more vested organisations (such as the labour unions and the environmental movement) wanted to focus on energy and climate and opted for a strategy of lobbying and coalition building around these themes, smaller organisations from the socio-cultural sector and some of the individual members involved defended that the diverse TNM coalition also had to develop a broad vision and had to opt for a diversified strategy. After five meetings, there was still no result on the table. The steering group now turned for support to a consultant with experience in future visioning, who had also been involved in the Flemish transition management processes. Interestingly, this support was possible though a budget for the promotion of ViA. The work of the consultant initiated a more creative process from September 2011 onwards, but the ideas still had to be translated in a common text. By January 2012, a far advanced working version of a common vision was on the table. However, to fit with the views of all participants, the text had gone through several rounds of amendments, additions and nuances, making it a difficult text to use and communicate with.

In early May 2012, Paredis was present at a TNM working group to prepare the first Transition Festival. The task of the working group was to propose on the basis of the vision a series of workshops for the festival and to invite exemplary, innovative local practices. However, the meeting did not pass smoothly, one of the main reasons being that the vision text did not provide enough guidance for the discussion. With frustrations growing, Paredis hinted that it should be possible to simplify and restructure the text and offered to give it a try by the next meeting of the steering group. The restructuring took the form of a mind map. The centre of the mind map defined TNM's core business as 'a transition for a just and sustainable society'. TNM's goals were formulated in six substantive branches and one strategic branch, with each branch further refined through more specific sub-goals. The mind map was presented and discussed during the steering group of May 2012.

Although not everybody was immediately convinced – some fearing that it might be too simplified and childish – most members present were enthusiastic. During ensuing discussions, some branches were reformulated and a few new ones were added. In the end, the mind map defined six main substantive ambitions for TNM: a societal embedment of the economy, realising quality of life,

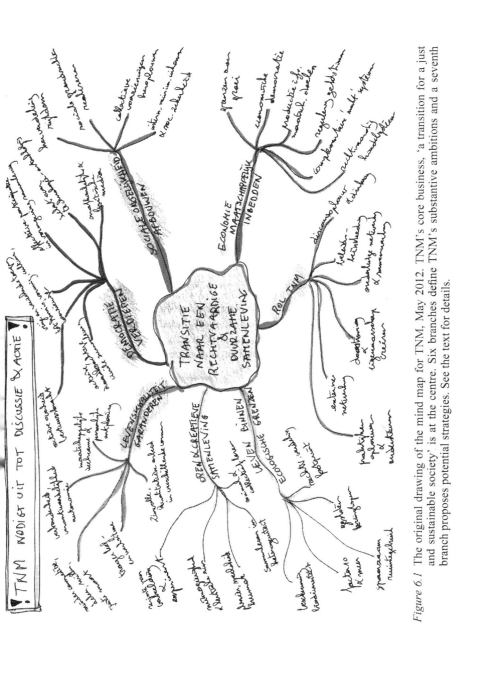

Figure 6.1 The original drawing of the mind map for TNM, May 2012. TNM's core business, 'a transition for a just and sustainable society', is at the centre. Six branches define TNM's substantive ambitions and a seventh branch proposes potential strategies. See the text for details.

cutting back on social inequality, deepening democracy, living together openly and creatively, living within ecological limits. The sub-branches made more explicit what the network stood for, e.g. limits to growth, redistribution of incomes and capital, 100 per cent renewable energy, a slower work and life rhythm. The final version of the mind map was handed to a graphic designer to turn it into a presentable and pleasant communication tool.

Over the following months and years, the mind map became the central discursive element in the discourse coalition that TNM had been aiming for. It gave organisations a better idea of what TNM stood for and explicated the vision, it informed discussions in the steering and working groups, and it facilitated communication. In that sense, action research had an impact in TNM. It was only a few years later, during the research for a learning history of TNM (see next paragraph) that two other, perhaps more important, effects surfaced. Somewhat unwittingly, the mind map had 'solved' the problem of how the smaller socio-cultural organisations could address the dominant framings and strategies of the more vested groups. First, the overview created by the mind map gave each organisation and its themes a place in a broader entity. It connected organisations and simultaneously created a sense of one's own place, identity and contribution to the whole. In that way, it literally built a discourse coalition. Second, the mind map does not work with full sentences, but with two- to four-word paraphrases. This makes it a relatively open vision, sticking organisations less to a fixed and negotiated text, and leaving room for interpretation and dialogue between member organisations and with the rest of society.

Learning as a group: the jointly told tale of a learning history

For the second episode, we turn to the development of a learning history with TNM. In late 2013 the researcher proposed the TNM steering group to develop a learning history of TNM. This idea had taken roots for several reasons. First, learning is considered an essential part of transition processes – 'learning by doing and doing by learning' is an often-repeated phrase in transition management. Still, in practice, participants seldom reserve time for common learning and it is mostly left implicit. That common learning could be useful, showed itself in how TNM was wrestling with some persistent topics that kept popping up on the agenda, in particular an ongoing discussion about what exactly the strategic goals should be of the network: should TNM focus on influence on policy, organising challenging niches, internal reorientation towards transition within member organisations, relations with and added value vis-à-vis other networks, or communication with a broad public, or perhaps all of that? A second reason for proposing a learning history was that it also fitted in the agenda of the TRADO research. It provided an opportunity to learn more about the main research questions such as better understanding how social movements try to play a role in transitions, which kind of change they strive after, how they define problems and solutions and how they try to gain influence.

Some TNM members were initially hesitant to step into the project, expressing a concern that the government might use the insights gained from the research against TNM. Most were, however, enthusiastic. It seemed a possibility to strengthen the network and become more reflexive and aware of what was happening, how and why. The condition for participation was, however, that the research would not interfere with planned activities and not push its own agenda. And indeed, the learning history was several times postponed because it did not fit in with the busy agenda of TNM. But this was part of the relational understanding that had been built up, namely to try to fit the research in with the rhythm of the process.

Paredis developed the learning history mainly between the Spring of 2015 and 2016. Reconstructing the story meant of course a lot of document study, but it also relied on interviews with ten participants and one ex-participant who left TNM because of disagreement with strategic choices. As is often the case, the interviews were not only a moment of information sharing, but also forced interviewees to reflect on their role, their relationship with other organisations, on what TNM had meant for them and what should be its role in the future. In June 2015, the steering group organised a group discussion about the first version of the learning history. The text was distributed beforehand and in preparation of the meeting, the researcher had drawn a timeline of TNM on an old roll of wallpaper. Steering group members were asked to answer two questions: 'What drew your (positive or negative) attention in the history?' and 'Which moment do you absolutely want to discuss with the rest of group?'. During a second group discussion in May 2016, when the learning history was almost finalised, participants were asked to answer two other questions: 'What are two learning points that you take from the history?' and 'Which conclusions do you draw for the future development of TNM?'.

The group sessions delivered some extra information for writing the history, but most importantly, they created space and time for a joint reflection on the process that participants had spent a lot of time and energy on during the previous years. The specific structure and lay-out of the learning history – with citations and comments of people on how they perceived certain episodes and developments of TNM – confronted participants with each other's opinions. This included some surprises, such as when people noted that one of the union leaders had consciously pulled out because he found that TNM did not deliver enough political results. Or when they learned that one of the socio-cultural members had thought about quitting (but did not in the end) because he had the idea that his voice was not taken seriously. The conversations during these group sessions were respectful and with a sense of trying to understand each other in order to strengthen the group and TNM.

The methodology of a leaning history is strongly relational in how it makes interaction possible between researcher and participants, but also serves critical purposes by allowing a critical dialogue about objectives and decisions taken. Several collective lessons learned emerged from the learning history, such as how the discourse coalition had been actively constructed. It brought the insight that the strategy discussion had been contained by opting for a pallet of strategies after a lot of trial and error, but also because some of the voices that pleaded for more radical, bottom-up strategies had left the network. It made participants also more aware that the activities of the network are still mostly outward-oriented, while also deeper changes in civil society organisations themselves are needed. Although members recognised the need to restructure their own organisations in order to work more integrated and transversal towards sustainability transition, a lot of organisations did not seem ready for such a change.[4]

Discussion and conclusions

In the introductory chapter to the book, Bartels and Wittmayer state that a sys-tematic understanding of the potential of action research for understanding and supporting sustainability is still missing. This chapter is based on action research with a network of civil society organisations that explicitly aim to influence sustainability transitions and Flemish policy in a series of transition domains. 'How can action research play a role for such a network and in such a context?', was the research question we tried to answer. We use the elements of the four-tier framework to reflect on this question.

Context and starting points obviously matter. That context matters is a long-established idea in policy analysis but the question is how it matters (Goodin and Tilly, 2006). Research never appears out of thin air. A combination of several elements created a favourable context for action research with TNM. 'Created' is perhaps the wrong word: a favourable context is at least partly constructed, and starting points have to be negotiated. In this case, context and starting points included: transition management that had made its way into sustainability policy and innovation policy, a demand to have scientists as active partners in the development of transition processes, civil servants and government representa-tives that were convinced of the important role of social movements in society, the personal convictions of the researcher and a relation of trust between TNM and the researcher. It is this particular context that explains what otherwise may seem paradoxical, namely that a network that is critical of government policy and wants to develop more radical ideas and practices of transition, is supported by action research funded through a policy programme. The starting points made a balance possible between relationality and criticality. Here, context seems to have mattered mostly through ideas (Rueschmeyer, 2006): ideas about the importance of transitions, sustainability, the role of social movements. In this respect, it is instructive to observe what happened when a new, more conser-vative government stepped into office in 2014, with dominant parties that have no affinity with sustainable development and that want to curb the influence of social movement organisations. At that moment, ViA was stopped and sustain-able development policy more or less suspended. Consequently, the new govern-ment also lost its interest in the TRADO Research Centre and decided in 2015 to abolish it. In this different context, it is inconceivable that the government would have agreed with action research for TNM.

There is another way in which context matters and that is in the approaches scientists use to develop knowledge. In a policy environment with contested concepts such as sustainability and transitions, the deliberative and co-productive approach of action research proves to be valuable. In particular, paraphrasing Roth and Bradbury (2010), the methodology of learning histories provided a structure to TNM that allowed a dialogue to be set up between organisations and support mutual learning in synergy between researcher and practitioners. We are charmed (and convinced) by Bradbury's argument that the ability 'to engage in dialogue, that is in developing an attitude of personal inquiry and social objectivity, may be thought of as the process equivalent of developing technological innovations to aid us in our quest for a sustainable state' (Bradbury 2006: 241).

What did we learn about how a researcher enacts multiple roles and relationships in action research? The account of two episodes of action research for TNM shows – as Wittmayer and Schäpke (2014) have observed for other processes – that researchers have to combine different roles during an action research process: it entails mediation between different perspectives (the role of knowledge broker), which alternates with and/or is combined with facilitation of learning processes (process facilitator), addressing problems (change agent), analysing and reporting (reflective scientist) and thinking about one's role and position (self-reflexive scientist). One could add that with the methodology of the learning history, a researcher is also an archaeologist of processes and a conservationist of insights and learning.

The TNM case reveals two other aspects of researcher roles. First, it shows how action research for sustainability transitions can be, what we termed, 'mildly interventionist', where the researcher does not have to be in one of the leading roles (as opposed to the more interventionist approach of transition management, which is the dominant approach to action research in the transition community). The intensity and forms of action research can vary during a process, in particular in a process that takes the form of a long-term cooperation network such as TNM, without a defined end point. In a mildly interventionist mode, action research develops partly on the rhythm of the process and the needs in the process, and partly on the rhythm of what the researcher can deliver. Sometimes, it can be restricted to participating in meetings, being part of the discussion, introducing different perspectives or helping the conversation along. At other times, it can take the more intensive form of a learning history (with its document study, interviews, reconstruction, writing up, facilitation of group discussions). We realise that such an approach may not always be possible. It demands some experience from the researcher to switch between methodologies and draw on different theoretical frames, while in practical terms flexibility is needed in research planning. Both are probably easier for a postdoctoral researcher who can alternate between agendas of different research projects (as was the case here). Furthermore, for the researcher it was only possible to exhibit this flexibility because long-term funding allowed it and because the board of the Policy Research Centre TRADO allowed flexibility in delivering results.

This last argument relates to a second point, namely that the case teaches that a researcher does not only play roles during the action research itself, but also in negotiating a space for that action research in between the policymakers and the practitioners. This concept of space (Wicks and Reason, 2009; Wittmayer and Schäpke, 2014), agora (Pohl *et al*., 2010) or arena (Greenwood and Levin, 2007; Loorbach, 2007) is often used to refer to the mental and physical space where scientists and practitioners meet to co-produce knowledge and develop understanding of problems and solutions. In the TNM-case, this would be the TNM steering group. However, with this idea of an in-between space we also refer to a more prosaic space, namely one where in a policy context interests can converge between the policymaker, the researcher and the participants in the research. That in-between space has to be actively negotiated so that the logics keep each other in check. We already mentioned this in the discussion of starting points. What we did not mention, is that such an in-between space also has to be actively kept open in a long-term process, e.g. by regular meetings to report intermediate results or to discuss the next research steps, by conference presentations, or by informal conversations about research activities to rub away tensions over progress.

Finally, we turn briefly to the elements 'impact' and 'addressing hegemony' of the four-tier framework, addressing them together because – at least in this case – they are strongly related. The action research for TNM seems to have been useful at the level of the network: it was important for uniting the network under a common vision and it reinforced the dialogue amongst its participants about how and why the network grew as it did. In order to do so, it had to address hegemonic framings and practices amongst social movements. In terms of vision and strategy, a balance had to be found between framings and practices of more vested organisations (such as the unions and the environmental movement) and the smaller socio-cultural organisations and engaged individuals in the network. In facilitating this dialogue, the action research strengthened the network and contributed to its objectives.

However, it takes of course a lot more to either change transition policy and influence sustainability transitions in Flanders – the original ambition of TNM – or to influence the member organisations of TNM in their discourses and practices. TNM has not had direct influence on policy, but it is meanwhile recognised as a new actor in the broad sustainability community. The translation of the transition idea into the working practices of the member organisations is still limited. In all this, an action research project is but one small factor amongst many. The impact of the research blends in with the impact of the whole set of activities of TNM on the one hand, and an almost intangible complex web of societal influences on the other hand. A self-reflexive researcher will realise that a bit of modesty in assessing the impact of research is no luxury. At the same time, what is considered relevant and useful knowledge also depends on a researcher's perspective: what he/she considers worthwhile research topics and concerns, what his theory of change is, how he wants to have impact. While it is often difficult to assess the impact of one particular research project, a combination of different research projects over a longer time period may have some impact. At least, that is one of the aims of our work.

Notes

1 The other was a government-driven transition process for sustainable housing and building, the so-called DuWoBo process.
2 In 2003–2004 the mentioned NGO network VODO was e.g. partner in a research project on ecological debt; in 2005–2006, VODO was involved in a research project on international climate negotiations.
3 The website of TNM is www.transitienetwerkmiddenveld.be/.
4 The learning history was published as a working paper for TRADO (in Dutch) and can be downloaded at https://biblio.ugent.be/publication/8102190/file/8102197.pdf.

References

Avelino F, Grin J, Pel B and Jhagroe S (2016) The politics of sustainability transitions. *Journal of Environmental and Policy Planning* 18(5): 557–567.
Bradbury H (2006) Learning with the natural step: action research to promote conversations for sustainable development. In: Reason P and Bradbury H (eds.) *Handbook of action research. the concise paperback edition*, London: SAGE Publications, 236–242.
Debruyne P and De Bisschop A (2013) Transitie, de meesterzet van de ideologie? *Oikos* 65(2): 46–62.
Dryzek J (2005) *The politics of the earth. Environmental discourses*, Oxford: Oxford University Press.
Friedman VJ (2011) Action science: creating communities of inquiry in communities of practice. In: Reason P and Bradbury H (eds.) *Handbook of action research. the concise paperback edition*, London: SAGE Publications, 131–143.
Furlong P and Marsh D. (2010) A skin, not a sweater: ontology and epistemology in political science. In: Marsh D and Stoker G (eds.) *Theory and methods in political science*, Basingstoke: Palgrave, 184–211.
Gearty M (2008) Achieving carbon reduction: learning from stories of vision, chance and determination. *Journal of Corporate Citizenship* 30: 81–94.
Geels F (2005) *Technological transition and system innovations. A co-evolutionary and socio-technical analysis*, Cheltenham: Edward Elgar Publishing.
Goodin RE and Tilly C (2006) *The Oxford handbook of contextual policy analysis*, Oxford: Oxford University Press.
Greenwood DJ and Levin M (2007) *Introduction to action research: social research for social change*, Thousand Oaks: Sage.
Grin J, Rotmans J and Schot J (eds.) (2010) *Transitions to sustainable development. New directions in the study of long term transformative change*, New York: Routledge.
Hekkert M, Suurs R, Negro S, Kuhlmann S and Smits R (2007) Functions of innovation systems: a new approach for analysing technological change. *Technological Forecasting and Social Change* 74: 413–432.
Hugé J, Block T, Waas T, Wright T and Dahdouh-Guebas F (2016) How to walk the talk? Developing actions for sustainability in academic research. *Journal of Cleaner Production* 137: 83–92.
Johnston H (2014) *What is a social movement?* Cambridge: Polity.

Jones PT and De Meyere V (2009) *Terra Reversa. De transitie naar rechtvaardige duurzaamheid.* Antwerpen/Utrecht: EPO/Jan Van Arkel.

Leach M, Bloom G, Ely A, Nightingale P, Scoones I, Shah E and Smith A (2007) *Understanding governance: pathways to sustainability.* STEPS Working Paper 2, Brighton: STEPS Centre.

Loorbach D. (2007) *Transition management, new mode of governance for sustainable development,* Utrecht: International Books.

Martinez-Alier J, Pascual U, Vivien F-D and Zaccai E (2010) Sustainable de-growth: mapping the context, criticisms and future prospects of an emergent paradigm. *Ecological Economics* 69: 1741–1747.

Meadowcroft J, (2009) What about the politics? Sustainable development, transition management, and long term energy transitions. *Policy Sciences* 42: 323–340.

Meadowcroft J (2011) Engaging with the politics of sustainability transitions. *Environmental Innovation and Societal Transitions* 1: 70–75.

Nevens F, Frantzeskaki N, Loorbach D and Gorissen L (2012) Urban transition labs: co-creating transformative action for sustainable cities. *Journal of Cleaner Production* 50: 111–122.

Nilsson M, Griggs D and Visbeck M (2016), Policy: map the interactions between sustainable development goals. *Nature* 534: 320–322.

Nowotny H, Scott P and Gibbons M (2003) Introduction: 'Mode 2' revisited: The new production of knowledge. *Minerva* 41(3): 179–194.

Paredis E (2013) *A winding road. Transition management, policy change and the search for sustainable development.* PhD dissertation, Gent: UGent.

Paredis E and Block T (2015) Transitiepraktijk van de Vlaamse overheid: meer dan een schijnbeweging? *Vlaams Tijdschrift voor Overheidsmanagement* (1): 11–18.

Pohl C, Rist S, Zimmermann A, Fry P, Gurung GS, Schneider F, Speranza CI, Kiteme B, Boillat S, Serrano E, Hirsch Hadorn G and Wiesmann U (2010) Researchers' roles in knowledge coproduction: experience from sustainability research in Kenya, Switzerland, Bolivia and Nepal. *Science and Public Policy* 37(4): 267–281.

Rip A and Kemp R (1998) Technological Change. In: Rayner S and Malone E, *Human choice and climate change,* Columbus, Ohio: Batelle Press, 327–399.

Roth G and Bradbury H (2010) Learning history: an action research practice in support of actionable learning. In: Reason P and Bradbury H (eds.) *The SAGE handbook of action research. participative inquiry and practice. Second edition,* London: SAGE Publications.

Rotmans J, Kemp R, van Asselt M (2001) More evolution than revolution: transition management in public policy. *Foresight* 3 (1): 15–31.

Rueschmeyer D (2006) Why and how ideas matter. In: Goodin RE and Tilly C (eds.) *The Oxford handbook of contextual policy analysis,* Oxford: Oxford University Press.

Sachs JD (2015) *The age of sustainable development,* New York: Columbia University Press.

Schot J and Geels F (2008) Strategic niche management and sustainable innovation journeys: theory, findings, research agenda, and policy. *Technology Analysis and Strategic Management* 20(5): 537–554.

Scoones I, Leach M and Newell P (eds.) (2015) *The politics of green transformation,* Abingdon: Routledge.

Senge PM and Scharmer CO (2011) Community action research: learning as a community of practitioners, consultants and researchers. In: Reason P and Bradbury H (eds.) *Handbook of action research. the concise paperback edition,* London: SAGE Publications, 195–206.

Shove E (2003) *Comfort, cleanliness and convenience. The social organization of normality*, Oxford/New York: Berg.

Shove E (2004) Sustainability, system innovation and the laundry. In: Elzen B, Geels FW and Green K (eds.) (2004) *System innovation and the transition to sustainability. Theory, evidence and policy*, Cheltenham: Edward Elgar.

Wicks PG, Reason P (2009) Initiating action research. Challenges and paradoxes of opening communicative space. *Action Research* 7(3): 243–262.

Wittmayer JM (2016) *Transition management, action research and actor roles. Understanding local sustainability transitions*. PhD Dissertation, Rotterdam: Erasmus University Rotterdam.

Wittmayer JM and Schäpke N (2014) Action, research and participation: roles of researchers in sustainability transitions. *Sustainability Science* 9(4): 483–496.

Co-inquirer reflection

Dirk Barrez

In 2009, I was one of the initiators of the Transition Network Civil Society (TNM) and I am still an active member. Next to working as an independent journalist at PALA.be (previously working for the public broadcaster), I am an author of non-fiction books mainly on globalisation, most recently about transition, and before about cooperatives.

When I look back at how the network started in late 2009 early 2010 and why we invited Erik Paredis to participate, this was not with the intention to develop research for or about TNM. We asked him to cooperate in developing the network in his role as an academic with previous working experience in the NGO-sector and with knowledge of transitions. Later on, in mid-2012, Erik saw an opportunity to set up action research with TNM. He presented this offer to the group with the question whether we were interested and what we expected from it. What persuaded us is that in network processes with civil society groups, reflexivity and a critical attitude towards formulated solutions and chosen strategies is seldom high on the agenda. It is then advantageous to have a critical insider-outsider who can analyse and confront you with your actions. Furthermore, we have the luck that members in the steering group of the network are open to such an approach and are willing to learn.

In spite of his research role, it did not feel like we were being observed. Everybody knew that a researcher was involved, but I do not think that this has at any moment influenced what people brought to the table or how they acted. In the relationship with the network members, he has always been considered as "one of the group", even at certain moments one of the more important figures because he played a central role in defining the vision of the network. He cooperated in writing the vision texts and translated them into our mind map. That mind map is probably the most essential document of who and what we are as a network. It still functions as a reference framework in our discussions.

Of course, action research confronts you with certain challenges. A lot of new and more sustainable practices are popping up everywhere, but social movements and civil society organisations do not seem to have the power and capacity to go beyond these practices and formulate and realise coherent, system-wide solutions, or to push the political and economic world into that direction. The financial system remains on the brink of collapse, but we are not capable of formulating an alternative and as a society reinforce our grip on the banking system. In the decades after the Second World War, social movements had a much stronger network in academia, where parts of the brainwork was being done and where movements found support for the development of a broad vision for the industrial and the social welfare state. If we want to topple systems towards sustainability, sooner or later we will again have to build such a supportive knowledge base. In my opinion, the best solutions for societal problems have in the past seldom come from the business world or even politics. So, civil society is obliged to keep on developing new ideas, formulating solutions and implementing new practices, from niche to stable new systems. This is where action research with its practice of cooperative knowledge creation can play a role.

Action research in TNM had an impact. I already mentioned the cooperation around the vision. The learning history helped to gain better insights in how the process has grown into where we are now, which hurdles we had to take, why we have taken certain decisions, what the meaning of a network is for us, and what different people thought about different episodes in our development. It showed how we have grown into a network that does not want to institutionalise, but works with a group of people that gets some autonomy from their respective organisations, and simultaneously leaves freedom to its member organisations to develop their own initiatives through TNM. It also shows that we have to be wary of focusing too much on information and awareness raising. You do not arrive at changes and transitions purely through such activities. We still have a long way to go in developing structural and viable alternatives practices. If you look at some of the attempts to develop more structural initiatives in Belgium – such as a cooperative bank, real influence for alternative media in the media system, or buying land for sustainable agriculture – all these initiatives have so far reached only very moderate results. There is some hope in the energy system where new ownership models are appearing, but the real challenge will lay in the next years: will we succeed in running energy distribution networks and energy production under a public-civil structure, or will it all be public–private or privately owned? Action research can contribute in detecting how and why these kinds of practices remain stuck, and how workable models might be developed. In my opinion, a lot of the money that is now spent on consultants, also by civil society organisations, could be more productively used in interaction with an action researcher. In the TNM case, the researcher's previous history in civil society organisations, his background in sustainability and transition research, and a social engagement, created added value: it delivered insights, opened up the horizon, confronted members with what remained under the radar, and identified processes that participants felt but could not name.

7 Soft resistance

Balancing relationality and criticality to institutionalise action research for territorial development

Ainhoa Arrona and Miren Larrea

Introduction

Within the innovation and regional development literature, interest has increased recently in how innovation and development policies can help respond to grand societal challenges, establish a more sustainable future and build more resilient places (Bristow, 2010; Morgan, 2004; Schot and Steinmueller, 2016; STEPS Centre, 2010).

Action research for territorial development (ARTD), the approach presented in this chapter, fosters more inclusive development and innovation policies and processes through social learning and the generation of participatory regional governance patterns (Karlsen and Larrea, 2014a). The specificity of ARTD is that it emerges as the result of praxis, as the transformation through the practice of pragmatic action research (AR) and the legacy of Paulo Freire in the context of the Basque Country. That is why ARTD is not presented as a normative approach to AR but as a way to share 'how we do' AR.

The main project in which ARTD has developed is Gipuzkoa Sarean ('Networking Gipuzkoa' in the Basque language) (GS), led by the Provincial Council of Gipuzkoa (council), one out of three provincial governments in the Basque Country. Started in 2009, GS is ongoing. One of its key features is its continuity throughout three different terms, with changes in the political party in the government. Action researchers (including the authors of this chapter) have participated in GS from its inception and have played a role in the resilience of the project, which has been recognised by policymakers. The primary aim of policymakers through the three terms has been to develop new patterns of relationship with territorial actors in order to have more democratic and efficient policy processes for territorial development.

Institutional change is the Holy Grail of AR, and the core argument in this chapter is that GS has achieved institutional change through *soft resistance*. This is the concept we use to describe the relationship between the relational and the critical dimensions within the co-generation process between policymakers and researchers in ARTD. The discussion leads to identifying this relationship as conflict-based and agreement-oriented. The awareness of having conflicting perspectives made the relationship between researchers and policymakers openly critical in both directions (the *resistance* dimension). But there has also been a steadfast prioritisation of action, one of the three cornerstones of AR, by both policymakers and action researchers. Action required agreement, and agreement required that action researchers and policymakers gave up part of their interests in order to act together (the *soft* dimension).

Our proposal of *soft resistance* derives from praxis, the continuous interaction between theoretical concepts and practice. The first part of the chapter discusses previously developed theoretical frameworks. Then the case is used to share the practice that inspired the concept. Relating the concept of soft resistance exclusively to theory or practice would conceal its inspiration from praxis. Consequently, the connections between different sections are as relevant in this chapter as the content presented in each of them.

Action research for territorial development (ARTD)

ARTD is a research approach developed within the context of the Orkestra Basque Institute of Competitiveness and its alliances with the University of Agder in Norway and the Praxis Institute for Technological and Social Studies for Territorial Development in Argentina. Orkestra is a university-based research institute in the Basque Country (Spain) specialising in the field of regional development. Its founding goal is to act as an agent of regional change and have an impact on the development of the Basque Country. Orkestra researchers work in collaboration with a great number of networks, businesses, governments, and other institutions with the aim to foster transformative research. AR was one of the approaches adopted by some of the researchers with that aim. The main theoretical background for ARTD includes regional innovation systems (RIS) literature and policy analysis together with AR literature (Arrona, 2017; Costamagna and Larrea, 2016, 2017; Estensoro, 2012, 2015; Estensoro and Larrea, 2016; Karlsen and Larrea, 2014a, 2014b, 2017).

The promotion of innovation has become a significant priority in the policy agenda of regional governments, stemming from the solid consensus that knowledge and innovation capacities are key to the progress of territories (Navarro, 2009). Especially influential has been the regional innovation systems (RIS) framework (Asheim and Gertler, 2004; Cooke, 1992, 1998; Trippl and Tödling, 2007), which, in a nutshell, sees innovation in a region as the product of the interactions among the production subsystem (firms), the knowledge-generation subsystem (universities and technology centres) and the policy subsystem (governments). Although ARTD considers the RIS framework useful, it places a stronger focus on micro-practices and social processes (including policymaking) that produce innovation in order to better understand and contribute to such processes. Moreover, micro-practices cannot be framed exclusively within a regional scale. Problems of specific actors are influenced by processes occurring at local, regional, national, and international levels. Hence, a multiscale concept of development is required. That is the reason why ARTD does not refer to regional development but to territorial development, interpreting the concept of territory as a space of mutual influence in which actors operate at different territorial levels.

ARTD also proposes that researchers should go beyond the normative position of proposing to foster interactions in order to promote innovation and offer methodologies to do so. In that sense, ARTD strongly resonates with developments in interpretive and collaborative approaches to policy analysis that argue that collaborative and participatory ways of policy analysis are needed for the complexity of today's world (Goodin *et al.*, 2006; Hajer and Wagenaar, 2003). ARTD proposes a hands-on strategy to foster collaborative policymaking processes that (unlike mainstream approaches to innovation and regional development policy analysis) not only acknowledges the complexity of policymaking but also delves into and interacts actively with it.

The ARTD framework

AR and its different approaches have already been presented in the introduction to this book. In this section, we describe how we started working with Greenwood and Levin's (2007) co-generative framework, a well-known framework in the literature of AR, to later develop our own, ARTD (Karlsen and Larrea, 2014a). ARTD is not presented as a normative model on how AR should be conducted but as how we did AR in GS, which is the context in which *soft resistance* and institutionalisation took place.

When the GS project began, the research team did not have a framework of its own to develop AR processes. We used Greenwood and Levin's (2007) co-generative framework to discuss the process and our roles with policymakers. We chose pragmatic AR because it evolved from workplace development to networks and regional processes (Gustavsen, 1992; Johnsen and Normann, 2004; Pålshaugen, 2013), which was consistent with our territorial approach.

Greenwood and Levin (2007) propose pragmatic AR as the way to produce *cogenerative learning* – that is, new actions that derive from collective reflections between researchers and local stakeholders. The key to building mutual learning is the creation of arenas for dialogue between local stakeholders and researchers. Greenwood and Levin (2007) propose a cyclical co-generative framework with two distinct phases for practising AR. First, researchers and stakeholders define and clarify a research question derived from local demands (problem definition). Then, researchers foster a meaning-construction process through reflection and action where researchers help local stakeholders to solve their problems and increase their problem-solving capacities.

At the initial stage of the GS project, the goal was to develop social capital among actors influencing the competitiveness of the province. Following Greenwood and Levin's (2007) framework, we assumed that policymakers were the problem-owners and it was their problem to develop social capital while we were outsiders helping them.

But praxis requires the continuous testing of theory in practice, and our experience of AR showed that some concepts in Greenwood and Levin (2007) matched our practice better than ours. In order to overcome this perceived mismatch we undertook the process of elaborating a framework that better represented our practice. We named the new framework 'action research for territorial development' (ARTD).

Figure 7.1 describes ARTD's cyclical process that takes place in the agora. The agora is the space where policymakers and researchers meet – the space in which societal and scientific problems are framed and defined and where what will ultimately be accepted as a 'solution' is negotiated. It starts with an initial negotiation between policymakers and researchers about the problem they want to solve together. A critical moment for this has been every last trimester of the year, as the relationship of Orkestra with the council materialises through a yearly agreement and during these months the goals for the next year are discussed and agreed upon. Then, cycles of reflection and action occur. Although workshops are a typical tool used for reflection, one of the main specificities of this approach is that dialogue and reflection mostly do not occur in ad hoc workshops outside policymakers' routine but that researchers are integrated into routine meetings of policymakers in the policy process.

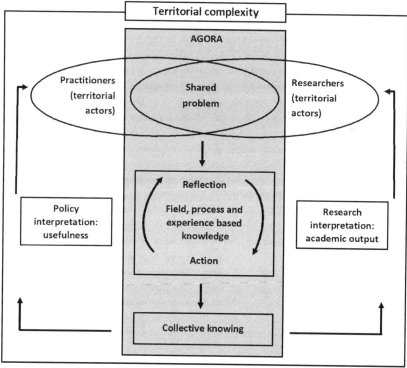

Source: Karlsen and Larrea (2014b, p. 100)

Figure 7.1 Co-generative framework for territorial development.

One example of this is the core group of researchers and policymakers who meet every Wednesday in the government premises to reflect and decide on the entire process. For specific goals, larger groups of policymakers and researchers meet in two- to four-hour workshops that take place either monthly or bimonthly. In these meetings and workshops, we help policymakers reflect on their challenges by introducing concepts and frameworks that help interpret the problem from different angles. Another feature of ARTD is that we make an effort to use the same language in academic and policy environments, contradicting the principle of adapting the language to each community and prioritising the construction of a shared language for all participants. After shared reflection, making and enacting policy decisions is the responsibility of policymakers, who then report that experience to the agora – and continue with new cycles of reflection and action.

In order to help the reader understand the connections between this framework and *soft resistance*, we focus on three features that influence the interrelation between the critical and the relational roles of researchers that emerged from praxis.

The first feature that distinguished ARTD from Greenwood and Levin (2007) was that we did not feel that we were 'friendly *outsiders*' to the process of constructing social capital for competitiveness in the province. Orkestra had been created not only to analyse but also to influence competitiveness. We felt that the development of social capital for competitiveness was also our problem and that we were not neutral regarding that goal. We stopped talking about insiders and outsiders and developed a new language with policymakers: we were all territorial actors and all problem-owners. Being accepted as problem-owners by policymakers empowered us to maintain our own positions. For instance, one of the aims of the main policymaker who led the project was to have an impact on the population through media and at a macro level. We offered resistance to this proposal, supporting the definition of specific problems and dialogue in micro-processes with the actors directly involved in their solution. We consider that evolving our status from outsiders to insiders created a context in which our critical positions were given more legitimacy to influence the process.

The second feature of ARTD was the explicit consideration of complexity. As problem-owners, we as action researchers had our own position on the issue that did not always coincide with those of the policymakers. In order to talk about it with policymakers, we framed the AR process as part of *territorial complexity* (Karlsen, 2010), a situation in a territory where various autonomous but interdependent actors might have different interpretations of the problems and the possible solutions to these problems. None of the actors had the hierarchical power to solve the problems using command and control procedures (Karlsen and Larrea, 2014a). ARTD proposed complexity, and thus conflict between policymakers and action researchers, was a natural situation. Having conflict at the core of the framework made some policymakers feel uncomfortable. They thought the conflict meant that something was not working properly in the project. But slowly, through the continuous use of the framework as our road map for the process, complexity and conflict were accepted as the natural state in our relationship and the departure point for dialogue and agreement for action. This shared understanding helped policymakers accept that our critical perspectives were a natural input into the process and thus generated conditions for the development of *soft resistance*.

Finally, Greenwood and Levin's (2007) framework did not address in an explicit way that the continued process of solving problems together generated a collective capability that was a strategic feature for territorial development. In our case, we felt that this collective capability was more relevant in the process than the specific solutions we constructed. We thus proposed the development of *collective knowing* as the main aim of ARTD and defined collective knowing as a capability, a learned pattern of collective action, where the actors systematically modify their actions over time through a dialogue and learning process. Collective knowing can only develop over time among actors who regularly meet and interact. It is a capability for knowledge in action, the capability of stakeholders and researchers to solve the problems of the territory together. We consider collective knowing as a basic condition for the institutionalisation of ARTD and thus *soft resistance*, as what is institutionalised are not the specific solutions but the mechanisms to construct such solutions together, namely, collective knowing. That is why we argue that the institutionalisation of AR occurs through collective knowing and, more specifically, through the integration of some features of AR – *soft resistance* among them – as intrinsic parts of the new governance that accompanies collective knowing.

Soft resistance

We had not systematically reflected on the interaction of the relational and the critical dimensions in ARTD until we started the writing process for this chapter. Still, we have found this relationship to be deeply embedded in our concepts and practice. We also think that one of the GS policymakers had already named it when, in an interview with a PhD student, he described our work as 'soft but continuous resistance'. These words served as inspiration for us to reflect on the relational and critical dynamic and to name such a dynamic *soft resistance*. As are the rest of concepts in this approach, *soft resistance* is not proposed as a normative concept but as part of 'how we do' ARTD.

We understand *soft resistance* as the mutually reinforcing relationship between the critical and the relational roles of researchers and practitioners in ARTD that can institutionalise new modes of governance among territorial actors. Soft resistance is conflict-based and agreement-oriented. The aim of having the mutual reinforcement of the critical and the relational dimensions does not mean there is no recognition of differences in policymakers' and researchers' frameworks. Conflict is understood as the natural state in this relationship. Still, the case shows that when there is a will to agree and act to improve the territory, the critical and the relational dimensions can reinforce each other and do not necessarily need to be interpreted as a dichotomy in AR.

Soft resistance has two main features. The first is that it is a dynamic concept. The dynamics of *soft resistance* have to do with stages in which the relational role generates a buffer of trust and the conditions to be critical without disrupting the process. When the moment to be critical comes, pressure is exercised by researchers in order to generate change. Policymakers accept this pressure because of the buffer of trust. But if pressure is exercised honestly and for the sake of shared interests, the critical role of researchers can also strengthen the buffer of trust in the medium to long term. This sequence generates in time the conditions to produce and institutionalise change.

The second feature of *soft resistance* is its steadfast focus on one of the cornerstones of AR: action. This focus is inspired, on the one hand, by the will of participants (researchers and practitioners) to prioritise territorial development beyond particular positions and, on the other hand, by the understanding that agreement is necessary in order to act. In ARTD, researchers and practitioners assume that they have different positions, but they also assume dialogue is a negotiation process in which they will give up some of their positions in order to reach action. We consider that this feature is what explains the longevity of the project presented in the chapter and, most relevant of all, its capability to reach the stadium of institutionalisation.

ARTD and *soft resistance* are frameworks developed in contexts in which change has been crafted within the system without radically challenging it but pushing it to slowly transform. They do not focus only on *what it is* or *what it should be* but on *what it can be* (Avelino and Grin, 2017). When proposing his pedagogy of the oppressed, Paulo Freire (1996, 2008a, 2008b) argued that the oppressed cannot initiate the process of liberating themselves nor helping others in their liberation until they recognise that the oppressor is partly inside them. Inspired by him, we approach change processes by considering that although many of us work to change the system, the system is also inside us and it is important to be aware of that. *Soft resistance* has more to do with generating this awareness in those in power than generating external pressure on them to change. But researchers can also be powerful and influential in change processes. This means that *soft resistance* requires that researchers are aware that they must change their research approach and their role in change processes in order to change the system.

Soft resistance in Gipuzkoa Sarean (GS)

Gipuzkoa Sarean (GS) is an action research project in which both authors have participated since 2009: one as research coordinator, the other in a technical facilitation role until 2016. The project has been extensively documented by meeting minutes and research diaries, which constitute the main data source. Different lessons from this experience have been presented in several publications (e.g. Estensoro and Larrea, 2016; Karlsen and Larrea, 2014a, 2014b, 2017).

This section focuses on the dynamic between the critical and the relational dimensions in GS. First, an introduction to the case is presented in order to briefly explain the project's substantive change within the context in which it has been developed. Then, in order to illustrate how we practise *soft resistance* in ARTD and reflect on its features in connection with the guiding framework presented in the introduction of this book, we focus on three lessons that represent three episodes within different periods of the project. These episodes do not explain the whole history, neither do they constitute one linear story. They are loose episodes that aim to help understand relevant features and results of *soft resistance* as we practise it.

Introduction to the case: context, aim and main results

GS was launched by the provincial government of Gipuzkoa in 2009. Its focus has been to develop new patterns of relationship with territorial actors in order to have more democratic and efficient policy processes for territorial development. In a nutshell, GS aims at fostering a new governance model for territorial development.

In administrative and political terms, the Basque Country has a regional government, three provincial governments and municipal councils. In the 1980s, most of the municipalities created county-level economic development agencies. Counties are supra-municipal territorial levels with no political representation, comprising several municipalities. Local economic promotion is made through county development agencies (11 in Gipuzkoa) that work on the application of programmes from other government scales and also articulate county-level projects and offer services to small firms and entrepreneurs.

Governance prior to GS. Prior to the action research process, the council and the 11 county agencies defined and developed their own strategies. Coordination among them was made only through one-to-one informal communication. The council did not formally involve counties in their policy definition processes.

Governance after GS. As a result of the action research process, in 2013 GS created new governance mechanisms through building collaborative spaces between the council and the county development agencies in order to foster more aligned territorial development processes and policies. Two of the mechanisms include the core dialogue spaces constructed through co-generation processes between researchers and policymakers working together to design, create and later manage the spaces. The InterCounty Table (ICT) is the space where policymakers of the council meet on a bimonthly basis with political representatives (mayors of municipalities) and directors of county agencies to decide and agree upon joint strategies. The county facilitators' action research process is the capacity-building space for technical staff of county agencies, currently focused on the creation of capacities for developing policies for Industry 4.0 (a strategy to use digitalisation to modernise industry) and coordinate actions linked to economic development programmes.

These spaces have been key in terms of changing governance and creating stronger relationships among local- and provincial-level policymakers, eventually leading to the empowerment of local economic actors, which now have a formal place in provincial economic development policies. They have also produced more concrete changes, such as the adaptation of some governmental programmes. The collaboration framework between local and provincial policymakers was institutionalised in 2017 with a formal agreement that defines the spaces and procedures of the collaboration (the details of this agreement are explained later in the chapter). This can be considered the main result of GS as it institutionalises a new governance (procedures and spaces) for territorial development in the province.

The need for building the relational base for practising soft resistance

Our first lesson learned when reflecting on our experience is that in order to generate the context for *soft resistance*, it is necessary to build a relational base on which to develop such a relational-critical dynamic.

In order to illustrate this lesson, we focus on the initial stage of the project in 2009–2010. In the initial months of the project, the main conflict (and later agreement) between policymakers and researchers was the research approach of the project. Building a trust relationship was necessary for us to negotiate the approach and to empower and legitimise ourselves to play a critical role.

GS was launched with the aim of strengthening social capital to improve competitiveness and well-being. The policymaker who launched the project was a university researcher on leave to undertake his political role. Although he had a real desire to do policy-relevant research, he defined a traditional linear research process in which he planned to interact with territorial actors in order to gather data and later share the results. We had a different approach based on AR: we wanted to build the solutions to problems based on dialogue with territorial actors. However, due to the imbalance of status between policymakers and researchers, the interpretation of the research methodology by policymakers prevailed.

Despite the differing visions, the team from Orkestra was committed to the process and performed the tasks assigned in the traditional design research process. This was our way to offer *soft resistance*. We knew that in order to develop AR in the long-term (*resistance*), we needed to be part of the team that implemented the policymaker's vision in the short term (*soft*).

This way, at certain moments we were able to solve some problems that were relevant process-wise. For example, the project director decided to produce four workshops (with approximately 70 territorial actors) to share the results of secondary data and interview analysis conducted about social capital. We helped him with the operational issues of organising the events (invitations, presentations, lists of participants), and this created the context to share with him some critical perspectives based on AR principles. One perspective was that instead of using the workshops only to present research results, they could also be used to reflect on future challenges and further define the actions to be implemented, using the analysis only as a means to start that discussion. This contribution was incorporated into the design of the workshops.

Our commitment to the process despite the differing views and our initial constructive critical contributions created trust between policymakers and our team. As a consequence, some months after the project had begun, one of the action researchers (one of the authors) was designated the research director of the project, which up to this point had been the exclusive responsibility of the policymakers. Through *soft resistance* we had changed the distribution of power and generated the conditions for us to be more openly critical about the research approach and push action research forward in the process.

One example of how action research started to emerge in this project is that policymakers started to regularly meet with researchers not to distribute work but to design the process together. This was a substantial change in the relationship and included, for instance, a discussion on the legitimacy of policymakers, researchers and participants in the workshops to influence the process. This specific discussion on legitimacy created a positive context in which to be mutually critical: researchers to policymakers and policymakers to researchers.

In sum, through probing effectiveness in problem-solving in the existing research framework, we could generate the conditions in which to be critical about such a framework and start changing it.

Contesting engrained habits in practice

The second lesson is that contestation when developing the critical dimension must focus not only on ideological or political discourses but also on concrete practices in which engrained habits emerge. This section shows that although a government may have a critical stance in ideological terms, it is the way in which these are implemented in practice that defines how the critical stance transforms policymaking. The role of action researchers was to make incoherencies evident and generate pressure to be coherent in actions that might seem small but in the long term made a difference. To elaborate, we use the period between June and December 2013 in which the process with county development technical staff was launched.

The coalition governing at the time (different from the one that launched the project) was leftist, with a critical stance toward traditional power structures. In the previous two years, policymakers and researchers had worked on a proposal for a new governance model for territorial development that was based on AR principles: dialogue, participation and research. The alignment of the research approach with some of the new government's principles, among others, contributed to building the relational base with the political team. But although there was an overall agreement on the governance model defined and how to methodologically develop it, several conflicts emerged when making concrete decisions on how to put it into practice. One such conflict occurred between June and September 2013.

We had explicitly discussed that governance spaces to be created with county agencies should not only include directors and political representatives but also the technical staff, since this staff facilitates economic promotion in their counties as their daily practice. When the (newly entered) policymaker in charge of the implementation of the process made a first design of the governance model, he included an initial design for a 'training programme' for county development technical staff. The policymaker had a coherent discourse on new governance and participation; still, possibly because of his own training and background, he had conceived of the training process in a linear way, consisting of a series of lectures from experts on territorial strategies, development, and participatory methodologies. This design was more connected to what Freire (1996) defined as banking approaches (depositing knowledge on those who do not have it) than a problem-posing approach (initiating the process based on what participants know and the problems they meet). This was not aligned with the philosophy of the governance model that we had discussed; moreover, the design gave a passive role to technical staff.

We made this contradiction explicit from the first day (*resistance*), and we had several discussions about it at the theoretical and methodological level. Among others, we discussed Freire's work and its alignment with the government's proposal: the principles of action research and dialogue. But the discussion at this theoretical level did not change the design of the training process made by the policymaker.

However, the policymaker had to meet a tight schedule to start the training process and asked our team to help him develop it. We accepted even though we had disagreed with his design (*soft*). But we also told him that our contribution would follow our AR principles (*resistance*). He accepted this because he needed and trusted us.

Now we had our space to be critical not in discourse but through a myriad of practical issues: who would participate, what concepts would be presented and discussed, how would discussions be generated, how would results from the discussions be taken to other spaces, and so on. Unlike with the theoretical discussion, the policymaker accepted our concrete proposals and let us implement them in workshops, in which he also participated.

The first four-hour sessions took place between 3 October 2013 and 14 November 2013. The group was formed by two staff members from each county agency (22 in total), the policymaker of the council in charge, and our team (the two authors). We discussed the building blocks of the territorial development and governance approach of the new government with the participants: inclusive and participatory territorial development, paradigm change and social innovation, and innovative governance models. Besides discussing and reflecting on ideas, staff from agencies discussed the proposal of the council for a new governance approach and we designed the sessions so the participants could jointly elaborate on: (1) concrete proposals to develop a participatory governance in our province and (2) a critical document about the government's model and the process we were developing.

On 5 December 2013, we organised a special feedback session to which policymakers from the council were invited. Five policymakers (politicians and civil servants) took part besides the policymaker in charge of the process. Technical staff of county agencies made presentations about the specific realities of each county. They also presented the proposal on 'things to be done', which they had worked on in previous sessions. This proposal included ideas such as the need to work on the political commitment to county development, the need to define the roles of different actors in territorial development and the need to improve communication patterns. Finally, they also shared their critical view of the project and the model proposed by the government. The document and presentation – literally named 'a critical view' – posed questions such as: are you/we really promoting a holistic development model or are we just focused on economic development? Why haven't we been included in the initial design of the process if the governance model is supposed to be participatory? We are asked to have a shared project in our counties, but is the model you propose a shared project in the council or is it just a project of one political party?

The participants and policymakers had a deep and honest dialogue around these questions. This was not a usual practice for anyone. Staff from development agencies used to fill out (anonymously) an evaluation sheet after every session, and the one from that day includes comments such as the following:

Without any doubt, [what I most liked from the session is] the participation of the members of the government. We should value a lot that they have sat down with us "face to face". It has been very useful for us to talk with them about all these issues. We should value a lot the humbleness that they have shown and the way they have reacted to our contributions and to our critiques.

It is clear that we are facing a new governance model. If all politicians would have an attitude like that....

Likewise, policymakers from the council recognised that the session had 'helped us have a map of the territory', and they 'realised that there is a lot of strength in counties', that 'we have seen diversity and that enriches the process' and that 'we are building the government together' (words of different policymakers, taken from the meeting minutes). The policymaker in charge of the process was of course very satisfied with the session and its results.

Moreover, the work developed in those first sessions had a real impact on the project. The proposal made by participants on 'things to be done' served as the base for defining and launching some months later 11 specific projects for experimenting a new governance model in each of the counties, with the involvement of technical staff, politicians and directors of county agencies.

The training space continued discussing other relevant issues of the process and after one year transformed explicitly into an AR process. When we initially offered resistance to the policymaker's design, we were ineffective in terms of generating any change. Still, we had a soft attitude by getting involved in the development of his idea and started to offer our resistance in apparently less relevant practical issues. In a few months, the process was completely transformed, becoming a dialogical process that impacted the new governance mode in ways that we could not have imagined when we initially resisted its design. The training process was created through *soft resistance*, and it later became itself a space for *soft resistance*.

Soft resistance and the institutionalisation of AR

Our third lesson is that *soft resistance*, and thus AR, can lead to the institutionalisation of more productive critical-relational dynamics in territorial governance. In the early stages of the AR process, we needed to play a proactive role to keep the process moving by engaging in *soft resistance*, but over the years, the need for such hands-on facilitation was reduced as we co-generated collective knowing and new rules of the game that made it possible for participants to express criticism and strengthen relationships. In line with our ARTD framework, the participants recognised that territorial development is a cyclical process of conflict and agreement and were empowered to accept, explicate, and manage conflict. In this section, we show how ARTD became institutionalised first in *experimental* practices and relationships of *soft resistance* and second in *formal* agreements and structures among the stakeholders.

We present two key episodes to illustrate this lesson. The first one (March and April 2017) illustrates how *experimental* practices and relationships of *soft resistance* became institutionalised in the AR process. The second (June 2017 onwards) shows how the AR process institutionalised to become a new mode of territorial governance.

Institutionalisation of soft resistance

At the beginning of March 2017, the research team facilitated a workshop with staff from development agencies and representatives of the council in order to agree on how to improve their programmes to support internationalisation of small firms. One of the main issues at stake was a programme in which the chamber of commerce, the council and the agencies had previously collaborated, but the council had stopped even though the agencies had a very positive evaluation. The proposal from the agencies was to resume this collaborative framework, and in order to orient reflection to action, a representative of the chamber of commerce was invited.

When introducing the workshop, one of us shared the news that the policymakers in charge of innovation programmes in the provincial council had positively reacted to a proposal to develop part of its Industry 4.0 programme through an experimental process of AR together with county agencies. Although we felt this to be good news, the following is what one of us wrote in her research diary that day:

> [...] I looked at them [facilitators from agencies] and realised some of them couldn't even keep eye contact. They looked down, none of them seemed

happy about the news. [...] when we stopped for the coffee break, I approached a group and [...] asked them directly if there was anything wrong. They immediately started talking about a programme of the provincial council they were implementing. [...] they saw a huge inconsistency between the discourse in the [AR] workshops and the "real relationship between them and the council."

(Research diary, 9 March 2017)

In response, we engaged in *soft resistance* to further make conflict explicit. We proposed to use the workshop evaluation system to gather information about this inconsistency and invited the facilitators to constructively suggest what could be improved in the programmes. We would then take this feedback to the next meeting with policymakers in the council, who were in charge of the programmes and would analyse the evaluations from the workshops. They agreed even though, as we gathered from informal conversations later, some of them felt anxious about the potentially negative consequences of voicing their critiques for us. Comments from participants included:

I think that, although our role is agreed on paper, we are being nullified in practice.

I feel frustrated. On the one hand we want to believe in the process [...] but the day to day attitudes are demotivating, as if nothing could be changed.

Many participants consider the provincial council the powerful actor compared with the collaborating county development agencies because the council decides on the funding that the agencies depend on to operate. The agency staff in charge of developing the collaboration programmes actually have limited space to directly discuss, and thus be critical of, these power structures.

While previously there were no mechanisms for constructively channelling such criticism, the new governance framework enabled the staff to have their voices heard. When we presented their feedback at the next regular meeting with policymakers of the council, the policymaker most directly involved in the programme immediately accepted part of the critique: 'our discourse is not paced with practice, the self-critique is that we need to adjust discourse and expectations' (Meeting notes, 14 March 2017). Yet, he also shared his own interpretation of the process: 'this is their truth, but it is not the truth' (ibid.). This response was echoed two days later at a regular meeting of the ICT, where policymakers of the council and the action researchers met the presidents and managers of the agencies. One of the agency directors commented:

What they [staff] presented were subjective experiences, they are legitimate, but we must not confuse them with the position of the agencies. This does not mean they are not important.

Maybe we have not acted properly in order to help the staff understand the context.

(Research notes, ICT meeting, 16 March 2017)

A couple weeks later, the stance of the staff had undergone a remarkable transformation. During a monthly workshop involving us, agency staff, and council members, one of us wrote the following:

In the coffee break I approached a group again. I did not mention the incident [...] but they started to talk about it. This time all comments were positive [...] and one of them thought their critique had had a positive effect [in how the project was developing].

(Research diary, 6 March 2017)

The change in the staff's stance probably had to do with their reflections on how *soft resistance* enabled them to constructively use their voice in the new governance model. After being critical with the programme, some of them expressed their worry, which we interpret to be linked to their fear of lacking the relational buffer for their critical stance. The relational base developed by others, such as the action researchers and directors and presidents of the agencies, helped the council to constructively integrate the critical perspective in their decisions. Hence, engaging in *soft resistance* helped to generate change without disrupting the process.

We argue that *soft resistance* was institutionalised because the use of the facilitators' AR process as a space for dialogue with asymmetric power was ingrained in the participants' habits and the less powerful actors, the agency facilitators, were empowered to speak in these spaces. Still, what was institutionalised at this stage of the process was *soft resistance* as 'the way we do ARTD'. What we share in the next episode is how ARTD was institutionalised as 'the way we do territorial development policy'.

Institutionalisation of ARTD

The second episode took place on 2 June 2017, when the new governance framework was institutionalised in a formal ceremony, presided by the prime minister of Gipuzkoa and with the participation of the 11 presidents (mayors) of the county development agencies. They signed a formal agreement that transformed the dialogue spaces created in the AR process into what was named the new governance mode for territorial development. AR was given formal recognition as the method to construct the new governance because, besides an invited external keynote speaker, the coordinator of the AR team (one of the authors) was the only additional person invited to sit at the table where the agreement was signed. She was, together with one of the policy-makers, the only one who had been part of the process since 2009. Policy-makers expressed gratitude for Orkestra's role:

The signature today is the result of a long process of years in the ICT [...]. At the starting point there was scepticism with the process. [...] with the help of Orkestra we developed a process where we developed trust and tested our patience. The process has given good results. [...] Today we formalise it.

(Director of Management of the Strategy of the Provincial Council, 2 June 2017)

The agreement commits all participants to a yearly cycle in which AR is integrated. An ICT meeting in July will set the priorities for collaboration between the council and the agencies. From July to December, the council will work on including these priorities in the budget. Once the budget is approved in December, ICT meetings will co-generate programmes that respond to shared goals and workshops of the facilitators will co-generate the conceptual frameworks and technical tools to make these programmes effective. A new ICT meeting will evaluate the one-year cycle and initiate a new one, reinforcing the goals already established or establishing new ones.

This process is already being implemented, and the main goals agreed upon in July 2017 relate to connecting the Basque Government to participate in these procedures, develop Industry 4.0. and coordinate economic promotion programmes.

Closing reflections

Throughout the chapter, we have introduced and discussed *soft resistance*, the concept that describes the critical–relational dynamic within the co-generation process between policymakers and researchers in ARTD.

ARTD is a hands-on research strategy to create collective knowing and foster more participatory and inclusive territorial development governance modes. In ARTD, as action researchers, we feel that territorial problems are also ours; hence, we do not think that we help policymakers solve *their* problems but that we are solving *our* problems together. We do so in "the 'mud' of policy practice" (Hajer and Wagenaar, 2003: 19): dialogue arenas in ARTD occur in hybrid spaces where not only research is developed, but also policies are enacted. Entering such spaces involves having to adapt the research practice to the constraints of the world of policymaking: we take the world as 'it is', and soft resistance is exercised in such a world, with all its opportunities, limitations, and contradictions.

Soft resistance is conflict-based and agreement-oriented. Conflict is the natural state of processes for ARTD, and we do not only acknowledge it but also actively manage it (Karlsen and Larrea, 2014a). However, soft resistance also relies on the idea that we need agreements in order to act and that it is possible to reach enough agreement between policymakers and researchers and among the several territorial actors despite our differing views.

The starting point of AR processes, as described in the guiding framework of the introduction of the book, is highly situational and dependent on the contexts it is developed. In our case, we have learned that it was necessary to first build a relational base between policymakers and researchers on which to develop the critical–relational dynamic. Only through that base did we negotiate the methodological approach of the project, gain space and recognition for action research in a project that initially had a traditional linear research approach and place ourselves in a position to play a more critical role.

As also pointed out in the guiding framework of the book, AR needs to simultaneously engage with and challenge the status quo. Through *soft resistance*, the critical stance does not only focus on programmatic ideas or general discourses but especially on concrete decisions and actions that materialise them. In our experience, it is in those micro-practices where engrained habits emerge and need to be challenged through continuous reflection. It is also in concrete practices that power imbalances occur and where learning that may affect practice can be co-generated: concrete micro-actions and decisions may be decisive factors in the ways policymaking and governance is developed in a territory.

Last, we have discussed how the critical and relational dimensions get embedded within the system once AR and, more specifically, *soft resistance* have been institutionalised as part of a new governance mode. In GS, not only the collaboration spaces have been formally institutionalised through an agreement between the provincial council and county agencies but also the relational–critical way of engaging in *soft resistance* has been institutionalised as part of the governance mode of these spaces. Consequently, process outcomes and impacts, following the editor's framework, are the main changes achieved by *soft resistance* in ARTD.

To conclude, we use this final section to respond to the invitation of the editors of the book to share reflections for anyone that would like to take up our approach to engage in *soft resistance*. Throughout the chapter, we have described why and how we practise it, but we cannot offer a how-to guide: *soft resistance* is praxis, and praxis occurs differently in every context. However, we do have a recommendation for those wanting to experiment with it: go into practice and develop your own way. It will not be easy. It is much easier to be critical in academic work than it is being critical in real-world practice. But knowledge co-generation and change do not occur on paper, they only take place through action. In your process, what we conceptualised as *soft resistance* will transform into something else, a new concept that will better suit your context. But if our concept inspired you to act, its mission will be accomplished. That is the way we believe we can better contribute to change.

Acknowledgements

We want to thank all the policymakers and territorial actors that have been and are part of the work we develop together. The learnings discussed in this chapter would not have been possible without their generosity and implication in this co-generation process and their trust in our work.

References

Arrona A (2017) Can interpretive policy analysis contribute to a critical scholarship on regional innovation policy studies? *Orkestra Working Paper Series in Territorial Competitiveness* No. 2017-R01, Vol. 1.

Asheim B and Gertler MS (2004) The geography of innovation. In: Fagerberg J, Mowery DC and Nelson RR (eds.) *The Oxford handbook of innovation*, Oxford: Oxford University Press, pp. 291–317.

Avelino F and Grin J (2017) Beyond deconstruction: a reconstructive perspective on sustainability transition governance. *Environmental Innovation and Societal Transitions* 22: 15–25.

Bristow G (2010) Resilient regions: Re-'place'ing regional competitiveness. *Cambridge Journal of Regions, Economy and Society* 3(1): 153–167.

Cooke P (1992) Regional innovation systems: competitive regulation in the new Europe. *Geoforum* 23(3): 365–382.

Cooke P (1998) Introduction: Origins of the concept. In: Braczyk H-J, Cooke P and Heidenreic M (eds.) *Regional innovation systems*, London: UCL Press, 2–25.

Costamagna P and Larrea M (2016) La gobernanza multinivel en los procesos de Desarrollo Territorial. *Revista Desarrollo Y Territorio* 0: 45–53.

Costamagna P and Larrea M (2017) *Personas Facilitadoras: Su Papel en la Construcción de Capacidades para el Desarrollo Territorial* (Serie Desa). Bilbao: Publicaciones Deusto.

Estensoro M (2012) *Local networks and socially innovative territories: the case of the Basque Region and Goierri County*, Bilbao: University of the Basque Country.

Estensoro M (2015) How can social innovation be facilitated? Experiences from an action research process in a local network. *Systemic Practice and Action Research* 28(6): 527–545.

Estensoro M and Larrea M (2016) Overcoming policy making problems in smart specialization strategies: engaging subregional governments. *European Planning Studies* 24(7):1319–1335.

Freire P (1996) *Pedagogy of the oppressed*, New York: Penguin Books.

Freire P (2008a) *Pedagogía de la Autonomía: Saberes Necesarios para la Práctica Educativa*. Buenos Aires: Siglo XXI.

Freire P. (2008b) *Pedagogía de la Esperanza: Un Reencuentro Con la Pedagogía del Oprimido*. Buenos Aires: Siglo XXI.

Goodin RE, Moran M and Rein M (2006) The public and its policies. In: Moran M, Rein M and Goodin RE (eds.) *The Oxford handbook of public policy*, New York: Oxford University Press, 3–35.

Greenwood DJ and Levin M (2007) *Introduction to action research. Social science for social change* (2nd edn), Thousand Oaks (California): SAGE Publications.

Gustavsen B (1992) *Dialogue and development: theory of communication, action research and the restructuring of working life*. T. S. C. for W. Life, Ed. Assem: Van Gorcum.

Hajer MA and Wagenaar H (2003) *Deliberative policy analysis: understanding governance in the network society*, Cambridge: Cambridge University Press.

Johnsen HCG and Normann R (2004) When research and practice collide: the role of action research when there is a conflict of interest with stakeholders. *Systemic Practice and Action Research* 17(3): 207–235.

Karlsen J (2010) Regional complexity and the need for engaged governance. *Ekonomiaz* 74: 91–111.

Karlsen J and Larrea M (2014a) *Territorial development and action research: innovation through dialogue*, Farnhman: Gower.

Karlsen J and Larrea M (2014b) The contribution of action research to policy learning: the case of Gipuzkoa Sarean. *International Journal of Action Research* 10(2): 129–155.

Karlsen J and Larrea M (2017) Moving context from the background to the forefront of policy learning: reflections on a case in Gipuzkoa, Basque Country. *Environment and Planning C: Government and Policy* 35(4): 721–736.

Morgan K (2004) Sustainable regions: Governance, innovation and scale. *European Planning Studies* 12(6): 871–889.

Navarro M (2009) Los sistemas regionales de innovación: Una revisión crítica. *Ekonomiaz* 70(1): 24–59.

Pålshaugen Ø (2013) Meta-theory and practice: a plea for pluralism in innovation studies. In: Pålshaugen Ø and Johnsen HCG (eds.) *Hva er Innovasjon? Perspektiver i Norsk Innovasjonsforskning*, Cappelen Damm Akademisk, 286–306.

Schot J and Steinmueller WE (2016) Framing innovation policy for transformative change: Innovation policy 3.0. Available from: www.johanschot.com/wordpress/wp-content/uploads/2016/09/Framing-Innovation-Policy-for-Transformative-Change-Innovation-Policy-3.0-2016.pdf (accessed 12 November 2017).

STEPS Centre (2010) *Innovation, sustainability, development: a new manifesto*, Brighton: STEPS Centre.

Trippl M and Tödtling F (2007) Developing biotechnology clusters in non-high technology regions: the case of Austria. *Industry and Innovation* 14(1): 47–67.

Co-inquirer reflection

Ander Arzelus

When today's citizens perceive political action from afar, it becomes clear that the search for new modes of governance is a must for every public institution. But what specifically drove the Provincial Council of Gipuzkoa (PCG) to launch a process of reflection and action for policymaking when it was aware that the process would not generate short-term results?

Historically, the Basque Country, particularly the province of Gipuzkoa, has been characterised by a significant development of initiatives based on deep community insight: for example, the co-operative movement, the promotion of the Basque school in reaction to dictatorship and the development of the public–private co-operation-based social sector, amongst others. However, in line with the global trend of the individualisation of society, several studies have observed a progressive weakening of these community values.

In this context, the political team leaders governing the PCG in 2009 understood that we needed to strengthen our traditional capacity for co-operation in order to better address the challenges of the future. Playing the institutional leadership role in such an endeavour would require us to be imaginative.

PCG launched a project with the aim to exploit new means of institutional action to strengthen the territorial capital of Gipuzkoa. Social and economic agents positively viewed the initiative and were actively involved in developing it, even though they shared an underlying scepticism because previous collaborative projects had not been successful.

Several universities – Basque Country University, Oxford University, Deusto University and Mondragon University – were also invited and became actively engaged. The relationship between PCG and the universities was based not only on trust but on personal complicity among their members. We had a history of developing relationships and projects together, but, above all, we shared the sense of possibility that we could improve processes and policies and contribute to the cohesion and welfare of citizens.

From the outset, we talked a lot, we talked clearly. The way forward was not clear, and we felt the political pressure of presenting tangible results in parliament within a reasonable period. At first, the choice of methodological approach was not clear. Fortunately, two circumstances guided the decision toward action research (AR). Orkestra had already been experimenting with this approach – they were collaborating with action researchers from Norway – and the policymakers trusted in their criteria and proposal. Moreover, AR fit the scope and spirit of the project. Strengthening the foundations for the future required us to do things differently: we had to abandon the traditional public administration 'island' logic, get over compartmentalisation and, above all, propose an effective participation scheme for all the different actors. New governance called for delving into democratic process and moving from a vision of politics from a sectoral prism to a regional perspective. Additionally, the policymaker who promoted and led the project was also an academic and had previously promoted research projects that did not get policy-relevant results. He believed previous experiences had been too theoretical and we could not do it in the same way again.

On this basis, we initiated the AR project, which combined action, research, and participation. The relationship between researchers and practitioners could be defined as a cross-border relationship. We permeate each other and when confrontation and separation occur, we meet. Meeting and working together, developing trust and actors' involvement have been a constant in the project.

In this process, knowledge acquired a transformational dimension. We 'mortals' see that our tacit knowledge and the skills we have been gradually incorporating are particularly valued in this methodology. For their part, the researchers enhance the process by providing theories, reflections, and analytical methods. Through collaborative work, each of us from our own positions and responsibilities, we analyse problems from new prisms and try to search for solutions. AR has allowed us to address problems that previously had become entrenched. The outsider perspective of researchers has helped us to talk frankly and even harshly about issues that previously were not treated successfully probably due to the fear of making explicit the existence of conflicting perspectives. We have brought about change and, together, we have managed conflict from a new perspective. We have also learned to deal with complexity: it is no longer valid to flee from it or simplify it. Hence, the scenario and the actors are the same, but the rules of the game have changed. The contributions of Orkestra's researchers have been essential to the process.

To conclude: is it possible to imagine a political action that, as an alternative to the progressive de-accountability of citizens for public action, is driven by shared work dynamics? In our view, it is, but we need to be aware that AR is a laborious process (it needs much dialogue and time), slow (tangible results do not come in the short term) and it requires patience. It also requires bridging different types of knowledge and much humbleness and generosity: for the general aim, we have to leave part of our power, be open to be influenced by others, and give up part of our goals. We need to leave the comfort and safety zones that the walls of our institutions give us in the name of hierarchical formal power. Thus, AR requires a sincere political commitment. In this line, the commitment of the policymakers of different parties during the last three terms is remarkable. The project has actively led to an agreement between the political parties to support it and leave it out of political disputes.

The PCG has now taken a new step forward through its 'Etorkizuna Eraikiz – Building the Future' strategy for the region. We aim to stress the importance of both the relational perspective and the sociocultural dimension in our policymaking through partnering agents, the administration and academics and working together to focus on 'how' things are done. The lessons from GS – which will be incorporated – have been crucial for it.

Part III

Approaches to critical-relational action research

8 Lipstick on a pig?

Appreciative inquiry in a context of austerity

Alison Gardner

'Austerity' policies pursued by the UK government since 2010 are driving extensive public service redesign and integration (Crewe, 2016; Hastings *et al.*, 2015). One consequence has been a re-appraisal of the opportunities for research collaboration between local authorities and universities. This has been motivated partly by local authorities seeking alternative sources of intelligence and analysis to inform policymaking, following reductions in funding for 'back office' staff and consultancy. At the same time, research councils and universities have sought fresh ways to demonstrate 'impact' on policy and practice, driven in part by the government policy and the Research Excellence Framework (REF) (Allen *et al.*, 2014; Ní Mhurchú *et al.*, 2017).

In this context, action research is sometimes perceived as a relational tool for building cross-sectoral engagement, delivering mutual benefits for researchers and research subjects. Relational approaches help to establish shared values to underpin collaborative research, including commitment and engagement, mutual trust, reflexivity, mutuality, egalitarianism, empathy, and an ethic of care (Kezar, 2003: 400). From a methodological perspective relational action research can also create collaborative and communicative space, building the conceptual understanding of connections between stakeholders and systems, and blurring distinctions between research subject and object (Touboulic and Walker, 2015: 312), enabling research findings to inform practice in a rapid and iterative cycle.

However, proponents of action research argue that, in addition to relational elements, action research should provide a critical challenge which can facilitate the 'flourishing' of communities, address imbalances in power relations, and stimulate reflection and transformative change (Gaventa and Cornwall, 2008; Gaya Wicks *et al.*, 2008). A similar impetus comes from the increasing influence of 'phronetic' social science (Flyvbjerg, 2001), based on 'practical reasoning' and 'practice-wisdom', which suggests that engaged research should deal with questions of the 'good life' (what we ought to do) and 'help people in ongoing political struggle question the relationships of knowledge and power and thereby work to produce change' (Schram, 2012: 19).

This transformative agenda presents tensions with relational aspects of action research, placing high demands upon action researchers to act as critical change agents, conveying 'truth' to wielders of hegemonic power, whilst also maintaining a dialogical engaged research relationship. Balancing these roles can be challenging: Bartels and Wittmayer comment that action researchers often walk a 'tight-rope' in seeking to create 'actionable' knowledge that is 'critical of the status quo in policy practice and academic research and is simultaneously used to act upon the problem(s) at hand and to advance academic debate' (2014: 399). They also argue in the introduction to this volume that action researchers must inevitably engage with these diverging elements in order to create dynamic research which can influence social and policy problems.

Yet although Bartels and Wittmayer's introduction refers to action research settings as 'concrete', the case of austerity incorporates a 'realpolitik' of diminishing resources and institutional flux which must itself be negotiated as the action research unfolds. This means that notions of what is 'critical', what is 'relational', and what constitutes 'change' and 'transformation' are likely to be fluid rather than fixed, contested rather than consensual. Resources to achieve change may also ebb and flow over time. What, then, are the implications of conducting research which aims to be simultaneously critical, relational, and transformative in this evolving context, and how might researchers manage these tensions?

This chapter explores these questions with reference to action research undertaken as part of a doctoral study into how English local public services were responding to austerity (Gardner, 2016). The research aimed to reconcile a critical investigation into responses to public spending cuts with a collaborative ethos that was sensitive to the particular strains and challenges of working in an organisation under sustained financial pressure. To facilitate this, the action research was informed by principles of 'appreciative inquiry', a technique which moves the focus of inquiry away from the action research emphasis on problem-solving to exploration of the 'life giving properties' of social systems (Cooperrider and Srivastva, 1987; Bushe, 2012: 9). Appreciative inquiry is sometimes associated with the 'unconditionally positive question' (Ludema *et al.*, 2001), and might therefore be seen as a curious methodology to inform a study of spending cuts, risking an accusation of positive bias, metaphorically putting 'lipstick' on the unappealing 'pig' of austerity.[1] However, this chapter shows that appreciative inquiry can help in making critical and relational research aims complementary, and holding them in productive, rather than negative tension; although the ability to negotiate transformation also rests upon the 'boundary spanning' role of the researcher, and the constraints of structural and institutional power.

The starting point: institutional dynamics and a collaborative research design process

The starting point for this research lay in a pre-existing research relationship between two senior academic staff in the schools of Politics and Sociology at the University of Nottingham and a local authority policy team. A previous short-term collaboration had explored neighbourhood-level effects of austerity in two electoral wards. Following this initial contact, the University sought funding for a collaborative PhD studentship which could extend and deepen the inquiry. The Labour-led council was in the midst of substantial spending reductions, implementing a cash-terms reduction in 'revenue spending power' of 22 per cent between 2010 and 2015,[2] which necessitated finding savings of more than £100 million over five years, in the context of an annual revenue budget of £273 million in 2010. The locality was also relatively severely affected by central government cuts, as it bore a historic legacy of poverty and deprivation placing it amongst the top 20 most deprived local authority areas in the country, and cuts impacted disproportionately on areas with higher levels of deprivation (Audit Commission, 2013: 23). Unemployment in the local area had risen sharply, due in part to a high reliance on public sector employers in the local economy.

The research brief set a broad intention of considering 'how public services are being re-designed to respond to a changing financial landscape', incorporating an action research approach as a means to 'generate significant findings alongside evidence and learning that is useful to those seeking to address public service challenges on the ground' (University of Nottingham, 2012).

It encompassed the ideal of mutual co-operation described at the start of this chapter, using the term "action research" as shorthand to signify an ethos of transparency, collaboration and shared aspiration. However, no attention was given at this stage of the project to identifying or managing potential tensions in the research.

One particularly pertinent issue was the conflicting status of the local authority as both a 'victim' of austerity and a mechanism by which austerity-related cuts were enacted and furthered. Janet Newman has captured this tension, highlighting that local government is characterised by "landscapes of antagonism" whereby local governments are not simply either agents of – or resisters to – neoliberalism, but instead ambiguously positioned, "constituted by and constitutive of the spaces of neoliberalisation", in a setting which is traversed by multiple political projects (Newman, 2013: 12–13). Thus, the local authority was in one sense engaged in a struggle against the power wielded by government, but also simultaneously left with few choices other than to displace the effects of austerity onto citizens and partners. This conflicted position was not fully acknowledged at the start of the research, but subsequently sat at the root of tensions which became significant in relation to the critical and transformational contribution of the work.

A PhD studentship, principally funded by the university but including a 7 per cent contribution from the council (totalling £1000 per year), was conceived as a cost-effective way for the local authority to monitor the effects of austerity, whilst providing an opportunity for the university to contribute positively to the community, and demonstrate research 'impact'. After a shortlisting and interview process involving both the university and the council, I took on the studentship, returning to an organisation where I had worked as a local government officer almost a decade earlier. My decision to undertake the PhD came at the close of a 15-year career in local government policy and consultancy, having accepted voluntary redundancy offered in response to the spending cuts. Concerns about the effects of the spending cuts were a motivating factor for my studies.

The research began with a series of informal conversations over a period of three months with council officials and partners, to identify key research themes. These iterative conversations shaped the research focus and questions, which were subsequently agreed with academic and council stakeholders. The main question centred on how English local authorities appeared, at least on the surface, to be 'coping' with spending cuts (Hastings *et al.*, 2013) despite experiencing reductions to central funding of around one-third between 2010 and 2015 (NAO, 2013). The challenge of this "austerity puzzle" (Gardner and Lowndes, 2016) was to open the 'black box' that lay between financial cuts and impacts upon services; acknowledging the felt and material impacts of the cuts, but also examining what factors were combining to mitigate those effects. The study focused principally on institutions of public service delivery rather than outcomes for populations, as – at the point when the study was initiated – there was a time-lag in the emergence of population-level effects.

Appreciative inquiry was included within the research design as a means to illuminate the "austerity puzzle" and as a contribution to improving organisational resilience. Appreciative inquiry originated within the action research movement, drawing on social-constructionist arguments that 'through our assumptions and choice of method we largely create the world we later discover' (Cooperrider and Srivastva, 1987: 129). A key tenet of appreciative inquiry is that the questions researchers ask can have a dynamic impact on the system they are trying to understand, arguing that "people invent and create their organisations and communities through conversation about who they are (identity) and what they desire (ideals)" (Ludema and Fry, 2008: 291). The inquiry and the specific questions framed therefore become part of an "engine of change" (Busche, 2012: 9), helping to achieve positive outcomes for research subjects alongside actionable knowledge for researchers. In UK public policy settings, appreciative techniques have been closely associated with asset-based theory, which advocates focusing on social and community assets (rather than deficits, such as spending cuts or deprivation) in formulating public policy interventions (see for example Foot and Hopkins, 2010; Rowett and Wooding, 2014; The Health Foundation, 2015).

From an appreciative perspective, there was an inherent risk to the research subjects participating in this study, in that dwelling on austerity might create a 'deficit'-centred vision of the future which could impact negatively on both individuals and the wider organisation. By contrast, through incorporating an appreciative approach, it was theoretically possible to shape the process so that it would deliver positive benefits for research subjects. This idea had ethical and relational attractions for work inside an organisation that was already experiencing considerable stress.

One common critique of appreciative inquiry is that early iterations required a relentless focus on optimism which might become a barrier to adopting a critical perspective. In the late 1990s appreciative inquiry became very strongly associated with the four and five 'D' models (see Bushe, 2011 and 2012 for a history of development.) A very brief summary is included in Box 8.1 below:

Box 8.1 Appreciative Inquiry: the 5 Ds

Define: agreeing a positive focus for the inquiry.

Discover: drawing out positive experiences and gifts – the best of what is – including common themes about 'what works' and what can be built upon.

Dream: what might be? Creating a shared vision of the future, presented in a series of 'provocative propositions' that have to be affirmative, challenging, innovative and based on real experiences.

Design: exploring how the ideal vision can be created.

Deliver: planning sustainable actions to deliver the dream.

However, recent methodological developments have seen a more nuanced emphasis on 'generative' inquiry rather than positivity, and a greater willingness to explore the learning potential inherent in the 'light and shadow' encountered within practice (Bushe, 2012; Johnson, 2013). In particular Johnson (2013) shows that by acknowledging challenging or difficult situations it is possible to incorporate emotions and contexts that would not be necessarily seen as 'positive' and draw strength and inspiration from re-framing them as stories of identity, resilience, and recovery. This flexibility can help with acknowledging critical perspectives, improving the technique's applicability to organisations under stress.

In the context of relational research into challenging and politically sensitive situations (such as governance under conditions of austerity) appreciative inquiry therefore provided a means to negotiate potential tensions arising from critical and relational elements of inquiry, whilst generating positive outcomes for the research subject. It moved away from the 'problem-solving' orientation of action-research towards identifying systemic sources of organisational strength and resilience which can promote 'flourishing' (Bushe, 2012). The intention was that this orientation could assist with building trust and acceptance for research findings, mitigate negative impacts arising from the research process, and potentially provide new inspiration to address the challenges of austerity.

The research design, based on a single exploratory and embedded case study, was shaped and agreed in conversation with project sponsors, with support given by the council for accessing key sources of information. The project had academic goals (answering core research questions concerning the austerity puzzle) and practical outputs, including fieldwork reports and presentations. Methods of data collection included document review, interviews, and collaborative workshops with frontline staff and participant observation. The research strategy incorporated generative principles rather than the full 5 Ds method, as it was felt that a mechanistic application of the model might negate the experiences of austerity experienced by research participants. In practice this meant encouraging interviewees and workshop participants to reflect on positive, as well as negative changes under austerity, together with examples of resilience, innovation and success. Whilst interviews and workshops acknowledged areas of work that had ceased or deteriorated, they also looked for strengths and aspirations.

Tensions in roles and relationships, and the benefits of appreciative inquiry

Despite the lack of focus on potential tensions in the research brief, there was from the inception of the project an implicit challenge to hold together critical and relational perspectives. Relationally, it helped that I was in a strong position to understand austerity, having directly experienced its effects. I was also familiar with the history of the organisation and fluent in local acronyms, comfortably part of the 'epistemic community' of local government officers. Practically, for the purposes of the research, I was embedded with the council's policy team, provided with access to IT facilities, email and telephone, a staff pass and access to meeting rooms.

In one sense this 'insider status' was an advantage for an action research, facilitating research access, and enabling informed conversations. However, I also found that as the research unfolded there were expectations from academic and local authority sponsors for me to take a 'monological' approach as an external observer, rather than the dialogical approach implied by the action research strategy. This highlighted my position on the boundary of two organisations: not fully embedded in my local authority setting, but equally, (as a PhD student) not yet established as an authoritative and independent academic voice.

Huzzard, Ahlberg and Eckman (2010) suggest that it is important to actively recognise and manage the boundary role of the researcher. They draw a distinction between researchers acting as a neutral, passive "boundary object" (an object which lives in multiple social worlds, with different identities in each) and an alternative conception of the researcher as active boundary subject, mediating across professional and organisational perspectives to actively construct collaboration (p. 293), and "shape alternative interpretations of reality" (p. 307). They also emphasise that the boundary subject's role is inherently political and connected to power relations between the researcher and the other participants (p. 310).

With this in mind, I found myself identifying more with the role of 'boundary object' than 'boundary subject', attempting to fulfil divergent roles and identities, but finding limited opportunity to construct collaboration. At that time, many posts across the organisation which had been connected with policy and research were being deleted, with considerable staff 'churn'. As one middle manager put it, there were "loads of redundancies, lots of people have gone, lots of change, lots of reorganisation … everything is in flux pretty much the whole time" (Interview Middle Manager, 2014). In this context I sometimes felt that I should provide an 'extra pair of hands' to complement the shrinking policy team where I was embedded (although as the co-inquirer reflection shows, this was my interpretation of the circumstances, rather than an explicit expectation). However, the pressures and timescales of the PhD meant that I could not participate directly in the work of the policy unit, limiting engagement in their day-to-day work to occasional contributions to requests for information, or presenting research in development for critique and feedback.

I was also conscious of being consulted on matters connected with the University as a whole, acting in an (unsought, and inadequately fulfilled) role as an unofficial ambassador for the University. There were sometimes awkward conversations, in the first year, as mutual expectations of obligations were explored and moderated – for instance how much time should I spend on site? How much access to facilities such as photocopying was acceptable? In terms of power relationships, I was treated on a par with other policy officers, but also seen as external to the organisational hierarchy of managers, senior managers, and councillors, with whom access had to be carefully negotiated. Thus, although the theory of relational research implied a blurring of the lines between researcher and research object, in practice the context and dynamics of the situation meant that separation and difference was frequently evoked. I was balanced uncomfortably on an organisational borderline, and my role sometimes seemed to be more about producing different types of knowledge for consumption or application within specific institutional constraints (which were either academic and practice related) rather than co-creating critical inquiry.

The appreciative basis of the project provided some initial benefits to deal with this separation, helping to build collaboration, allowing deeper exploration of emergent research themes, and strengthening the validity of the research. For example, appreciative questions offered a way of building trust with individual interviewees and workshop participants by eliciting positive stories of creativity and hope. In a workshop session for frontline staff, combining appreciative exercises with more traditional critical perspectives, there was a notable change in energy and engagement, between the 'shadow' focused parts of the session, focusing on challenges and concerns faced by teams; and more 'positive' parts of the session, which explored questions such as 'what do you believe is the single most important thing that positively influences this area?' and 'tell a story of how you involved others in bringing about real and sustainable change. When was it? What were the practical actions? What qualities helped you to respond?' Observations about organisational strengths were also well-received as part of an initial fieldwork report, for their value in assisting the council with balancing the challenges it faced.

Although these benefits were mainly relational, the process of building a stronger relationship also enhanced the capacity for criticality, as effective and transparent communications meant that the research could explore critical issues in greater depth. For example, the initial document review and participant observation uncovered evidence about the impacts of a new council commis-sioning system on the local voluntary and community sector, which had not been anticipated at the research design stage. These issues were subsequently pursued in further detail, with the agreement of project sponsors. Furthermore, although it may appear counter-intuitive to suggest that an appreciative perspective increased critical awareness, it arguably offered a mechanism to offset my own potential negative bias concerning impacts of austerity. A conscious emphasis on drawing out positive stories emerging from the stress of austerity acted as a counter-balance to my own innate negativity about the effects of the spending cuts.

Appreciative inquiry also helped in addressing the specific research challenge of the austerity puzzle (understanding how services were maintained despite the cuts) by enabling the research to acknowledge the local problems created by aus-terity, whilst enhancing understanding of how they were being mitigated. This helped to close the gap in literature between critical academic perspectives (which tended to focus on historic service provision, and concentrate on what was being lost) (for instance Davies and Pill, 2012; Davies, 2016; Levitas, 2012) and more practical practitioner perspectives evident on the ground, which focused on pragmatic approaches to moving forward with available resources (e.g. Lyall and Bua, 2015).

Finally, a strong relationship between the researcher and research sponsors was essential to the critical analysis and validation of research findings, which were checked for resonance, both through informal 'feedback' conversations with project sponsors and formal presentations to team members and managers. Following Lather's (2003) principles for establishing validity in qualitative research, this helped to create 'face' validity for fieldwork reports, although maintaining dialogue became more challenging in relation to the production of academic research products, as busy practitioners had limited time for engage-ment with academic debate.

However, there were also tensions, compromise, and limitations within this research strategy, particularly in relation to its ability to claim the 'catalytic validity' that arises from transformational impact, and it is to this challenge that the chapter now turns.

Negotiating the 'landscape of antagonism': encounters with structures, cultures and practices in a local authority under austerity

The central dilemma as the study unfolded, lay in responding critically and rela-tionally to two different viewpoints of the local authority which emerged from the research, consistent with Newman's concept of 'landscapes of antagonism' (Newman, 2013). On one hand the local authority was structurally a 'victim' of austerity itself, having been subject to a disproportionately high level of spend-ing cuts which were driving bitter compromise in long-established political ideals, as well as increased workloads and growing levels of staff stress. One elected member spoke of frustration in being unable to prevent welfare reforms and seeing diminishing opportunities to protect the poorest: "there's charging as well, categories of social care that are sliding away from us, that hurts. Also help for the homeless, the loss of 'Supporting People' [a homelessness prevention fund]" (Interview Elected Member, 2014). At the same time, the authority was not powerless, and there was a cultural undercurrent of overt and covert resistance in some quarters: epitomised in the repeated statement 'the whole city isn't just lying down and taking it' (Interview Housing Manager, 2014; Middle Manager, 2014). Wherever possible in line with its political aims and ideals, the Council was deploying multiple measures to mitigate the impact of cuts: "people think local government has these edicts they have to work to, but if they are not locally appropriate you can find a way around them. It's a huge misconception, we have more power than people believe" (Interview Council Director 1, 2014). Yet on the other hand, it was clear that the local authority was also implicated in implementing austerity, through the transmission of spending cuts and supporting practices which impacted upon citizens and other service delivery partners. The clearest example of this was in relation to the aforementioned revised funding system for the voluntary and community sector, which had replaced the preceding grant-based regime with a competitive bid-based system. Although the council had little choice under English law over balancing its budget, some officers and members saw the pressure of austerity as a positive opportunity to embed neoliberal practices such as contracting and commercialisation. One Director described the promise of additional income from commercialised services as a 'Trojan horse', to engage councillors in 'sensible' discussion:

> I think we need to move towards having a greater focus on commissioning, enabling the role of the business sector and voluntary sector. We need to be less about direct delivery (and I don't mean this in any political ideology sense, it's just reality) and thinking more about early intervention so that we change – lessen – future demand.
>
> (Interview Council Director 2, 2014)

Thus, the 'landscape of antagonism' was reflected in the contrasting ways that individuals exercised their agency across fissures in ideology which had been opened and deepened under the stress of austerity. (Further discussion of the differing agential responses to institutional change under austerity in this case can be found in Gardner 2017). There was not a single hegemonic structure and set of power relations governing responses to austerity, so much as a multitude of actors attempting to implement differing ideological and practical responses, with certain tactics becoming more politically palatable as spending cuts accumulated over time.

This meant that although the adoption of the appreciative inquiry approach had assisted with establishing relationships, there were competing and shifting interpretations of what would actually constitute 'organisational flourishing'. Essentially this point was politically contested, and any critical messages were likely to fall on one side or another of an ideological conflict, creating a dilemma for the researcher on what constituted transformative change, given the differing perspectives of interviewees. There was also a debate on how best to balance inquiry into generative, strength-related topics with the need to highlight points of internal conflict. Was the priority to protect organisational systems (and core action research relationships) by softening critical messages; or to provide an external challenge to the organisation, producing conclusions which might be unpalatable to some but potentially carried greater insight?

These tensions impacted both on the operationalisation of the research and the presentation and communication of results. From a practical perspective, there was a tension between serving the requirements of a time-poor workforce and gathering the data required for critical reflection. For example, when planning the two collaborative workshops with multi-agency teams described earlier, it became apparent that research participants were more interested in the applicability of the workshop for organisational development purposes (in this case, informing future team and neighbourhood planning) than the need to understand from a critical perspective how local partnerships were experiencing and responding to austerity. Team leaders decided that they could spare, at maximum, 90 minutes, which acted as a constraint on critical discussion, preventing exploration of some experiences of austerity raised by participants. Although the workshops produced material which was useful and relevant to organisational planning, the teams involved would also have needed to reflect further on findings in order to integrate them into future strategies, which limited the impact of the exercise (one might link this problem to Argyris and Schön's (1996) conception of single versus double-loop learning). Therefore, there was some limitation in the 'actionable' knowledge created for both relational and critical research aims.

Interviews were more successful in eliciting critical information, albeit because they were sometimes instrumentalised by research respondents as a means of engaging in their own negotiation of power-play (see Henderson and Bynner's chapter for a discussion of 'benign instrumentalisation'). Sometimes respondents appeared to be using the research as a means to convey messages which would be difficult to communicate face-to-face, reflecting the reality of power dynamics between the council and partners. One senior partner who was frequently in public conflict with council leadership took the opportunity to emphasise his respect for the leader of the council, whilst also promoting radical transformative change. Meanwhile a policy officer from a housing organisation that had struggled under the new voluntary sector grant regime was positive about her direct connection with the council, but keen to send a message that communications had suffered: in her terms "something is not quite working" (Interview Council Partner, 2014). In bearing these messages, the research became a valuable medium for communicating the "unsaid", but this instrumentalisation also highlighted the extent to which the research and researcher were incorporated within institutional power-play.

There was also critical reflection from within the council, partly due to the high level of staff churn in the organisation, prompted by the extensive re-organisation following the spending cuts. Senior managers who were either recent ex-employees, or about to move on, were generous in both their time and personal opinions, and open about policy successes and failures (perhaps more than they would have been had they been remaining with their employer). In these cases, the interview process was often used by participants as a final means of delivering personal impact, by recording frank accounts of their experience. In some ways this strengthened the critical messages of the research, but again reflected a wide range of consciously and unconsciously-held ideological perspectives.

Whilst a number of strong critical themes started to emerge, the task of interpreting and conveying these messages was made more complex by the rapid staff churn. By the time fieldwork was completed, the three layers of management that had originally co-designed and sponsored the project had all moved on. Despite the steps I had taken to collaboratively establish the project focus, and validate early findings (through conversations with the original project sponsors) there was some challenge to the focus of the research when findings were presented. This came principally from two senior managers who had not originally been involved in designing and sponsoring the research, but had formulated some of the institutional processes critiqued in interviews. These individuals were understandably keen to justify their position and contest certain findings and recommendations. Although no attempt was made to amend the conclusions in the final report and subsequent thesis, it is possible that communication and discussion of the most challenging conclusions was limited by this point of contention.

The local authority was also overtly politically led, with relatively stable policy agendas that had in many cases been developed over a long period of time. Whilst it was clear that there were a range of different views emerging (even within the Council's cabinet) on specific policy questions, critical viewpoints from officers were unlikely to sway political opinion in the short term (one director even went as far as to describe certain policy proposals as 'career limiting' red lines which could not be crossed) (Interview Council Director 2, 2014). Furthermore, the council was also subject to wider forces for ongoing change, such as the inception of devolution policies. These demanding new agendas, coupled with the imperatives of the budget cycle, clamoured for the scarce attention of policy professionals and further detracted from attempts at organisational review and reflection.

Reflexivity, impact and change

Given the conflicting discourses and pressures within the council's 'landscape of antagonism', it is perhaps understandable that the ideal of the research as a catalyst for transformation was only realised in modest ways. These included the appreciation interviewees showed for the opportunity to reflect on recent history, as well as their hopes and fears for the future. A key manager insisted that findings were important, and ensured they were conveyed to senior officials, even when she anticipated that some messages would be difficult for the individuals concerned to hear. But overall, rather than providing a decisive critical intervention, the main achievement of the research was to hold up a mirror to demonstrate where and how policies were shifting, subtly highlighting how this was – or was not – in line with the council's previous policies and democratically mandated agenda.

The challenges with achieving acceptance for research findings also highlighted the institutional and political constraints of the boundary role, as identified by Huzzard, Ahlberg, and Ekman (2010). I was institutionally situated by externality to the council hierarchy, and my status as a doctoral student. Access and opportunities to influence key stakeholders could be denied by gatekeepers. For example, although one important stakeholder had agreed in principle to be interviewed to help test the findings, seven appointments were cancelled, sometimes at very short notice, and eventually the research was completed without that interview. As a student there was a need on my part to build credibility, and the ambiguous position of being neither the 'insider' nor a 'fully-fledged' academic perhaps impacted on my confidence to engage key stakeholders. I was increasingly aware of my boundary position as sponsors from the council left the organisation. Rather than the active role of boundary subject, then, shaping inter-organisational relations (Huzzard *et al.*, 2010) my role was more akin to that of a boundary object: being neutral, recognised by both academics and practitioners, but part of a much wider landscape of conflict and interaction, which sometimes shaped the way I was perceived by either side.

Conclusions

The research question at the start of this chapter questioned the implications of conducting research which aims to be simultaneously critical, relational, and transformative in a fluid context such as austerity, and how researchers might manage resulting tensions.

This case study shows that there is no sharp division between critical and relational aims, finding that attention to relational issues could also enhance critical objectives. However, consensus on what is deemed 'critical' 'relational' and 'transformative' may not be present in large institutions under financial pressure, and the ability to pursue these goals in parallel can also vary according to the researcher's position and circumstances.

From a relational perspective the combination of action research and appreciative inquiry assisted with establishing principles for collaboration, built trust and energy for engagement, and helped in closing a gap between critical perspectives and practice, by encouraging reflection on the 'survive and thrive' factors that were coming to the fore as spending cuts impacted the organisation. In turn, the practice of building relational strength helped to elicit constructive critical reflection, assisted with validating messages arising from the research (in some cases) and offset potential negatives. Appreciative inquiry, in summary, was much more than 'lipstick' for the 'pig' of austerity. It helped to make critical and relational research aims objectives complementary, holding them in productive, rather than negative tension.

However, this research was not transformative, at least in relation to the institutional setting where it took place, and probably the starting point for this research meant that the study was never destined to deliver that goal. The genesis of the research within the large and complex institutional context of the local authority, without enduring sponsorship to provide 'sanction and sanctuary' for the work (see Henderson and Bynner's chapter), and amidst conflicting ideological undercurrents, meant that it was always going to be challenging to have critical viewpoints accepted and acted upon.

One recommendation for future practice might be that researcher and host organisation reflect at the outset on the role and position of the researcher, including the tensions which might emerge through the action research process and expectations around the degree of critical challenge raised by the research. Perhaps we as action researchers need to emphasise that in complex and contested settings, the contribution we bring from a dialogical perspective is not necessarily to be a critical purveyor of truth, able to judge what is (and is not) to be challenged, but to present our findings clearly situated in the context of the myriad influences shaping their production and communication. In doing this, we should particularly reflect upon different potential interpretations of 'transformation' within the institutional setting. This conversation may need to be repeated at several points in the research journey in order to ensure that opportunities for learning are maximised.

We also need to consider the role of the researcher working across organisational boundaries and the degree of transformational influence one might expect to exercise in a highly institutionalised context already subject to strong (and contending) forces seeking to direct the paths of change. In a political context, in particular, we frequently deal with 'landscapes of antagonism', where the 'correct' goals for the exercise of power are themselves unclear and contested. As researchers we offer one perspective among many, akin to what Shdaimah and Stahl call a 'polyphony of voices'. Within this polyphony some discord needs to be expected, and engaging with that conflict – rather than just seeking to mitigate it – can enhance collaborative practice (Shdaimah and Stahl, 2012: 124). However, the extent of that conflict engagement, and its eventual impact will be dictated by issues of power and position. Unless specifically briefed and empowered to deliver change, we are perhaps more realistic to offer our research within the spirit of 'reflective thought aimed at action' (Schram, 2012: 19).

Acknowledgements

I am grateful to the University of Nottingham and to the local authority featured in this chapter for funding my PhD studentship. Special thanks go to Liz Jones, for her support and guidance during the research, and for taking the time to (critically and relationally!) reflect on our experiences and learning, a process which I have found to be rich in sympathy, humour and insight.

Notes

1 'Lipstick on a pig' is a colloquial term implying that a particular topic or subject has been artificially enhanced in a way that is unconvincing. The phrase caused controversy in the US presidential campaign of 2008 when Barack Obama used it in a speech to criticise the policies of Republican rivals (the 'pig' was taken as an oblique reference to republican vice-presidential candidate Sarah Palin).

2 Revenue spending power represents UK Government's assessment of funding available to each local authority to spend on core services. It rests on a contested formula, but is recognised by the National Audit Office as the most reliable means for wider financial comparison (NAO, 2014b, 24).

References

Allen T, Grace C and Martin S (2014) *From analysis to action: connecting research and local government in an age of austerity*. Available from: www.solace.org.uk/know ledge/reports_guides/LGKN_Analysis_to_Action.pdf (accessed 19 April 2018).

Audit Commission (2013) *Tough times 2013*, London: Audit Commission.

Bartels KPR and Wittmayer JM (2014) Symposium introduction: usable knowledge in practice. What action research has to offer to critical policy studies. *Critical Policy Studies* 8(4): 397–406.

Bushe GR (2011) Appreciative inquiry: theory and critique. In Boje D, Burnes B and Hassard J (eds.) *The Routledge companion to organizational change*, Oxford: Routledge, 87–103.

Bushe G (2012) Foundations of appreciative inquiry: history, criticism and potential. *AI Practitioner* 14(1): 8–20.

Cooperrider DL and Srivastva S (1987) Appreciative inquiry in organizational life. *Research in Organizational Change and Development* 1: 129–169. Available from: www.centerforappreciativeinquiry.net/wp-content/uploads/2012/05/APPRECIATIVE_ INQUIRY_IN_Orgnizational_life.pdf (accessed 19 April 2018).

Crewe T (2016) The strange death of municipal england. *London Review of Books* 38(24): 6–10. Available from: www.lrb.co.uk/v38/n24/tom-crewe/the-strange-death-of-municipal-england (accessed 19 April 2018).

Davies JS (2016) Austerian realism and the governance of Leicester. In: Bevir M and Rhodes RA (eds.), *Rethinking governance: ruling, rationalities and resistance*. Oxford: Routledge.

Davies JS and Pill M (2012) Empowerment or abandonment? Prospects for neighbourhood revitalization under the big society. *Public Money and Management* 32(3): 193–200.

Flyvbjerg B (2001) *Making social science matter: why social inquiry fails and how it can succeed again*, Cambridge: Cambridge University Press.

Foot J and Hopkins T (2010) *A glass half-full: how an asset approach can improve community health and well-being*, London: Improvement and Development Agency.

Gardner A (2016) *How are local public services responding to austerity? English local governance between 2010 and 2015*. PhD Thesis. University of Nottingham, UK.

Gardner A and Lowndes V (2016) Negotiating austerity and local traditions. In: Bevir M and Rhodes RA. (eds.), *Rethinking governance. Ruling, Rationalities and resistance*, London: Routledge, 125–143.

Gaventa J and Cornwall A (2008) Power and knowledge. 2nd edn. In: Reason P and Bradbury H (eds.), *The Sage handbook of action research, participative inquiry and practice*, London: Sage, 172–188.

Gaya Wicks P, Reason P and Bradbury H (2008) Living inquiry: personal, political and philosophical groundings for action research practice. 2nd edn. In: Reason P and Bradbury H (eds.), *The Sage handbook of action research, participative inquiry and practice*, London: Sage, 15–30.

Hastings A, Bailey N, Gannon M, Besemer K, Bramley G (2013) *Coping with the cuts? Local government and poorer communities.* York: Joseph Rowntree Foundation. Available from: www.jrf.org.uk/publications/coping-with-cuts (accessed 19 April 2018).

Hastings A, Bailey N, Gannon M, Besemer K and Bramley G (2015) Coping with the cuts? The management of the worst financial settlement in living memory. *Local Government Studies* 41(4): 601–621. Available from: www.tandfonline.com/doi/full/10.10 80/03003930.2015.1036987 (accessed 19 April 2018).

Huzzard T, Ahlberg BM and Ekman M (2010) Constructing interorganizational collaboration: The action researcher as boundary subject. *Action Research* 8(3): 293–314. Available from: http://arj.sagepub.com/cgi/doi/10.1177/1476750309335206 (accessed 19 April 2018).

Johnson PC (2013) Transcending the polarity of light and shadow in appreciative inquiry: An appreciative exploration of practice. In: *Organizational Generativity: The Appreciative Inquiry Summit and a Scholarship of Transformation. Advances in Appreciative Inquiry*. http://dx.doi.org/10.1108/S1475-9152(2013)0000004007 Emerald Group Publishing Limited, 189–207 (accessed 19 April 2018).

Kezar, Adrianna (2003) Transformational elite interviews: principles and problems, *Qualitative Inquiry* 9(3): 395–415.

Lather P (2003) Issues of validity in openly ideological research: between a rock and a soft place. In: Lincoln YS and Denzin NK (eds.), *Turning points in qualitative research: tying knots in a handkerchief*, Walnut Creek, CA: AltaMira Press, 185–215.

Levitas R (2012) The just's umbrella: Austerity and the big society in coalition policy and beyond. *Critical Social Policy* 32(3): 320–342.

Ludema JD and Fry RE (2008) The practice of appreciative inquiry. 2nd edn. In: Reason P and Bradbury H (eds.), *The Sage handbook of action research, participative inquiry and practice*, London: Sage, 280–296.

Ludema JD, Cooperrider DL and Barrett FJ (2001) *Appreciative inquiry: the power of the unconditional positive question*. Monterey, California. Available from: https://calhoun. nps.edu/bitstream/handle/10945/40458/Barrett_Appreciative_Inquiry_2001.pdf? sequence=1& isAllowed=y (accessed 19 April 2018).

Lyall S and Bua A (2015) *Responses to austerity: how groups across the UK are adapting, challenging and imagining alternatives*. London: New Economics Foundation. Available from: www.neweconomics.org/publications/entry/responses-to-austerity (accessed 19 April 2018).

NAO (2014) Financial sustainability of local authorities 2014, NAO, London. Available from www.nao.org.uk/report/financial-sustainability-of-local-authorities-2014/ (accessed 19 April 2018).

NAO (2013) *Financial sustainability of local authorities*, London: The Stationery Office. Available from: www.nao.org.uk/wp-content/uploads/2013/03/Local-Authority-Full-Report.pdf (accessed 19 April 2018).

Newman J (2013) Landscapes of antagonism: local governance, neoliberalism and austerity. *Urban Studies* 16(1): 1–16.

Ní Mhurchú A, McLeod L, Collins S, Siles-Brügge G (2017) The present and the future of the research excellence framework impact agenda in the UK academy: A reflection from politics and international studies. *Political Studies Review* 15(1): 60–72.

Rowett R and Wooding N (2014) *Appreciative inquiry: using appreciative inquiry to make change happen*, Cardiff: Public Service Management Wales. Available from: http://researchdevelopment.academiwales.org.uk/uploads/attachments/rGGWZa3QZ.pdf (accessed 19 April 2018).

Shdaimah C and Stahl R (2012) Power and conflict in collaborative research. In: Flyvbjerg B, Landman T, and Schram S (eds.), *Real social science: applied phronesis*, Cambridge: Cambridge University Press, 15–26.

Schram S (2012) Phronetic social science: An idea whose time has come. In: Flyvbjerg B, Landman T, and Schram S (eds.), *Real social science: applied phonesis*, Cambridge: Cambridge University Press, 15–26.

The Health Foundation (2015) *Head, hands and heart: asset-based approaches in health care*, London: The Health Foundation. Available from: www.health.org.uk/sites/default/files/HeadHandsAndHeartAssetBasedApproachesInHealthCare_InBrief.pdf (accessed 19 April 2018).

Touboulic A and Walker H (2015) A relational, transformative and engaged approach to sustainable supply chain management: The potential of action research. *Human Relations* 69(2): 301–343.

University of Nottingham (2012) *Research brief: provision of local citizen-focused services in a changing policy and financial context*, Nottingham: No longer available online.

Interviews

Interview (2014) Council Director 1
Interview (2014) Council Director 2
Interview (2014) Council Partner
Interview (2014) Elected Member
Interview (2014) Housing Manager
Interview (2014) Middle Manager

Co-inquirer reflection

Liz Jones

In 2010 the UK Coalition Government's 'emergency budget' cut core funding to English Local Government by 28 per cent. Our council was amongst those hardest-hit, with cuts falling first on regeneration programmes, which relied on central funding. It was a big shock, loads of people left, there were masses of redundancies, change after change. From the inside, it felt like we were pulling back quite a lot from non-essential services, focusing on core business, whilst also trying to think about transformation.

The ability to change was limited by an inevitable obsession with financial planning rounds, because budgets had to be balanced every year. The cycle consumed an enormous amount of energy, it was exhausting: budgets were confirmed in April, and then we would start again in August. There was not much time for thinking about what we were doing, it was mostly about what we should stop (or do differently), but always with diminishing resources and people.

The City Council had a longstanding research relationship with the University, working with senior academics from Social Sciences. Our contacts offered a PhD student to explore what these changes meant. There were really strong partnerships in the City, so asking the University to help seemed important. There was also a drive for re-framing the challenges we were facing.

So that is how it felt from the inside, but we were not really sure how it looked from the outside. Were our perceptions of where impact was greatest in the right territory, or was it just that everybody really was doing more for less? There were policy changes that had not yet come through, particularly welfare reform. We could see some real pain coming to some of our poorest citizens, like watching a car crash going in slow motion.

But although our policy teams were shrinking, we were not really looking for an extra pair of hands. What we needed was a critical, observational, interrogating eye, asking things that would never occur to anyone else. This perhaps made an interesting tension with the action research. Action research can be great, it can give you a real in-depth understanding of the personality, the psyche, and culture of an organisation. But there is a risk that action researchers are too partisan, which does not really help because sometimes we need to step back, we need another pair of eyes to make us think differently.

There is value in objective distance. Having a tentative relationship – rather than a close and embedded researcher – is not bad; it brings that external viewpoint and different skills. Research does not have to be controversial, but it does have to be objective. The value comes in putting different lenses on a situation. Sometimes, part of you wants to feel that the research will justify your approach, but you can always respond in a better way. You need someone who can structure that thinking, who has not got a loyalty.

There is also something about making sure researchers have permission to challenge. When we commission research, we need to document it to say 'it is your job to make sure that I am not complacent'. The researcher has to get involved, but not sign up to the club; they must not subscribe to the instant response, the groupthink. They must provide critical and constructive challenge.

The environment shifted during the time of the study, as the degree of external pressure on budgets became more challenging. Eighteen months is a long time in local government, especially at such a time of change. We provided access to people, and data, which for us was honouring our side of the bargain, but people were getting busier, the project sponsors were moving on, and the budget rounds were tighter and more constrained every year.

It is possible that evidence from the action research was not as influential as other types of inquiry might have been. But perhaps the organisation's readiness to receive the messages arising from the research had also shifted, and the extent of choices over policy and action became more limited. Speaking 'truth' to power, in terms of critical challenge, when you are not sure they want to hear it, is always hard. Most organisations have a part that is happy to listen and a part that is not. The ability to learn is based both on the strength of evidence and the willingness to accept it – that is true everywhere. And perhaps you also need to have a real choice to do differently: did we have that given the pressures of austerity?

There was also a practical challenge for us in carving out time to keep in touch with the PhD. The academic outputs produced as part of the research were not always very accessible. There is a need for a critique back to the academic world: is that really necessary, or is it simply pontificating? Do you really need that? Is it a bit of vanity – could you have had an easier single product, just as insightful in a different style? Maybe, at the frontline, we need to up our game in terms of the complexity of the argument that we are prepared to examine. But academia also needs to flex – it does not matter if it is 5000 or 7000 words.

Ultimately the main value of this work lay in the conversations. Asking people some in-depth questions, looking at their motivations and behaviours. Trying to understand how we had moved so quickly from one philosophical position on public spending to another, and what it really meant for communities. And reflecting, 'if you could do it again, would you have done it like that?' Those conversations raised fundamental questions about relationships with communities, about what a local authority should or should not be doing. Having to create time for those structured conversations was important, it is the reflective challenge that is needed, because we do not usually have much time to reflect on these things.

9 Getting unstuck

The reconstruction clinic as pragmatic intervention in controversial policy disputes

Martien Kuitenbrouwer

Introduction

Policy conflicts and disputes have always been part of the daily practice of policy practitioners, but arguably, the nature of these policy disputes seems to be changing. Global challenges such as global warming, waves of refugees, and labour migration and the like become concrete and tangible when they touch down in local communities, e.g. as a need for siting wind mills, carbon storage, or refugee shelters, causing new challenges for local policymakers. At the same time, local problems of planning, land use or social policy issues seem to become more complex as well: "the number of players are higher, the venues are bigger, the resources at stake are typically bigger and the level and depth of emotional intensity can be greater as well" (Forester, 2013: xiv).

An increasing number of stakeholders seems to be involved in policy issues in an increasingly networked structure. At the same time, authority of government and policymakers in general is withering. New 'spaces of politics' are needed where differences are more important and acknowledgement of, and acting upon, interdependence is a must (Hajer and Wagenaar, 2003 Van den Brink and Kneyber, 2012; Karsten and Jansen, 2012; Hajer, 2013). Instead of interest-based bargaining, Hajer and Wagenaar see policymaking more and more as – referring to Hannah Arendt – "communities of action, able to arrive at shared problem definitions and to agree on common paths of problem resolution" (Hajer and Wagenaar, 2003: 11).

The Netherlands has a long-standing tradition of collaboration among different stakeholders on complicated policy matters. Dutch society is characterised by a hybrid structure. Governmental and non-governmental stakeholders seek to find agreement on complex societal issues in what has become famous as the 'poldermodel' where consensus via compromise is the dominant model of agreement-seeking (Prak and Van Zanden, 2013) When policy disputes become 'messy', 'unstructured', 'constitutional' or 'controversial', however, seeking consensus via compromise has its limits (Ury and Fischer, 1986; Susskind and Cruikshank, 1987; Hoppe, 2011; Schön and Rein, 1994). Controversies tend to be immune to fact and reason (Schön and Rein, 1994). As 'wicked problems', the definition of the problem is often the problem (Rittel and Webber, 1973).

Even more important is that the interests and beliefs that lie at the heart of policy disputes are not static but a dynamic part of an ongoing process of framing and reframing (Schön and Rein, 1994).

Alternatives to a static compromise-based agreement-seeking process can be found in the pragmatist tradition that can be traced back to the work of Peirce (1877), Dewey (1910, 1913) and Follet (1918). In the pragmatist tradition, understanding the ever-changing dynamics of interaction among stakeholders, and between stakeholders and their environment, is essential. Dewey speaks of a 'pragmatic procedure for inquiry' as a way to address problems in society. A pragmatic procedure for inquiry is "less a solution than a program for more work, and particularly an indication of the ways in which existing realities may be changing" (Dewey, 1913: 310). Changing realities occur in active interrelations, where thought and ideas are not abstractions but "knowing is literally something which we do" (Dewey, 1913: 332).

In their quest for pragmatic action research, Greenwood (2007) argues for the importance of diverse stakeholder participation in inquiry. The participation of diverse groups is not so much as a political or moral statement as a necessity in light of the complexity at hand:

> Participation is key to successful AR because the complexities of the problems addressed require the knowledge and experience of a broad and diverse array of stakeholders including academic experts and local stakeholders who have their own forms of intellectual/experiential expertise to contribute. Without participation, the research cannot be done well enough to have the desired results.
>
> (Greenwood, 2007: 134)

This kind of practically oriented action research approach to unravelling public disputes and controversies is at the heart of the Public Mediation Programme (PMP) based at the University of Amsterdam. The programme is rooted in the Dutch tradition of collaborative policymaking and seeks to design interventions that can assist policymakers and other stakeholders in policy disputes that seem to be immune for more traditional settlement. One recently designed intervention, the reconstruction clinic, is designed to assist in situations of messy or controversial policy disputes where stakeholders find themselves stuck. Experiences with the reconstruction clinic are explored in this chapter, starting from the question: How can a pragmatic action research based intervention like the reconstruction clinic facilitate a process of stakeholders who are stuck in complex or controversial policy disputes to get 'unstuck'? 'Unstuck' refers to the situation where stakeholders are able to move on, without the necessity of reaching agreement or finding a solution to the problem at hand. Stakeholders can get unstuck when they have found a frame-for-action in a congruent fashion (Grin and Van de Graaf, 1996).

To provide answers to this question, two experiences of the reconstruction clinic in two complicated policy disputes are explored. The first policy dispute unfolded in an urban neighbourhood where local planners and residents argued over playgrounds. The second dispute is set in a rural area where private developers, landowners, different layers of government, and NGOs argue over the development of wind turbines.

The exploration of these two settings is not aimed at drawing general conclusions, but rather to both contribute to a broader discussion about the opportunities for a pragmatic repertoire in complex, messy, and even controversial policy disputes as well as to improve the design features of reconstruction clinic itself. As is illustrated in the two settings, the key design features of the reconstruction clinic provided stakeholders with a safe and structured setting where truth-finding or agreement-seeking was not the aim, but finding a congruent frame for action was possible. The setting of the reconstruction clinic allowed stakeholders to scrutinise their own situation as if they were researchers in a non-judgmental way that assisted them to focus upon underlying patterns of disruptive inter-action, opening up opportunities for remaking and reframing the situation while staying away from quick solutions.

The reconstruction clinic: theory and practice

The reconstruction clinic was developed at PMP out of the work we had done with different practitioners – policymakers, street level bureaucrats, NGO representative, citizen initiatives, who find themselves *sucked into* difficult, messy and sometimes controversial policy disputes.

The reconstruction clinic is rooted in three distinctive approaches to action research. First is the *clinical* approach to action research, as can be found in the work of Edgar Schein (Schein, 2006). *Clinical* action research, a term borrowed from the medical profession, takes the (problematic) situation as defined by stakeholders themselves as a starting point, alike medical practice (Schein, 2006). In policy disputes, a clinical approach offers a non-evaluative way to reach diagnostic insights into their situation. These insights, in turn, can provide the basis for a pragmatic way of dealing with the situation. When these elements come together, the stakeholders can address the dispute through a process of collaborative learning and capacity-building.

A second important approach is the idea of *Learning History*, as developed by Kleiner and Roth (1998) with an emphasis on personal narratives, and as demonstrated by Cobb (2013). By combining personal narratives on a shared timeline, a common context can be created from which *"people can draw their own answers"* (Kleiner and Roth 1998: 44).

The third basis is Argyris and Schön's work on *reflection-in-action*, which stresses the importance of practitioners reflecting on their work while they are doing it (Schön, 1983; Argyris and Schön, 1996). It is not so much learning *about* practice that may provoke change, but learning *in* practice that may lead to new patterns of behaviour (Schön, 1983). *Frame-reflection*, as introduced by Schön and Rein is a specific form of reflection-in-action, aimed at developing a better understanding of underlying frames and the process of framing and reframing that occurs in interaction and interdependence between stakeholders in dispute (Schön and Rein, 1994).

Building on these insights, we have designed the reconstruction clinic with three distinctive features: the use of narratives to explore perceptions and beliefs (Cobb, 2013), the use of timelines to understand critical moments and conflict dynamics (Kleiner and Roth, 1998; Langley, 1999; Leary, 2004; Verloo, 2015), and the presence of outside reflectants as a way of organising structured back-talk (Schön and Rein, 1994; Laws and Rein, 2003).

The reconstruction clinic usually starts with a request for help by street-level bureaucrats from governmental institutions who find themselves stuck in their dealings with other stakeholders. From their wording of the issues at stake, the notion of 'stuckness' becomes clear. In the words of one participant, for instance, it entails that "people are afraid to make another move" (area manager, Amsterdam), while another described how "the options are limited, and all of them seem problematic" and "it's a game of chess" (project manager, Ministry of Economic Affairs). Such statements provide the starting point for further exploration. This starts with an inventory of potential participants in a reconstruction clinic. We ask the policymakers to think about the question: Who would you like to be there for us to gain a deeper insight into the situation? We then ask each member of this initial list the same question and supplement the list based on their answers. Sometimes, we suggest other participants who have not yet been named, based upon information we have about the dispute.

The reconstruction clinic is designed in four steps. The first step is collecting different narratives on the situation at hand. We do this by conducting narrative-style interviews with a selection of invited participants. A narrative-style interview is essentially unstructured, with only one set question at the start: Where did this story start? From thereon, the interviewer facilitates the interviewee in structuring his or her 'side of the story' (Cobb, 2013). We explain at the beginning of each interview that we are not after the truth, but gathering different perspectives on the situation at hand.

As a second step, we construct a rudimentary timeline of past events, based on the interviews conducted. At the start of the clinic, all participants are invited to complete the timeline in a plenary session, to add events that seem to be left out, and to add comments on the events that are laid out.

In a third step, outsider-reflectants are invited to help the situation 'talk back' (Schön and Rein, 1994). One, two or in rare circumstances three reflectants are invited to comment on the timeline as well as on the conversation that took place in making the timeline. These reflectants may be expert practitioners or fellow-researchers. Their contribution is not to evaluate, judge, or advise, but mainly to contribute to inciting a 'reflective conversation with the situation' (Schön, 1983: 135). By describing, interpreting, and summarising the current state of affairs and pointing out the unintended consequences of actions laid bare in the reconstruction process, the external reflectants can initiate a process that leads to reframing.

In the final step, all participants try to tease out common threads from the underlying dynamics that seem to be driving the dispute. The final aim of the reconstruction clinic is not so much to reach consensus about what is right or wrong or to reach agreement about future steps, but to get to a state of 'congruency' among stakeholders. 'Congruency' as defined by Grin and Van de Graaf (1996) is a state where actors who may be heterogeneous in their roles, ideas, and values, and even different in the problem-definition they use, manage to jointly define a meaningful line of action that will help them move out of the problematic situation they experience (cf. Loeber *et al.*, 2007: 90).

Two researchers are responsible for facilitating the reconstruction clinic: a main facilitator who structures the overall process of reconstruction, while the other captures the comments of participants in quotes that are added to annotate the timeline. The main facilitator steers the conversation through the sequence of events and invites participants to make observations on these events. The facilitator may ask clarifying questions or point out the seemingly critical moments in the process, where the different frames and perspectives seem to clash. The other facilitator mainly assists in the process, but may join in the inquiry and clarification process. The facilitators thus take an active part in the process, structuring, seeking clarification, inviting participants to join in to offer their perspectives and reflect upon others, and sometimes offering alternative frames. In the cases discussed below, I was the facilitator steering the main process. In both cases, the assistant role was taken by a PMP colleague.

Two cases further explored

Case 1: "a bowl of spaghetti in an urban neighbourhood"

The first case evolved around the planning of public space in a newly built urban neighbourhood. The local area manager brought the case to the PMP. He was worried about a number of conflicts in the area, especially because additional new developments were going to take place soon. If old disputes would not be settled, he was worried things could get rough. He briefly explained the situation. The local council, the central city administration, and different groups of local residents had been arguing about the quality of public space in the neighbourhood, issues of traffic safety, and the development of a number of playgrounds. Even though several plans had been made and the local council had presented designs, developments seemed to have come to a standstill because nobody seemed to be able to agree about what should happen. The area manager described the conflict as a relatively structured, albeit complex, problem: a conflict of interest between different groups of citizens and different departments of the city administration. "There are many players involved and there are so many different interests and I do not see how we can make them meet". He expressed a sense of confusion as well as the necessity to make a move: "something has to be done". The area manager suggested organising a joint session with all key players to discuss options. I suggested talking to the key players involved in advance in order to find out about their view of the situation as well as whether they would be interested participating in a joint session.

Setting the stage. To prepare the clinic we started with five names given to us by the area manager. The list included citizens and civil servants who were involved. We started out by contacting these five people and were pleasantly surprised to find that everyone seemed to be keen to talk about the situation. After each interview we were referred to someone else, with the notion that they too would have important issues to share. We ended up doing ten interviews, five citizens and five civil servants, some individually, some in groups. The interviews, conducted in narrative-style, were open and revealing. Each interview felt like a *piece of a puzzle*, and only after the last interview, the complexity of the case became somewhat clear. Whereas the area manager who initiated the reconstruction clinic in the first place described the dispute as a problem in which different groups with different interests were clashing, the interviews suggested a more complex situation with many underlying issues, interests that seemed changeable, dynamic, and ambiguous. There were different expectations about who should do what and a lack of transparent communication. Not only were there disagreements about what should happen, it struck us that, seemingly, no one involved had an overview of what was at stake. Hence, different issues and projects got blurred together. People were irritated by the situation, but willing to engage with each other.

In the interviews, citizens emphasised their frustration about the fact that everything seemed to have come to a standstill: "everybody seems to be waiting for everybody ... we have been waiting for so long for things to become clear" and "that is how it goes, wait, wait, wait ..." (local resident). They emphasised the lack of communication and transparency by the decision-makers: "we were never invited to talk about it. The council did not tell us. We could have sat around the table and talk about it" (local resident).

The civil servants had mixed feelings about the conflict. Some acknowledged the need for residents to be heard: "I think the main thing is that people feel taken seriously and that they can talk to us about that" (project manager). Others framed the situation as NIMBY-problem: "this whole playground discussion is just ... this whole NIMBY-attitude. This place should be right and then some people just say no" (planner). Overall, civil servants emphasised the need to provide clear information about what they could and could not do, rather than leaving things open:

> this is an important problem. We do not yet know if this part of the road is going to be part of the main traffic access system ... this depends upon the need and necessity for the free bus lane. We need the figures from the traffic department for that ... they should come soon.
>
> (Planner)

They also worried that citizens would want things they could not afford or that were out of their scope: "anyway, we need money ... for everything people want" (planner) and "there's a lot of costs, it sort of oversteps the scope of my project" (project manager).

We identified a number of key moments or events from the interviews. These events were described, to the extent possible, in factual, non-controversial terms such as "the council made a decision" or "the fence was placed". These statements were used to construct a rudimentary initial timeline of eight critical moments.

The reconstruction clinic. The clinic was organised together with a local debating centre, to emphasise the independent character of the evening. Invitations were distributed in the neighbourhood. We also invited the people we interviewed to attend and to bring whomever they thought might add to the discussion. Based on prior experience, we did not expect a huge turnout and were taken by surprise when over 50 people turned up.

The timeline of events was put in the middle of the room on the wall.

We started the evening with a question: Is this were the story starts?. A citizen we had not interviewed responded immediately: "Oh no, that was not the beginning, it started in 2008 when we had to wait for our apartments to be finished!" (local resident). His comment struck a chord that would become important. It displayed feelings of disappointment, rather than of anger or disbelief. I took the group through the timeline and my colleague captured important quotes on differently coloured post-its and annotated the timeline with them. As we worked our way from the beginning to the end of the timeline, we asked people to add events that were critical in their mind and to comment on the events on the wall. The discussion was captured by quotes (each party in a different colour), which were added to the timeline.

We were finished when none of the stakeholders wanted to add events or comments on the events in the timeline. The stakeholders present at the meeting agreed that the picture before them was *the story*.

Reflectants' backtalk. Two external reflectants with an interest in urban conflicts – colleagues from the university (reflectant 1 and 2) – were invited. The external reflectants briefly commented on the story that was now laid out on the wall. They tried to tease out the key features in terms that showed why they were essential for understanding what had happened and how it led to the current impasse. They also pointed to unintended consequences and the influence that they had. "How come so many well-intended people can end up in such a mess?" (reflectant 1); or "it seems like a bowl of spaghetti, yet all of the stakeholders seem to be reasonable people" (reflectant 1). They emphasised the overall paralysis that developed without intention, seemingly from the degree to which everything was intertwined: "It seems as if 'when pulling one thread, everything moves, so that no step is undertaken" (reflectant 1). They observed how the process seemed to keep restarting, without acknowledging what had happened before – "How come so much knowledge seems to get lost?" – and pointed out the consequences – "new events seem to have been taken hostage by the past" (reflectant 2). This backtalk opened interpretive space in which participants could start to remake and reframe their situation. Rather than looking for ways to blame the other party, this 'reflective talk with the situation' led to the collective insight that the situation that they were in was something they were in together and that they created *together*.

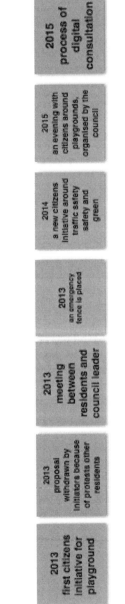

Figure 9.1 Extract of the timeline as prepared by the facilitators before the start of the reconstruction clinic.

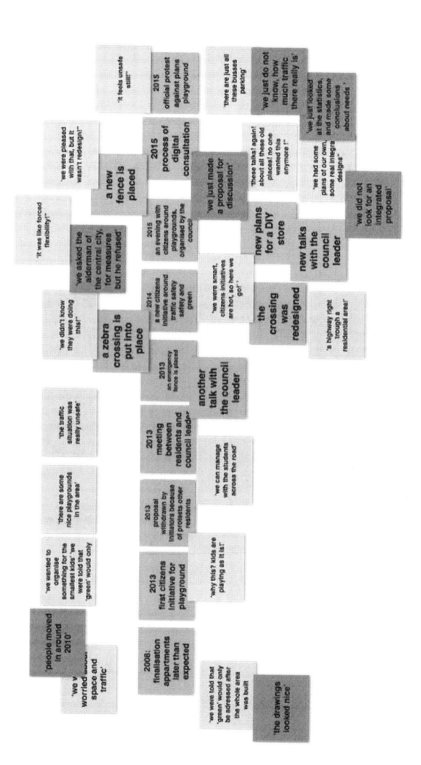

Figure 9.2 Extract of the timeline produced during the reconstruction clinic.

Joint insights: remaking and reframing. The discussion then turned back to the participants in the room. We asked them to reflect on the timeline and on the reflectants' comments. The participants recognised how the reflectants' comments drew out the essence of the situation: *"a good summary"* (planner) and *"It is a bowl of spaghetti indeed"* (local resident). The discussion among participants then focused on three shared key insights:

- There was a difference in the ways groups approached the situation. Planners regarded the area as 'not finished' and emphasised upcoming decisions regarding traffic, access, and use of public space that were connected to broader planning in the city. Citizens stressed the lived quality of daily experience and argued from the 'here and now' for immediate change ("this is where we live" – local resident).
- This linked to a contrast between government's need to provide clear answers and perfect long-lasting solutions and citizens' focus on action and movement ("we do not want perfect solutions" – local resident).
- Policymakers framed the situation as conflict of interests whereas citizens emphasised the need for creativity and co-production to make things work: "we do not mind a playground, we would like to be involved in the design and the search for locations" (local resident).

During the final part of the evening we proposed to extend the discussion by mapping an imaginary timeline for the future. We asked them "What will this timeline look like, if we were to look back one year from now?" This opened the door to broad participation as those in the room engaged each other, not so much focused on a search for solutions, but in a search for practical ways to foster a joint process as things moved ahead. Plans were made to set up a joint group of citizens and civil servants to work out different possible scenarios for the children's playground.

Reflection on the reconstruction process. The session took two-and-a-half hours. The discussion was lively, sometimes critical when people felt their part of the story did not receive sufficient emphasis. The discussion became more emotional when one of the citizens and one of the civil servants argued and then blamed each other for not listening. The heat dissipated when the civil servant apologised for making a faulty assumption. This seemed to create a turning point in the discussion. The public apology was accepted, and the tension broke. It was not easy to conduct a conversation with 50+ participants, and this immediately raised questions about the setting of the reconstruction clinic. The benefits of the public setting were clearly the transparency and opportunity for many people to join in. The practicality of conducting a reconstruction with 50+ participants proved challenging. The participants stressed the importance of making the collective timeline as it was the revealing part of the evening. Even those who advocated action – as opposed to investing time in looking back – said things like: "It was revealing, looking back like this made things a lot more clear" (local resident) and "everybody's perspective was added to the timeline, this way the puzzle became complete" (planner) and "It was good that we could all tell our story and were being heard" (local resident) and "it feels like a fresh start, we can leave the past behind" (area manager).

In sum, the story that unfolded turned out to be far more complex than initially perceived by policymakers. This is perhaps not surprising. What seems revealing, however, is how combining the divergent, even conflicting, perspectives of the participants led to a shift from blaming – 'the opposites parties fault' – to seeing the situation as a collective mess that needed collective action in order to move forward.

Several months later, we asked the project manager and the area manager how they looked back at the evening. "It really felt like a fresh start", the project manager stressed: "we regained some of the trust we lost and it felt as if we could let the past be the past" and "I have a better sense of what is important now and why people were so angry" (project manager). At the same time, the area manager expressed his worries about holding on to this moment: "we have to find a way to capture that spirit of the evening into a new collaborative process, otherwise we'll lose it again" (area manager). These remarks are important. They indicate the importance of getting unstuck and gaining active trust among stakeholders who seem to have become aware that trust is about "a bet about the future contingent actions of others" (Sztompka, 1999).

Case 2: "a game of chess in an area for wind turbines"

The second case evolved around a complicated and controversial rural development project for wind turbines in a province in the north of the Netherlands. The project manager – based at the Ministry of Economic Affairs and new to the project – asked us for help to address a conflict that had developed between two private energy developers who disputed each other's right to develop wind turbines at one specific location. The Ministry was held by a tight deadline for reaching the national goals as laid down in the national Energy Agreement for the development of wind energy in 2020. The conflict had been going on for five years and attempts by the Ministry to mediate had failed. The project manager gave us her view on the situation: "It's a game of chess ... we have been trying to get parties to agree, but it did not work out" (project manager, Ministry of Economic Affairs). She emphasised the Ministry's urgent need to find a solution to comply with targets for 2020 laid down in a national Energy Accord that had been signed by over 50 different private and public stakeholders, including the Ministry: "We are in a hurry, we are losing momentum" (project manager, Ministry of Economic Affairs). She expressed feelings of anger and disappointment and questioned why the developers could not come to an agreement. We suggested starting with interviews with the key players to get background on the history and to see if a joint session would be feasible.

Setting the stage: preparation for the clinic. During the initial interviews, we felt that some of the parties were a bit reluctant to talk to us. Most of them wanted to know why we were approaching them and what lay behind our efforts.

We responded by emphasising our independent role. We acknowledged that we had been asked by the Ministry to assist them in designing a process in which the parties could see if they could reach an agreement, but we could only do our work if we took – and kept to – a role that all the parties accepted.

We interviewed the key stakeholders, 15 in total. These interviews presented a complex story. Each time we thought we understood the situation, the next interview would reveal new events and new stories about these events. At the end of the 15 interviews, we got the feeling that we were looking at the world through parallel universes that had been created over the last few years. In these universes, things happened alongside each other, each according to its own logic and without regard for the often-deep conflicts this created with other perspectives and positions. When we interviewed the project leader from the Ministry, she seems to be even more irritated than she had at the beginning of the initiative. "We want to give them one last chance or we'll have to make the decision for them" (project manager, Ministry of Economic Affairs). The developers instead emphasised the need to clarify this history and its implications: "We want to develop, not go to court, things have to become clear" (developer 1). Four different layers of government were involved with unclear division of responsibilities for the project: "it is not clear who is responsible now" (civil servant, representative for the province) and "I went to the council, but they do not decide, I went to the province, several times ... this whole procedure puzzles me, there is always a new something new pulled out of a hat" (landowner).

In addition to responsibilities not being clear, the different government players took different positions and pursued different strategies: "They (the Ministry-sic) are pushing this situation so it fits to the planning, that just makes things worse" (civil servant province) and "the province just wants to create a fourth and fifth row of turbines, but there is already so much noise pollution, we don't want it" (civil servant, representative for the local council) and "we decide what happens to the dikes" (civil servant, representative for the Water board). The landowners we interviewed emphasised the importance of finding a solution and for the two parties to work something out and they emphasised the need for government to push for action: "the province has left it for too long, these parties need to agree amongst each other" (landowner). Overall, feelings of distrust dominated the scene: "we only agree on one thing, that trust in this project is below zero" (developer 2) and "so much has happened, there is just so much distrust now" (civil servant, representative of the province).

Even the preparations for the reconstruction clinic were confusing. While we were drawing the initial timeline, not one, but two timelines developed. We invited three external reflectants; one academic colleague (reflectant 1) and two private consultants – one experienced in environmental projects (reflectant 2) and one as public mediator in infrastructural projects (reflectant 3) – to offer an 'external view' during the reconstruction clinic to help the group to see through the complexity and bring out the essentials of the case.

The reconstruction clinic. On the day of the clinic the situation was tense. We had agreed to meet on 'neutral' terrain, in a conference room, in the middle of

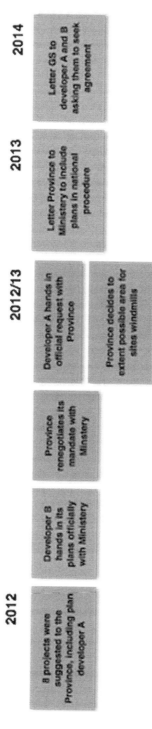

Figure 9.3 Extract of the timeline presented at the start of the meeting.

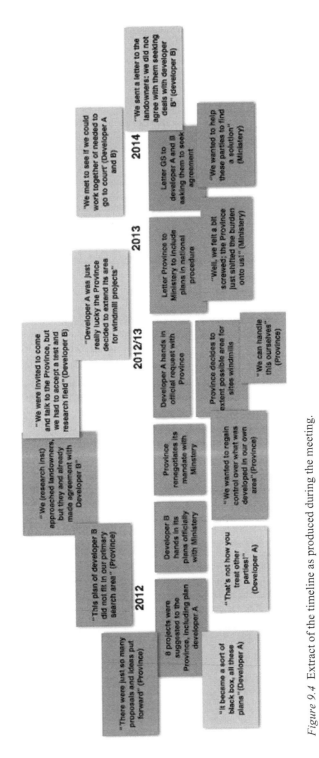

Figure 9.4 Extract of the timeline as produced during the meeting.

the country. As we all had our morning coffee, we were already wary of how we would be perceived and made sure that we did not spend more time with one party than another. It also came out that this was actually the first time that these people had met, all together in one room.

From the start we made clear to all participants – from the representatives of the four tiers of government involved, to the representatives of the private companies, the landowners and several NGOs – that this session was not about finding the truth, evaluation, or allocating blame. Our focus would be on unravelling the current situation and making sense together in a manner that could help us define next steps, and seeking congruent action, rather than an agreement. I conducted the meeting while my colleague captured quotes and used a selection to annotate the timeline. Not only points of view and remarks were added, but also many new events appeared to have been key to some of the participants.

Reflectants' back talk. We asked the reflectants to comment on the timeline, the quotes, and the events that were added while participants remained silent and listened. We could see it was not easy for them, and every now and then someone wanted to react and add something. We explained to them again that the reflectants add a perspective; it is not the truth they are seeking. After some initial discomfort, the participants remained silent and listened. "The complexity and especially the lack of transparency of this case is enormous, this must be threatening to all parties", reflectant 1 commented and "It seems difficult to create a setting for negotiation when the different roles and responsibilities of parties involved are unclear" (reflectant 1). They wondered why it is that "if the BATNA to all parties seems to be a legal procedure, this has not happened so far, what is keeping them?" (reflectant 1 and 2). They reflected on the role of the Ministry; "the Ministry has its own interests, there they should not seek the role as mediator" (reflectant 3). Finally, they wondered where the protesters were; "everybody seems to agree on the need for wind on land, where are the protesters?" (reflectant 2).

Joint insights. The discussion was brought back to the participants, and a lively conversation followed. Participants reflected on the timeline, quotes and comments of reflectants. The discussion focused on three insights:

- The revelation of two separate storylines, that added to the feeling that both developers stood in their rights whereas the ministry sought to mediate;
- The desire to have a transparent process while sharing information was experienced as threatening and undermining the different legal positions;
- The need for a process design where all participants could be at the table while formal positions are not clear.

Reflection on the process. The session took an entire day. Here, again, participants suggested beforehand that they wanted action rather than more talking. At the end of the day, however, the group emphasised that together going through this process of joining stories and events into one history had been important and revealing. "This was for the first time that we were sitting together in one room to hear the complete story" (civil servant, representative of the province) and "everybody looked at the problem together, now we can no longer deny it" (developer 1). A key insight that contributed to reframing the situation was the insight that emerged that the case was not so much a conflict between two private developers each claiming its own rights, but a problem that developed because the rules of the game were unclear and because government attempts to solve the conflict had instead contributed to it. "Because we tried to mediate as a government we made the problem worse" (project manager, Ministry of Economic Affairs). Whereas the day started as an attempt to bring two developers together, at the end of the day, the problem was reframed as a question about joint responsibility: "we were all responsible for the problem, and now we are all responsible for finding a solution" (civil servant, representative of the province).

Shortly after the reconstruction clinic, the project manager called us again: "we feel we are close to a breakthrough, but things are fragile". She asked us, on behalf of all other parties, if we would be willing to do another session, this time focusing on the problems we had disentangled in the reconstruction clinic. We prepared a process in which we would revisit the timeline we had created, focus on the critical moments that had been discussed previously and forecast a timeline while asking: What needs to be done to prevent that same entanglement from happening [again]? At the end of this session, an agreement seemed to be emerging. The stakeholders agreed that they were close, and proposed to continue in a third session to see if they could reach agreement on the issues that they had identified as critical. As we prepared the third session, it became clear that there was not going to be an agreement any time soon. The representatives of the private developers kept threatening each other with lawsuits and fights broke out among the different layers of government that were at the table. Months later, the project leader told us that the particular problems around this case had not been resolved, but that the different layers of government had begun to sit together on a regular basis to discuss and try to design a new approach to collaboration that would help prevent repeating the mistakes of the past. The insights produced during the reconstruction clinic helped the different government actors understand the importance of coordinating their policies and actions in efforts to develop wind-on-land. Even though their policies might have been formally aligned, the reconstruction revealed how interpretations of general policy lines varied across the levels of government involved. The capacity building that developed contributed to a breakthrough in this project and provided insights for other projects that were at risk of suffering similar problems.

Key findings

Two key findings arise from the exploration of these two settings. First, the specific design features of the clinic provided a safe setting for participants that was structured in a way that helped them conduct research into their own situation and do so in a non-evaluative way. Second, the switch in emphasis from immediately seeking agreement on action to providing space for making sense together, finally led to the possibility of finding a congruent proposal for action that would help stakeholders get themselves unstuck.

The first design feature of the reconstruction clinic – the use of narratives – illustrates how the use of quotes as short narratives contributed to a tangible sense of the "felt needs and experienced sufferings of the agents involved" (Laws and Rein, 2003: 173). The quotes that were appended to the timeline were concrete and tangible. They translated the needs and suffering into understandable and tangible language.

The perception and acknowledgement of the different narratives within the timeline sparked a process of narrative braiding (Cobb, 2013). Practitioners became engaged in a collaborative process in which different stories and pieces of information were plotted together on a single timeline. This practice revealed the sequence of events, but also helped those involved discover that their information, ideas, opinions, and positions were highly interrelated, and were anything but static. This, in turn, led to reframing within the stream of events. Narrative braiding describes a process in which individual stories are 'braided' together in a shared storyline.

> The 'braid' is the story about the problem, told collectively, that includes the terms of legitimacy offered by each of the parties to the conflict. It is the set of narrative strands that are inflected, or articulated to each other.
>
> (Cobb, 2013: 14)

This braiding initiated a process in which history was remade as was made collective. Instead of different storylines, one story about a shared history emerged.

The use of a timeline – a second important design feature – structured the discussion in a non-judgmental way that made the process of narrative braiding workable. The timeline helped to reveal how events developed along a line that had its own logic that was punctuated by the story. Austin (1962) describes punctuation as an important part of interpreting conversation: "where the story starts defines for an important part how we understand it" (Austin, 1962). In both cases, practitioners involved in the reconstruction clinic punctuated their stories differently. For example, the stories regularly did not have the same starting point. The narratives (captured in the quotes from practitioners that annotated the timeline), underlined the importance of seeing their own logic in two ways. The narratives that were captured were, as much as possible, answers to the question "what happened?". John Forester (Forester, 2009, 2013; Laws and Forester, 2015) explains the important difference between that question and the questions "why did it happen?" or "what did you think that happened?". As Forester argues, the latter questions may pre-empt the learning of the researcher about the course of action (Forester, 2013: xviii). Here, it may have also pre-empted the process of collaborative learning.

This process of remaking history is essentially what Dale (1999) has described as a process in which participants work to create a story that they can all agree on, which is fundamentally different from a story in which everybody agrees. "As such, it is very different from 'consensus' as in sameness of meaning, but precisely reflects the real meaning of 'consensus' as making sense together" (Cobb, 2013: 14). This idea of integrating different stands, ideas, or positions rather than seeking agreement as an important way to find breakthroughs can be traced back to the work of pragmatists such as Mary Parker Follet. In her work on community building, the concept of integrating plays an important role: "When you get to a situation it becomes what it was plus you; you are responding to the situation plus yourself, that is, to the relation between it and yourself" (Follet, 1924; cf. Whipps, 2014: 133). Follet's ideas on integration echo's Dewey's sense of experience: "Experience as interaction includes the possibility to adjust and mentor change on both sides of the experience, thus opening the door for personal and social reconstruction and evolution" (Whipps, 2014: 410). In short, it supports the possibility for stakeholders that disagree to change, or adjust their ideas and perspectives in a process of interaction, thus opening the door to transformation. Narrative braiding, integration, and experience as interaction are highly relational processes of continuous dynamics that may open up situations that are stuck and possibly create opportunities for breakthroughs.

The process of narrative braiding eventually leads to some sense of joint history. Dale's rich account of a negotiation process over the Future of Haida Gwaii shows that process of (re)making history together is a powerful way of reshaping options for the future (Dale, 1999). This feeling of joint history is echoed in both cases, and perhaps best formulated by the representative of the Province in the wind-turbine case: "we were all responsible for the problem, and now we are all responsible for finding a solution". This process of remaking history can be understood as a process of framing and reframing, as "the interplay between belief and doubt within a frame viewed as a struggle that generates effort to make sense of a changing situation and to coordinate action" (Laws and Rein, 2013: 174). As the details of the cases have shown, frames were not static but rather dynamic and fluid belief systems that "intertwine with identity and social action" (Laws and Rein, 2013: 174). The process of remaking provided practitioners as well as the researchers with insights into how existing frames may have been formed. At the same time, it facilitated a process of seeing and understanding things in another way.

The remaking of a joint history is what seems to have opened the door to efforts to reframing the problem or the conflict. The process of reframing was triggered by the backtalk provided by the external reflectants. Organised backtalk – the third design feature of the reconstruction clinic – introduced a more critical conversation about underlying patterns of disruptive interaction that (re)created the dynamics of the conflict. The reflectants were able to comment not only on the past events, but also to point to underlying patterns in institutional structures, processes, and procedures that might present obstacles for working together in the future. By describing, interpreting, and summarising the current state of affairs and pointing out the unintended consequences that had surfaced during

the reconstruction process, the external reflectants offered openings for participants to review their situation in light of possible future actions. This last step
opened up opportunities for finding new frames as well as finding a congruent
frame for action

Conclusions

The design features and outcomes of the reconstruction clinic reveal some benefits
and constraints of a pragmatic and relational approach to action research in policy
disputes. First, the clinical approach emphasises that the starting point is defined by
the stakeholders themselves. The clinical approach underscores the importance of
self-insight and the responsibility of each stakeholder for his or her own contributions to the diagnosis of the situation (Schein, 2006). As a result, the knowledge
about the situation as diagnosed by the stakeholders in their collective process was
not only a *shared understanding*, but also a *joint transformation* (Wagenaar, 2012),
for which the stakeholders could take responsibility.

The limits of a clinical approach also became clear. Since we conducted our
reconstruction clinic in response to a request from stakeholders that were stuck,
we finished our involvement as soon as the stakeholders felt the situation needed
no more facilitation. In both cases, we were no longer actively involved after the
clinics were finished, even though we were of course interested in the further
developments. In both cases, we have occasionally asked for updates from the
stakeholders involved, which are still given to us albeit on an irregular basis. It
may be worthwhile to develop a sequel or a series of sequels to see how the
cases develop in due course.

Second, the highly pragmatic and relational nature of the reconstruction clinic
highlighted the character of this process as "ever-changing and unfolding"
(Emirbayer, 1997: 289). The highly relational process of *joint transformation*
however demanded a highly reflective stand from the researchers and reflectants.
Within the settings of the reconstruction clinic, the roles were clearly defined
and structured. Key here seemed to be the division between the facilitators who
were steering a highly *relational* process and the reflectants, who provided *critical backtalk*. The separation of these roles resembles Vickers' distinction of two
typical researcher roles: the *spectator-manipulator* who observes and remains
distant from the situation and the *agent-experient* who locates him/herself within
the problematic situation (Vickers, 1968; cf. Argyris and Schön, 1996: 36). The
findings of the two cases indicate that the separation of these two roles seemed
to work. More work is however needed to understand and describe this separation more clearly.

Third, reconstruction is a voluntary process, most often initiated by a governmental institution. This itself contributes to creating a context in which policymakers are open and willing to participate in a process of collaborative learning.
This move seems to fit very well with the Dutch culture of collaborative policymaking and is important to the success of the reconstruction clinic. Bringing the
reconstruction clinic to other countries might provide interesting insights to this

specific feature: the willingness to engage in a collaborative process in policy disputes as a prerequisite for getting unstuck.

Finally, the two experiments of the reconstruction clinic have demonstrated opportunities for operationalising pragmatism for new global challenges in local settings. In order to avoid *getting stuck in a search of certainties*, settings such as the reconstruction clinic can offer concrete and practical opportunities in *"active experimentation"* (Dewey, 1913: 332) that are needed to deal with today's radical uncertainties.

Acknowledgements

I would like to thank all participants in the reconstruction clinics for their collaboration, confidence and openness. Their willingness to be part of this adventure was remarkable and courageous. I am grateful to Hendrik Wagenaar and David Laws for their constructive critique and suggestions; to Anne Loeber and John Grin who have read and commented on many versions. Their suggestions have greatly helped to shape the final product. Finally, my special thanks to Karima Arichi, who has, as a key participant in several reconstruction clinics, provided very valuable feedback on the design of the actual clinic in order improve its performance.

References

Austin JL (1962) *How to do things with words*, Boston USA: Harvard University Press.
Argyris C and Schön D (1996) *Organisational-learning II*, Reading USA: Adison Wesley Publishing Company.
Cobb S (2013) Narrative braiding and the role of public officials in transforming the public's conflicts. *Conflict and Narrative: Explorations in Theory and Practice* 1(1): 4–30.
Dale N (1999) Cross-cultural community-based planning: negotiating the future of Haida Gwaii. In: Susskind L, McKearnan S and Thomas-Larmer J *The consensus-building handbook*, Thousand Oaks: SAGE Publications Inc.
Dewey J (1910) *How we think?* Lexington USA: D.C. Heath.
Dewey J (1913) *Essays in experimental logic*, Chicago USA: Chicago University Press.
Emirbayer M (1997) Manifesto for a relational sociology. *American Journal of Sociology* 103(2): 281–317.
Follet M (1924) *Creative experience*, New York: Peter Smith.
Follet M (1918) *The new state*, New York USA: Longman, Green and Co.
Forester J (2009) *Dealing with differences*, Oxford: Oxford University Press.
Forester J (2013) *Planning the age of conflict*, Chicago USA: American Planning Association.
Greenwood D (2007) Pragmatic action research. *International Journal of Action Research* 3(1 and 2): 131–148.
Grin J and Van de Graaf H (1996) Technology assessment as learning. *Science, Technology and Human Values* 20(1):72–99.
Hajer M (2009) *Authoritative governance*, Oxford: Oxford University Press.
Hajer M and Wagenaar H (2003) *Deliberative policy analysis*, Cambridge: Cambridge University Press.

Hoppe R (2011) *The governance of problems*, Bristol UK: Bristol University Press.

Karsten N and Jansen T (2013) Veranderend Lokaal Gezag. *Beleid en Maatschappij* 40(4): 378–400.

Kleiner A and G Roth (1998) Developing organisational memory through learning histories. *Organisational Dynamics* 27(2): 43–60.

Langley A (1999) Strategies for theorizing from process data. *Academy of Management Review* 24(4): 691–710.

Laws D and Rein M (2003) Reframing practice. In: Hajer M and Wagenaar H (eds.) *Deliberative policy analysis*, Cambridge: Cambridge University Press, 172–201.

Laws D and Forester J (2015) *Conflict, improvisation, governance*, Milton Park UK: Routledge.

Leary K (2004) Critical moments in negotiation. *Negotiation Journal* (4): 143–145.

Loeber A, Van Mierlo B, Grin J and Leeuwis C (2007) The practical value of theory: conceptualising learning in the pursuit of a sustainable development. In: Wals A (ed.) *Social learning towards a sustainable world, principles, perspectives and praxis*, Wageningen: Wageningen Academic Publishers, 83–97.

Peirce C (1877) The fixation of belief. *Popular Science Monthly* 12(11): 1–15.

Prak M and Van Zanden J (2013) *Nederland en het Poldermodel*. Amsterdam: Bert Bakker.

Rittel H and Webber M (1973) Dilemma's in a general theory of planning. *Policy Sciences* (4): 155–169.

Schein E (2006) Clinical action research. In: Reason P and Bradbury H (eds.), *The SAGE handbook of action research, participative inquiry and practice*, Thousand Oaks: SAGE Publications.

Schön D (1983) *The reflective practitioner*, New York: Basic Books.

Schön D and Rein M (1994) *Frame reflection: toward the resolution of intractable policy controversies*, New York: New York Basic Books.

Susskind L and Cruikshank J (1987) *Breaking the impasse, consensual approaches to public disputes*, New York: Basic Books.

Sztompka P (1999) *Trust: a sociological theory*, Cambridge: Cambridge University Press.

Ury W and Fischer R (1986) *Getting to yes*, Boston USA: Houghton Mifflin Harcourt.

Van den Brink G, Kneyber R and Jansen T (2012) *Gezagsdragers*, Amsterdam: Boom Uitgevers.

Verloo N (2015) *Negotiating urban conflict. Conflict as an opportunity for urban democracy*. PhD Thesis, University of Amsterdam, Netherlands.

Vickers G (1968) *Value systems and social processes*, London: Tavistock.

Wagenaar H (2012) *Meaning in action. Interpretation and dialogue in policy analysis*. New York: M.E. Sharpe.

Whipps JD (2014) A pragmatist reading of Mary Parker Follett's integrative process. *Transactions* (50) 3: 405–424.

Co-inquirer reflection

Karima Arichi

I am area manager in an Amsterdam city district, responsible for coordinating policy interventions and activities in a specific geographical area. I also act as a kind of 'mediator' between different stakeholders, making sure everyone's input is heard. I have been working with the Public Mediation Programme (PMP) at the University of Amsterdam (UvA) for several years. The collaboration started out of a joint interest in settings for collaborative learning in difficult policy situations. I have participated in several reconstruction clinics and in a year-long collaborative action research project on conflicts around urban planning of playgrounds.

We talk a lot with our stakeholders. There are many of them: groups of citizens, entrepreneurs, etc. Often there is a lot going on, a lot of activity. Sometimes, things get stuck. For example, when there are not only many different community stakeholders but also many stakeholders from our own organisation, different civil servants, different departments. We can get stuck after trying many different interventions, which do not really seem to work. People get frustrated and feel powerless. We (area managers) always have an urge to try and resolve things, to find solutions. But sometimes we need to take a step back. Ever since our first reconstruction clinic around the 'playboat' (an idea for a floating playground at the waterfront), we are capable of better recognising when we need to step back, when there is a need for us to understand different perspectives on the situation.

The action research-based partnership with the UvA is of great value to us. It is about real, relevant, unfolding cases. It is a way to learn while we are working. We have really explored this together. Civil servants are experts in their own field. The action researcher is like a critical reflectant observing what we are doing, without having any interest or judgment about the outcome. That is also a real difference in roles between practitioners and researchers. Everyone is looking at the process from a different role. I like that. The action researcher does not judge or evaluate but just asks questions. We (civil servants, policy-makers) feel safe because of that. It provides us space to talk and ask each other questions. The researchers are not there to undermine what we do. We do not feel threatened in our own field of expertise.

We asked PMP to organise a reconstruction clinic around a public space where residents wanted more room for kids to play as well as greenery such as trees and bushes. This clinic was organised together with citizens and civil servants. It went really well. There were a lot of citizens that evening. What really helped were the interviews the researchers did with key participants before the clinic. To me, the key insight of the evening was to really understand how citizens experience their contacts and interaction with us, the government. We have this term we like to use a lot: "working integral, or cross-domain". But it is sort of an empty phrase when you do not have a feeling for the people you are doing this for. This reconstruction clinic really made it clear that we have organised ourselves in silos. Also, we have a high turnover of civil servants. The historical knowledge of what happened before is limited. So, citizens have to tell their story again and again. They feel they have to continuously start the conversation with the government all over again. What was also an important insight for us is that we are not articulate about what we want as a government.

What I find really difficult is that we have promised we would do better. We want to learn from the insights from the reconstruction clinic. We really mean that. In the end, I have to conclude that we have only succeeded partially. Even though there is great willingness amongst the participants of the reconstruction clinic to do things differently, it has proven hard to change 'the system'. The way we have organised our work leaves us little room to be flexible. Only now (two years after the reconstruction clinic) we have found a way to organise ourselves better.

The role division between the outside reflectants and the process facilitator within the team of researchers was not always clear to me and even a bit confusing: who talks from what role? In one specific reconstruction clinic, the language of the outside reflectant did not really match with the group. The process facilitator combined both roles, which actually worked well, I would recommend keeping it that way. In another case, the outside reflectant role did work well though. The reflectants were colleagues who were not involved in the case. They provided a rich outsider perspective yet close enough in language and understanding of the participants.

Engaging in a reconstruction clinic has great added value for us. It provides breathing space and can relieve us from a sense of failure. For instance, in one of the reconstructions, there was a planner who carried the weight of a failed project on his shoulders. It made him lonely and he felt a lot of pressure. By engaging in more than one reconstruction clinic, my colleagues and I are starting to see underlying patterns that occur in other conflicts we have with citizens.

The reconstruction clinic is in itself – because of its simple and accessible structure – quite a brilliant way to learn while working. What I miss is having a sort of reflection upon the impact of reconstruction clinic after a few months or years. I would like to look back and gain insight about its impact on our work, on our practices: what have we really done differently? I am really curious to understand the long-term effects of the reconstruction clinics. Another thing I would really like is to broaden the scope of our insights: how can others who were not present profit from the insights we have had as participants?

10 Exploring the use of audiovisual media for deliberation

Reframing discourses on vulnerabilities to climate change in Nepal

Floriane Clement

Introduction

Experts have largely framed international debates on climate change (Jasanoff, 2010), contributing to (re)produce the dominance of a 'risk-hazard' perspective in the design of climate change adaptation programmes and policies (Bassett and Fogelman, 2013). This perspective establishes a linear causal linkage between climatic risk and vulnerability and tends to disregard other non-climatic factors producing vulnerabilities. Furthermore, dominant international discourses have framed climate change as a universal threat to humanity at large, concealing the structural inequalities that create different vulnerabilities to the same risk (Ribot, 2010; Swyngedouw, 2010).

This dominant perspective to understanding vulnerability has called for 'development as usual', missing to consider the political-economic structures that hinder 'transformative adaptation' (Bassett and Fogelman, 2013, Smucker *et al.*, 2015). Much climate change adaptation initiatives in the rural South indeed propose a similar package of techno-managerial interventions than earlier development programmes. The latter tend to provide 'quick fixes' without challenging the hegemonic structures that create vulnerabilities.

As the positivist approach to climate change adaptation legitimises technocratic and managerial interventions, moving towards transformative policies and programmes becomes particularly challenging (as Westling and Sharp remark for the water sector, Chapter 2). It requires confronting expert-driven climate change discourses by opening up discursive space, to integrate a more diverse range of voices and framings on what constitutes vulnerabilities across geographies and social groups. However, despite the rhetoric around participation in climate change adaptation programmes, the voices of vulnerable people have had a limited inclusion in policy arenas. The dominance of experts' contribution to international debates has been justified by the fact that climate change is a global complex phenomenon that can only be adequately addressed by scientific knowledge. Yet, many scholars observe that the deficiency of local voices and knowledge in climate and environmental policy processes has much to do with unequal governance mechanisms (Forsyth, 2003; Yates, 2012) and the political-economy of aid (Keeley and Scoones, 2003).

This research stems from the assumption that the production of scientific knowledge through conventional research is not sufficient to trigger transformative change in environmental policies (Forsyth, 2011, 2003). Instead, we explore the potential of an art-based, critical, and relational approach to action research in supporting transformative change. Particularly, we used participatory video and the media to initiate a series of deliberative events in Nepal with the objective to bring in discursive change that would acknowledge the structural causes of vulnerabilities. This chapter aims to answer the following research question: how does an art-based, critical and relational approach to participatory action research influence deliberation and discourses? Our approach to deliberation is based on a substantive rationale: we did not seek to achieve a priori defined outcomes, but rather explored the value of combining deliberation with participatory video to open up discursive space (Blue, 2016). Our aim was to create opportunities to voice a diverse range of values and meanings and to develop counter-narratives to apolitical discourses on climate change adaptation. The next section introduces the theoretical premises underlying the potential opportunities and limitations of using participatory video and deliberation to challenge hegemonic discourses. The following sections present the context of the research in Nepal and the methodology adopted for the action research project. We then move on to the research findings and conclude with a discussion on the main lessons for action researchers and development practitioners.

Participatory video and deliberation for transformative change

Participatory action research is a set of tools and approaches 'that involves researchers and participants working together to examine a problematic situation or action to change it for the better' (Wadsworth, 1998 in Kindon *et al.*, 2007: 1). Participatory video is a method of participatory action research that has been extensively used to give political voice to marginalised or underrepresented citizens (Milne *et al.*, 2012). Raising voices is seen as a critical foundation to enhance the downward accountability of policymakers (Gaventa and McGee, 2013). Participatory video is rooted in Freire's (1970) work on conscientisation. Freire defends that oppressed people have the right to voice their perceptions and experiences and that doing so supports challenging oppressive and hegemonic structures. In this chapter, we did not envision participatory video as a tool to enhance accountability, but rather as a process that enables opening discursive spaces whereby plural perceptions, claims and forms of knowledge can be voiced (Dutta, 2011). We also posited that the process of participatory video would help re-balance positions of power by enhancing what feminists call 'the power within' (Rowlands, 1995), that is the critical consciousness that help people realising the structural causes of oppression and taking actions against them (Freire, 1970).

Deliberation can strongly support to achieve the ideals of participatory video. By deliberation, we mean that the participants 'carefully examine a problem and arrive at a well-reasoned solution after a period of inclusive, respectful consideration of diverse points of view' (Gastil, 2008: 8). There are different views on whether and how deliberation can lead to transformative change, especially in settings characterised by unequal power relationships, divergent interests, and low prior level of trust and interaction among stakeholders. The use of deliberation as a tool for policy learning and policy change is rooted in the writings of Habermas (1987), who argued that political deliberations are biased in the favour of the elite who depoliticise debates to conceal social and political conflicts. His work was pioneering in emphasising the role of citizens and interest groups in policy change and the social construction of reality. However, Habermas' theory has been criticised for its exclusive focus on bourgeois and liberal public spheres and its lack of attention to discursive and institutional mechanisms of exclusion within these spheres (Fraser, 1990; Young, 2000). More pervasive forms of power can also shape deliberation, by implicitly giving legitimacy to certain types of knowledge, norms of discussion, and authority to certain social groups within the deliberation arena.

It is this pervasive form of power that we are interested to observe in discourses. We see discourses as both an instrument and a manifestation of power, shaping institutions, behaviours, and practices (Foucault, 1975). For post-empiricists, language, discourses, and narratives are central in framing social and environmental problems and how problems and their solutions are discussed in policy debates (Hajer, 1995). In this perspective, knowledge production and use are inherently political, especially in situations characterised by a high degree of complexity and uncertainty and when strong economic and political interests come into play (Forsyth, 2003).

In theory, in a deliberative process, the validity of one interpretation is tested against earlier interpretations and is accepted or rejected through reasoning with problem-solving as the main objective. A dialogue might be a useful preliminary step to deliberation to bridge linguistic and epistemological differences between them (Levine *et al.*, 2005). However, in practice, deliberative processes might also support the entrenchment of hegemonic discourses. For example, in the case of climate change debates, the use of deliberation to reach consensus has resulted in the exclusion of actors and demands that are not conforming to dominant discourses and actually reinforced the hegemonic discourse on the 'post-political condition' (Swyngedouw, 2010). We relied on several assumptions in choosing to use participatory video to initiate deliberative processes. We felt its artistic dimension was pertinent in two respects: first, its evocativeness, i.e. the strength with which it makes the audience feel emotions for the issues and challenge entrenched beliefs (Harris, 2009), and second, its action orientation, i.e. the extent to which it calls the audience for reflection and potentially for action (including verbal reactions), for example through self-identification (Mitchel *et al.*, 2012; Wheeler, 2012). We posited that evocativeness has the potential to enhance among the audience empathy, listening, and opening towards different perspectives and framings. The film was also to offer a buffer zone between farmers and policymakers by presenting farmers' views in a non-confrontational way. In their films, interviewed farmers raised their concerns to policymakers but the various claims were not directed to the specific individuals present in the audience – though they might have felt concerned by the nature of the claims. Last, the content of the film was also important. We compiled the films directed by farmers and experts' responses to highlight the multiplicity of framings of vulnerabilities and the importance of structural political-economic factors in producing vulnerabilities. Our hypothesis was that combining participatory video and deliberation holds the potential to develop counter narratives to hegemonic discourses as a first step towards transformative policy change (Castells, 2009). At the same time, we were aware of the need to consider the contextual factors that can limit the potential of participatory video to enhance social power (Shaw, 2012; Plush, 2015).

Climate change policies and discourses in Nepal

Nepal is one of the 16 countries listed globally as being at 'extreme risk' from climate change over the next 30 years and ranks fourth in a recent global Climate Change Vulnerability Index (CCVI), prepared by Maplecroft. The country has been the target of major international climate change adaptation programmes and is notably one of the nine pilot countries for the Pilot Programme on Climate Resilience (PPCR). At the national policy level, climate change has received strong political attention, visible in recent policy development, notably through the National Adaptation Programme of Action (NAPA) to Climate Change (GoN – MoE, 2011). The NAPA offers a framework for adaptation programmes in Nepal whereas the Climate Change Policy was developed to comply the institutional developments requested from all signatory parties of the Climate Change Convention.

Both the NAPA and Climate Change policy exhibit discursive features that fit with the risk-hazard approach. The NAPA establishes a linear linkage between projected climate change, climatic variability/hazards, and their potential impacts on a range of sectors/domains (public health, food security, energy, shelter, etc.) and proposes adaptation options to address these impacts. In the NAPA, vulnerability is rooted in the natural environment, poverty, and the heavy reliance on small-scale agriculture (GoN – MoE, 2010: 14). It points to structural factors when referring to gender and the lack of basic services and livelihood options, but the analysis stops here – for instance, it does not mention why the provision of basic services is lagging behind and for whom. The Climate Change policy is framed around identifying climate change impacts on different socio-economic sectors and depicts an apolitical narrative on vulnerability. The solutions advocated to reduce vulnerabilities lie in science and technologies and in the capacity building of the actors who can help farmers to adapt. None of the documents mention important structural factors shaping vulnerability such as high agrarian stress and levels of migration, processes of systematic exclusion of several social groups or the absence of locally elected government bodies.

Action research process

Research area

Most of the research took place in Dhanusa District, in the Tarai-Madhesh region, the southern lowland belt of Nepal. Only 31 per cent of the agricultural land is irrigated in Nepal and farming is particularly sensitive to change in rainfall patterns. Farmers in the region have also been facing a range of non-climatic processes creating vulnerabilities, notably a rise in male out-migration. The latter is both an indicator of agrarian stress and a producer of new forms of vulnerabilities, differentiated by gender, caste, and class (Sugden *et al.*, 2014). With the monetisation of the economy and reduced profits from agriculture, migration, increasingly long-term and overseas, has become a foremost livelihood strategy in the region. The absence of a large share of the male working force has in turn strongly affected rural areas and farming, leading to labour shortages and to rapid changes in gender roles and relationships. Last, the region has also been the site of Madhesi-led social uprising and political contestation for the last decades, related to issues of cultural discrimination and economic neglect of the region, weak political inclusion and representation, and more recently over the delineation of province boundaries following the 2015 Nepal's Constitution establishing a federalist state. There is therefore a certain resentment and lack of trust from Madhesis towards the national government and the bureaucracy.

Starting point

The action research was initiated as a pilot project to explore the potential of participatory video to capture and convey non-expert perceptions of climate change. It started with the allocation of seed money (US$10,000) by the Consortium Group on International Agricultural Research (CGIAR) Program 'Climate Change, Agriculture and Food Security' (CCAFS) to IWMI to conduct research on climate change and gender. The IWMI human geographer and author of this chapter opted for an action research approach, using participatory video. Conducting action research for transformative change is not very common in the CGIAR system. This choice was therefore an individual choice that was motivated by three reasons: a commitment to go beyond conventional extractive approach with a greater emphasis on the relational aspects of producing knowledge, an interest to bring local voices to national climate change debates, and a personal exposure to participatory video as a tool to bring transformative change. The project team was composed of two South Asian male and female professional film-makers who were familiar with participatory video, one male Nepali research assistant, one local female development worker who was respected by the community, and the author of the chapter. We used participatory video to engage with a group of eight women farmers in Dhanusa District over three days. We alternated training sessions on how to use a video camera, focus group discussions around a seasonal calendar, and video practices where women video interviewed themselves first on their daily lives and then on the effect of climatic variability and extremes on their livelihoods. Some of the interviews touched upon very intimate moments of their lives and the three days were punctuated with tears, laughs, and songs.

Thanks to additional funding from the same programme, we extended the use of participatory video to support a process whereby farmers reflected on and produced audiovisual material about local perceptions and framings of vulnerability over the course of ten months. The same project team interacted with two groups of six men and women farmers from two adjacent village development committees (VDCs), including several of the women who had taken part in the first phase. The farmers' participants were selected by the local co-operative committees, but we ensured there were participants from a higher and lower caste in each group and representing a wide age range, from 16 to 47 years old.

The process started with focus group discussions about the most meaningful and important social and climatic changes for them, with the objective for farmers to identify and reflect upon the issues that they would like to develop in a film. The two professional filmmakers trained farmers to use the camera, to frame questions, and to interview other farmers in their community. Farmers were also trained on how to do simple editing of audiovisual material so that they could have control over the overall production process. They were given the film and editing equipment (a handycam and a computer) against a small contribution of the local farmers' cooperatives towards the equipment costs. Once the training was over and the project team left, farmers interviewed on their own other farmers from their villages and produced 12 films on ten different topics related to vulnerabilities. Each film consisted of four to five interviews. We had asked the farmers-filmers to interview farmers of different social groups, and, although the group of farmers interviewed was overall dominated by middle-class/caste farmers, it included men and women of different caste, class, gender, and age. Our original intention that the farmers edit their films proved in practice difficult to implement as editing required sitting for an extended period of time, which was difficult especially for the women involved who had a high daily workload. Unreliable electricity supply was also a major constraint.

Seeking experts' responses

The research team partnered with the Nepal Forum of Environmental Journalists (NEFEJ) to show farmers' films to experts and policymakers in the headquarter of Dhanusa District, Janakpur, and in the capital city, Kathmandu. The first film was shown to the chief secretary of the Government of Nepal and the secretary of the Ministry of Science, Technology and Environment (MoSTE[1]) during a public launching event of the TV programme, organised in the premises of NEFEJ. Other films were shown in private to a range of experts, from civil society organisations, national and district level government agencies, researchers, and journalists and a journalist video-documented the experts' responses.

Two experts' interviews were compiled with each of the 12 films made by farmers and edited as a TV episode for a new programme produced by NEFEJ called 'Samudayako Aawaj' (Communities' Voices). The programme was broadcasted weekly on a national TV channel between July and December 2013. The participatory video process allowed creating new knowledge on vulnerabilities and raising farmers' voices. Policymakers and experts listened to these voices, but the research team and the farmers-filmers found their response and the overall outcome disappointing. Most of the policymakers and experts either repeated the issues raised by farmers or adopted a defensive stance to defend the actions already in place. Although films might have raised their empathy, there was no direct relation between the experts and the farmers in the approach adopted. There was however one instance of a policy action taken locally that farmers-filmers reported as potentially resulting from their film. Interestingly, the action taken was related to the only instance when a few of the farmer-filmers came with the journalist to show the film to the policymakers, in that case the local development officer. It suggested that the relational element of the communication – between those raising voices and those in power to address some of their claims – was a critical feature of participatory action research. Reflecting on the outcomes of this first round of action research, the research team and the farmers planned for the next steps, following an iterative process (Kemmis *et al.*, 2014: 18).

Deliberative events

The next step was to engage with policymakers following a relational approach using face-to-face and deliberative interactions. The deliberative events took place in 2014, first among farmers from the same district, and then among farmers, government officials, politicians and representatives from the civil society in Janakpur and in Kathmandu. The events were organised jointly by the research team, Nepal Madhesh Foundation (NEMAF), a national advocacy NGO working on governance and human rights in the region, Panos South Asia, a regional media organisation, and the Southasia Institute of Advanced Studies (SIAS), a national research institute working on natural resource and climate change governance. The four partners had several meetings prior to the events to view farmers' films and discuss the structural causes of vulnerability and learning process. Each event started with the screening of a documentary that collated extracts from the 12 films produced by farmers and the interviews of the experts conducted by NEFEJ. The format for the events differed, as we did not seek to adhere to one specific format but rather attempted to test different formats for initiating dialogue and deliberation.

The deliberation among farmers were organised in six VDCs in Dhanusa District and facilitated by NEMAF. Some of the farmers participating to these local events were invited in Janakpur to a dialogue with local government officials, which was mostly based on small group work discussion and facilitated by NEMAF. Panos South Asia organised another event between the farmers-filmers and district-level officials and facilitated by a local respected journalist. The discussion was recorded, edited, and broadcasted a few days later on local FM community radios. In Kathmandu, we organised two events, gathering the farmers-filmers from Dhanusa and representatives from the civil society, national and district-level government agencies, and from local government and political parties. The first event was organised by the research team and Panos South Asia and facilitated by a renowned Nepali journalist. It was recorded, edited, and broadcasted a few days later on national and local FM community radios. The second national-level event gathered a similar but slightly larger group of stakeholders (Table 10.1). It was jointly organised with SIAS and facilitated by a senior Nepali researcher.

Following the events, the research team, PANOS South Asia, and the journalist who had facilitated the national radio discussion met with a senior government official from the Department of Irrigation and a senior politician, ex-Minister for Environment, Science and Technology. They reflected on the outcomes of the deliberations and discussed possible ways forward.

Assessing impact

The journey that we undertook aimed at changing the beliefs and attitudes of policymakers, to result in policies that would better acknowledge and address the structural causes of vulnerabilities. We reflected during the process on the extent to which our actions and knowledge production could actually lead to such impact, and the extent to which we could assess this impact amidst the many other factors that might have influenced stakeholders' attitudes during the process. We decided that changes in policy debates, particularly, in how climate change adaptation is framed, would be an important first step in this direction and would be relatively more straightforward to pin down. The research team therefore conducted a discourse analysis to understand the impact of the debates that took place, from a discursive, relational and critical perspective. We developed our analysis around two major scientific approaches to define, conceptualise, and assess vulnerability (O'Brien et al., 2007): the risk hazard (or natural hazard) approach and the political-economy approach (Adger, 2006; Bohle, Downing and Watts, 1994). Scholars have evidenced how these approaches significantly frame debates and policy responses to climate change (e.g. Fussel, 2007; McLaughlin and Dietz, 2008; Ribot, 2010; Bassett and Fogelman, 2013). The risk-hazard approach understands vulnerability as primarily produced by natural and climatic factors. Adaptation is dependent upon local people's choices over a range of livelihood and adaptation strategies. Contrastingly, the 'political-economy' approach views climatic factors as only one of the multiple causes of vulnerability and locates vulnerability primarily in the social, economic, and political structures across multiples scales. Our analysis of discourses examined the reliance on one or the other approach in the narratives. We considered that discourses framed around a political-economy approach were more conducive to bring transformative change than discourses framed around a

Table 10.1 Characteristics of the events organised

Location	Format	Number of participants for each type of organisation	Organised/facilitated by	Other
6 VDCs, Dhanusa District	Facilitated discussion based on a set of questions defined by the research team, in small groups of around seven persons disaggregated by sex	Farmers: 185 (in total, for six dialogues) Sex: 97 men, 88 women	IWMI and NEMAF / NEMAF	
Janakpur, Dhanusa District	Facilitated discussion upon the discretion of the facilitator	Farmers: 17 Journalists: 2 District government agencies: 4 Sex: 14 men, 9 women	IWMI and Panos South Asia/A journalist	Recorded, edited and broadcasted on the radio
Janakpur, Dhanusa District	Facilitated discussion in small groups with representatives from each type of participant around three pre-defined themes	Farmers: 12 Civil society organisations: 8 District government agencies: 6 Sex: 17 men, 9 women	NEMAF/ NEMAF	
Kathmandu	Facilitated discussion upon the discretion of the facilitator	Farmers: 10 Civil society organisations: 1 Media organisations: 2 National government agencies: 2 District government agencies: 2 Sex: 10 men, 7 women	IWMI and Panos South Asia/A journalist	Recorded, edited and broadcasted on the radio
Kathmandu	Workshop style, facilitated discussion on relevant themes selected by the facilitator	Farmers: 10 Civil society organisations: 3 Politicians: 1 National government agencies: 2 District government agencies: 3 Sex: 12 men, 7 women	IWMI and SIAS/ SIAS	

Note

risk-hazard perspective, because the former recognises and stresses the social limits and structural constraints to adaptation. As the risk-hazard perspective is the dominant framing of climate change vulnerability in international and national policy debates in Nepal, we explored to which extent the political-economy perspective was present and potentially influential in the deliberation.

We relied both on an analytical and interpretive approach to analyse the material. We linked discourses to actors and their positions, to assess whether influential actors, who usually rely on a risk-hazard framing, engaged in a deliberation that integrated a political-economy framing. Our analysis relied on the English translation of the transcript of the four debates that included both government officials and farmers. For the analytical approach, we coded quotations according to the two main types of vulnerability discourses (risk-hazard/political-economy) and to the position and sex of the speaker, using Atlas TI, a qualitative data analysis software. We classified quotations under the 'political-economy' perspective when they referred to political-economic drivers, social inequalities, governance failures such as lack of accountability, etc. We classified quotations under the 'risk-hazard' perspective when they referred to proximate causes of vulnerabilities, and pointed to techno-managerial causes of vulnerabilities. It was sometimes difficult to neatly categorise some quotations into one or another category, e.g. when speakers where referring to lack of government budget or the poor provision of services. We classified as 'political-economy' when they were linked to structural factors (e.g. misuse of public funds, exclusion from and unequal access to public services) and as 'risk-hazard' when they were linked to proximate causes. For the interpretive analysis, we followed a grounded theory approach, based on notes and comments from in-depth and repeated reading of the material.

For the interpretive approach, we examined the overall dynamics that took place during three of the events in terms of both critical and relational aspects. We simultaneously examined the extent to which discourses shifted or not to a critical framing and the type of relations among the participants. For the latter, we looked not only at the extent to which a dialogue and deliberation took place but also at the visible and discursive power dynamics among participants, for instance, related to voice, inclusion, and exclusion. We adopted a reflexive approach on the deliberation process by examining the exclusionary mechanisms that obfuscate some views and voices (Pepermans and Maeseele, 2014). In particular, we looked at the discourse features that increased or reduced the legitimacy of certain forms of knowledge during the debates and the authority of specific actors. These included the degree and kind of agency given to different stakeholders in the statements, the type of argumentation used and the lexico-grammar (Scollon, 2010).

Findings

Analysing discourses

We first analysed the distribution of the two types of discourses (risk hazard and political-economy) according to the position and sex of the participants in the four events that took place in Janakpur and Kathmandu (Table 10.2). For this, we counted the number of quotations coded under each type of discourses. Each statement was counted as a different quotation. We also looked at the repartition of non-farmer participants according to the scale of influence related to their position (district or national).

These findings are to be interpreted with caution due to the difference in the number of quotations for each category. For instance, there were no representatives of civil society organisations and politicians in one event in Janakpur, hence the relative lower number of quotations coded. Also, some of the quotations from the second debate held in Janakpur were not attributed to any position in particular when these were part of the presentations of the working groups. There are however a few gross patterns that are useful to note.

First, the analysis evidences the dominance of civil servants and men in terms of spoken time over farmers and women respectively. Representatives of civil society organisations and farmers relied on both types of discourses with a slight dominance of the political-economy perspective. As expected, the discourse of civil servants draws more heavily on the risk hazard than on the political-economy perspective. On the other hand, politicians mostly relied on arguments that could be linked to a political-economy perspective. Last, national level participants mostly relied on a risk-hazard perspective whereas district level participants (some of whom also attended national level events) were much more balanced between the risk-hazard and political-economy perspective. This is in line with our expectations that national level actors' knowledge and beliefs are more heavily influenced by national policy discourses and rely less on direct experiences of the ground reality than district level actors. These findings also indicate the need to move beyond monolithic representations of 'the state' and differentiate between civil servants and politicians, and between national and lower administrative level actors.

We also examined the occurrence of the two discourses across the different debates (Table 10.3).

Table 10.3 indicates that the dialogues were quite balanced between the two types of discourses. The group-based discussion organised in Janakpur was however the most successful in bringing discursive change towards a greater consideration of the structural causes of vulnerability. We now turn to a more interpretive approach to analyse the discursive dynamics that took place during three of the dialogues that we convened.

Table 10.2 Number of quotations for the two types of discourses among participants

	Representative civil society organisation	Farmer	Civil servant	Politician	National	District	Female	Male
Risk hazard	7	16	60	5	46	26	16	76
Political-economy	12	20	20	25	28	29	12	67
Total	19	36	80	30	74	55	28	143

Source: Transcripts from the four events held in Janakpur and Kathmandu in November and December 2014.

Table 10.3 Percentage of quotations for the two types of discourses across the different debates organised

	District group discussion	National roundtable	District radio roundtable	National radio roundtable	Total
Risk hazard	30	54	51	50	49
Political-economy	70	44	49	50	50

Source: Transcripts from the four dialogues held in Janakpur and Kathmandu in November and December 2014.

Deliberations from a critical and relational perspective

District radio roundtable. The first debate that was organised in Dhanusa District gathered a small group of senior government officials and farmers-filmers. Such encounters are relatively rare in rural Nepal, and in the climate change adaptation/development sector in particular, where meetings are usually held separately with farmers and with district-level government officials. They listened to and responded to each other in a reasoned and respectful manner. If the relational component led to deliberation, it however did not lead to discursive change because the critical perspective was missing in the facilitation. The facilitator, who was a journalist, inadvertently created a discursive closure by asking farmers to raise their problems and the government officials to respond on how they have addressed these problems. By doing so, he did not acknowledge the existence of multiple framings nor asked farmers and government officials to jointly reflect on what could be the causes of the problems faced by farmers. As a result, the causes of farmers' problems were not discussed. Farmers largely relied on the risk-hazard perspective to frame the causes of their vulnerability, which they identified as the lack of borewells for irrigation, lack of agricultural extension services, etc. and framed solutions in a wish list: 'we want dams', 'we want bore wells', 'we want good roads', etc, focusing on the provision of facilities and technologies without acknowledging the broader political-economic issues that affect who might be able to access and benefit from these. The government officials reacted with a defensive stance, stressing that all these services were available but that farmers needed to 'be aware' and approach the district level agencies with their requests. The discussion therefore did not really see emerging a reflection on the underlying causes of vulnerabilities and on structural inequalities, with the possibility to develop an acceptable framing. The participants remained largely entrenched in antagonistic positions and did not find a common discursive space where joint solutions could be discussed. Farmers came out of the roundtable relatively disillusioned in regard to the prospects for change. They also felt they could have better prepared their arguments before the debate, which was a lesson for the project team. It revealed the importance for researchers to engage a critical reflection with farmers on argumentation and deliberation prior to opening up the discussion to other parties – thereby re-working on both the critical and relational components of our approach.

Despite this limited discursive shift, the art-based approach we had adopted however led to slightly redefine gender and power relationships among participants, by defining new identities to the women farmers-filmers, as acknowledged by the journalist facilitating the debate:

> We saw the documentary. Definitely, Nepalese women were categorised as marginalised in the past. They were defined as second-class citizen. But in my view, after watching this video, not only Nepalese women, but also Madhesi women who used to believe in pati-parmeshwar,[2] are now walking towards progress, prestige and competition. They are talking about Internet; they are handling a movie camera by themselves, taking interviews. I am also impressed as you stand with a camera here in this room. Women are not anymore confined inside ghumto (veil) and inside four walls.
>
> (Male journalist, Janakpur, November 2014)

Women farmers also recognised during the roundtable that holding a camera made them feel 'empowered' in the sense that it enhanced their self-confidence and agency: '*Earlier, we hadn't handled movie cameras. We used to watch videos of marriage ceremonies. We used to watch only with our eyes, now I can use my hand. Now I can handle a camera for any function*' (female farmer-filmer, November 2014, Janakpur). Although this woman does not associate the use of the camera with transformative change, the quote testifies of her enhanced sense of agency. The female farmers-filmers who participated to the debates reported having more confidence in engaging in deliberation with government officials thanks to their experience of filming. In Kathmandu, the two groups of farmers-filmers spontaneously brought their camera for the event and some of them were standing and filming the discussions and the participants on their own initiative, thereby reversing traditional participation roles: the central government officials were those sitting and participating and the farmers were standing above them to record and document their responses.

District group-based deliberation. In the next event organised at the district level, which gathered more participants, it was decided to use a different format whereby farmers and government officials would sit in small groups to reflect on specific topics, guided by questions provided by the research team. The three topics were: roads, agriculture and irrigation, and education. The research team therefore had a greater control over the relational and critical components of the deliberation process, by defining who would sit with whom, providing questions that clearly asked the discussants to relate to the film and to reflect on the structural causes of vulnerability and giving an explicit problem-solving orientation to the discussions.

The group dynamics worked relatively well in the sense that we observed engaged and inclusive discussions from all the participants sitting at one table. The discussions were probably the most deliberative with a reasoned and joint reflection on the causes of the issues met by farmers that led to the joint development of action points that seemed acceptable to the discussants. However, despite the deliberative forms of engagement that took place, there were some entrenched power mechanisms that could not be addressed. Only the low-rank and middle-rank government officials accepted to sit with the farmers for the group discussions. The senior level officials who were present at the beginning of the event found an excuse to leave the meeting just when the group discussions started, eventually coming back once these were over. This is in line with hierarchical norms in Nepal that require maintaining distanced relationships between individuals holding different positions in the social structure along lines of gender, caste and ethnicity. Therefore, those who had the most authority and influence to take policy actions refused to engage in a deliberative process with farmers.

As indicated earlier in Table 10.3, there was a clear discursive shift towards the political-economy perspective. Except for the topic of agriculture, the action points proposed by the two other groups addressed several of the structural factors raised in the films. For instance, the group that reflected on how the lack of proper roads created vulnerabilities proposed to form a committee comprising of representatives from the civil society and local civil servants to jointly discuss road development activities. They also defined clear responsibilities for both government agencies and farmers, e.g. whereby farmers should report irregularities to concerned agencies, who would then conduct proper and fair investigation. Beyond the relational component (group dynamics), another supporting factor for the discursive change was the ability for critical reflection that these farmers had developed when discussing the structural causes of vulnerability among small groups in their village, during the earlier debates organised by NEMAF.

National roundtable. At the national roundtable organised and facilitated by SIAS, the setting gathered a larger number of participants and national-level senior government officials, which led to different relational features and power dynamics. In this case, the identity of farmers as filmers was not sufficient to give farmers the authority to actively engage in the discussions. Farmers' speaking time represented around 1.5 per cent of the discussion content (as per the number of words). This happened despite several of the research team's requests to the facilitator to involve farmers in the discussion – and the facilitator genuinely tried to do so.

There was no real deliberation, in the sense that each participant offered his or her personal view without responding to the previous speaker. For instance, at the end of the event, one farmer asked two very specific questions to the Department of Irrigation representative:

> The director general of the Department of Irrigation said that they have allocated around 20 Crores[3] for the Kamala Irrigation Project. [...] May we know for which district is the budget allocated? If it is for Dhanusa district, our VDC Thadhi Jhijha will surely get water. Furthermore, we have heard

about the intention to construct a dam on the Koshi River [...]. What is the progress of this project?

(Male farmer, Kathmandu December 2014)

These questions were important for the farmers, as the two projects mentioned in the quote above could have a direct and substantial impact on their livelihoods. The questions also touched upon the lack of information farmers have on national level planning. A female irrigation engineer, from the Social, Environmental and Climate Change Section of the Department responded, as the director general had already left the meeting. She did not acknowledge in some way she had heard the question and made a very lengthy statement that was not addressing the question in any way. She grounded her arguments in scientific knowledge, thereby challenging the validity of farmers' claims and the legitimacy of their knowledge:

We should not rely on subjective judgments. We need solid objective evidence to design something [...] I found that the temperature trend is increasing at the rate of 1.85°C till 2050 which will cause around 7% increase in water requirement and erratic rainfall patterns.

(Female government officer, Kathmandu, December 2014)

The facilitator, a researcher from SIAS, however overall brought up very well the critical component through its facilitation and a very open discussion took place, whereby several politicians and civil society representatives radically framed their response around issues of social inequalities and justice:

The central government urges local bodies not to invest money for teachers. Few well-off families send their children to private boarding schools, but for the poor farmers, the central government does not want to invest a minimum proportion of local budget on education.

(Male politician, December 2014)

Several discussants made explicit references to the content of the film and reflected on the use of the film as a means to communicate between farmers and policymakers. It was the case notably of a senior government official that the research team had regularly met before at several occasions. He had in the past held rather conservative discourses where he identified farmers' laziness and lack of entrepreneurial skills as the causes for the lack of irrigation development and low agricultural productivity. He was the first to speak after the film was screened, as he was the most senior person in the audience. Although his overall response was very much in line with the techno-managerial arguments, he had a very unusual reference to unequal access to government services at the end of his speech, which was one of the key arguments of farmers highlighted in the film '*in the current situation, only people with power and influence are getting support and the poor are not benefitting at all*' (male senior government official, Kathmandu, December 2014).

Reflecting on roles, hegemony and impact

The research team played multiple roles during the action research process – from a reflective scientist role to a process facilitator, knowledge broker, and at times, change agent role (Wittmayer and Schäpke, 2014). As reflective scientists, we analysed situations, farmers' knowledge and narratives and provided conceptual frames to guide the discussion. As process facilitator, we jointly designed with the media, civil society, and research partners, learning and communication processes related to the debates. As knowledge brokers and to some extent change agent, we created the space for farmers to voice their views through participatory video and partnered with media organisations to bring these voices to experts, policymakers, and the general public.

There were however tensions between these roles and between a critical and a relational approach. As remarked by Shaw (2012), there is, in participatory video, an inherent tension for action researchers between giving voice to marginalised people (change agent) and having control over the audiovisual product to increase its impact (knowledge broker). In our case, our position was first to have the least influence on the filming process. We let farmers choose the topics of the films, with the risk to receive critics from our funder, as many of the topics went far beyond agriculture and climate change. Farmers were also free to decide who and how to interview other villagers and we made very minimal edits to the video footages, mostly solely clipping them together. However, when researchers and journalists showed the farmers' films to experts and policymakers, many of them responded in a defensive way that closed possible opportunities to engage in a dialogue. They often commented that it was not 'representative' and 'scientific'. Solely empowering farmers (to the extent that the participatory video project did) did not serve our purpose of shifting discourses and supporting transformative change.

Reflecting on this, we acted as a knowledge broker by compiling the 12 films produced by farmers into one documentary that also incorporated some of the experts' interviews, an interview of the lead researcher and author of this chapter, and a narrative underlining the multiplicity of framings and experiences of vulnerability. Our objective was to include 'expert's knowledge' to increase the legitimacy of farmers' knowledge and frame it according to a powerful narrative. The documentary was better received, in the sense that it did not trigger defensive postures among the audience and was well acknowledged by many participants, including senior engineers from government agencies:

> The way farmers raised themselves the problems of their village by making films is the best medium to share problems to the centre, otherwise it is always a difficult task to tell people in the centre about the problems of rural communities. I feel the ways problems are raised in farmers' own way and language is very effective.
>
> (Male senior government official, Kathmandu, December 2014)

The learning was that incorporating voices from different stakeholders increased the legitimacy of the voices of the most powerless and reduced defensiveness among policymakers.

There was also a tension between the researcher's normative critical orientation to highlight the structural causes of vulnerabilities through discursive means and farmers-filmers' aspirations for the infrastructures and technologies that would support a 'modern' agriculture. Although farmers stressed the structural inequalities and political-economic drivers in their narrative, the farmers-filmers also legitimately had expectations of rapid changes in their livelihoods as a result of their films and the dialogues that followed. To address this tension, we regularly engaged with farmers to confront our own normative expectations related to social justice and transformative change with their expectations. Fortunately, the local government took a couple of concrete development actions after they saw the farmers' films during the first phase of the project – so at least part of farmers' expectations were met before they engaged in the debates.

Conclusion

By using participatory video to support deliberation, we aimed at creating new knowledge and narratives to challenge hegemonic national policy discourses on vulnerabilities in Nepal. We followed a process-oriented approach to science (Wittmayer and Schäpke, 2014) by temporarily creating parallel discursive spaces to the mainstream policy sphere (Fraser, 1990), where marginalised farmers could engage in deliberation with the help of facilitators either among themselves or with external stakeholders. The originality of the approach was to use farmers' knowledge and narratives, conveyed by a film, as a starting point for the discussion. The research findings highlight the need to combine a relational and critical approach in a context characterised by apolitical discourses on climate change adaptation, by a high level of distrust between farmers and government officials and by rigid social hierarchies.

Participatory approaches have been criticised for their neglect of entrenched structural and social inequalities and for reproducing existing power structures (Cooke and Kothari, 2001; Hickey and Mohan, 2005). In this project, our approach to criticality was precisely to bring the participants to reflect on the social inequalities and hegemonic political and economic structures that create farmers' vulnerabilities, using audiovisual media. We found that the art-based approach supported critical reflections but was not sufficient to lead to discursive shifts towards more critical perspectives. Similarly, the relational approach did not necessarily bring in changes in discourses. Even when the interaction among stakeholders was close to deliberation, where government officials and farmers listened to and responded to each other with reasoned arguments, the debate led to few critical reflections and no joint re-framing of the causes of farmers' vulnerabilities. Stakeholders' engagement into the debate remained largely framed within the dominant risk-hazard perspective. Our findings indicate that the role of the facilitator is crucial to bring in criticality into the debates by framing the terms of the discussion. Another lesson we learnt while engaging in the process was the importance to build the capacity of farmers to critically reflect on their claims and on the root causes of their vulnerability before they engage in deliberations with other stakeholders.

We however also found that criticality was not sufficient to lead transformative changes. In some instances, the debate triggered very critical reflections but there was no real deliberation, in the sense that there was a lack of respect and acknowledgment of farmers' perspectives during the debate. This indicates the need to combine a critical perspective with a relational approach that is attentive to group and power dynamics. Again, the role of the facilitator is key in shaping group dynamics and controlling the distribution of speaking time among different participants, especially in settings characterised by high differentials among participants in terms of power and position in the social structure. Even in the case of one event that led to a critical deliberation, with a list of concrete action points for transformative change jointly proposed by farmers and government officials, the prospect for change remained low, as the senior officials who had the most influence to implement these changes refused to engage with farmers as part of the working group discussions.

As Kuitenbrouwer (Chapter 9) remarks, this leads us to conclude that participatory action research requires for the researcher to take on distinct roles – not only facilitating but also at times intervening by re-framing the discussion and by setting the rules of the games for the debates. It brings us to reflect on the potential tensions between participation and criticality and on the importance of reflexivity. On the one hand, as researchers we wanted to play a minimal role in stirring the debates and leave space for local farmers to raise their voice. On the other hand, we did not want criticality to get lost – yet was this really important for farmers?

Reflecting on the methodology we used, we found that participatory video helped challenging existing power relationships within hegemonic structures in unexpected ways. The new identities that farmers gained by becoming filmers reversed actors' positions among the facilitator, farmers-filmers, and government officials – e.g. as active or passive participants, as object of observation or observers. While filming the dialogues in which they were also participating, farmers could adopt a different body posture that allowed them to look down on other participants, including those in higher positions of power. Although this is not necessarily effective in deliberative arenas with high power asymmetries, for instance in the events when farmers participated in debates with central level senior government officials, it can be a starting point to challenge entrenched authorities.

Funding

This research was funded by the Climate Change, Agriculture, and Food Security (CCAFS) and the Water, Land, and Ecosystems (WLE) CGIAR programmes.

Acknowledgements

My sincere thanks go to the book editors for their supportive encouragements and critical feedback along the writing process and to two anonymous reviewers for their extremely useful comments on earlier drafts of this chapter. Deep gratitude goes to those who have contributed their creative ideas, energy and heart to this participatory action research, and in particular, Prajjwal Kumar Dahal, Hari Dhungana, Damakant Jayshi, Beena Kharel, Pawan Kumar, Preeya Nair, Ashok Rai, Tula Narayan Sah, and Lalita Sah.

Notes

1 The MoSTE is now the Ministry of Population and Environment (MoPE).
2 This refers to Nepali women's faith for the long life span of their husband, which is expressed in different rituals and practices, such as fasting.
3 A 'crore' denotes ten million in the Indian/Nepali numbering system. Twenty Crore Nepali Rupees is equivalent to US$1.9 million as per the exchange rate of 3 September 2017.

References

Adger WN (2006) Vulnerability. *Global Environmental Change* 16(3): 268–281.
Bassett TJ and Fogelman C (2013) Déjà vu or something new? The adaptation concept in the climate change literature. *Geoforum* 48: 42–53.
Blue G (2016) Framing climate change for public deliberation: what role for interpretive social sciences and humanities? *Journal of Environmental Policy and Planning* 18(1): 67–84.
Bohle HG, Downing TE and Watts MJ (1994) Climate change and social vulnerability: towards a sociology and geography of food insecurity. *Global Environmental Change* 4(1): 37–48.
Castells M (2009) *Communication power*, Oxford: Oxford University Press.
Cooke B and Kothari U (2001) *Participation: the new tyranny?* London and New York: Zed Books.
Dutta MJ (2011) *Communicating social change: structure, culture and agency*, Hoboken, NJ: Taylor and Francis.
Forsyth T (2003) *Critical political ecology. The politics of environmental science*, New York: Routledge.
Forsyth T (2011) Expertise needs transparency not blind trust: a deliberative approach to integrating science and social participation. *Critical Policy Studies* 5(3): 317–322.
Foucault M (1975) *Surveiller et Punir. Naissance de la prison*, Paris: Gallimard.
Fraser N (1990) Rethinking the public sphere: a contribution to the critique of actually existing democracy. *Social Text* 25/26: 56–80.
Freire P (1970) *Pedagogy of the oppressed*, New York, NY: Herder and Herder.
Fussel H-M (2007) Vulnerability: a generally applicable conceptual framework for climate change research. *Global Environmental Change* 17(2): 155–167.
Gastil J (2008) *Political communication and deliberation*, Thousand Oaks, CA: Sage.
Gaventa J and McGee R (2013) The impact of transparency and accountability initiatives. *Development Policy Review* 31(s1) 3–28.

GoN (Government of Nepal) – Ministry of Environment (2010) National Adaptation Programme of Action (NAPA) to Climate Change. Kathmandu: Government of Nepal, Ministry of Environment (MoE).

GoN (Government of Nepal) – Ministry of Environment (2011) Climate Change Policy. Kathmandu: Government of Nepal, Ministry of Environment (MoE)

Habermas J (1987) *Theory of communicative action volume two: liveworld and system: a critique of functionalist reason*, Boston Mass: Beacon Press.

Hajer MJ (1995) *The politics of environmental discourse: Ecological modernization and the policy process*, Oxford: Oxford University Press.

Harris US (2009) Transforming images: reimagining women's work through participatory video. *Development in Practice* 19(4–5): 538–549.

Hickey S and Mohan G (2005) Relocating participation within a radical politics of development. *Development and Change* 36(2): 237–262.

Jasanoff S (2010) A new climate for society. *Theory, Culture and Society* 27(2–3): 233–253.

Keeley J and Scoones I (2003) *Understanding environmental policy processes: cases from Africa*, London: Earthscan Publications Ltd.

Kemmis S, McTaggart R and Nixon R (2014) *The action research planner: doing critical participatory action research*, Singapore: Springer.

Kindon S, Pain R and Kesby M (2007) *Participatory action research approaches and methods. Connecting people, participation and place*, New York: Routledge.

Levine P, Fung A and Gastil J (2005) Future directions for public deliberation. *Journal of Public Deliberation* 1(1): Article 3.

McLaughlin P and Dietz T (2008) Structure, agency and environment: towards an integrated perspective on vulnerability. *Global Environmental Change* 18(1): 99–111.

Milne E-J, Mitchell C and de Lange N (2012) *Handbook of participatory video*, Plymouth, UK: AltaMira Press.

Mitchell C, Milne E-J and de Lange N (2012) Introduction. In: Milne E-J, Mitchell C and de Lange N (eds.) *Handbook of participatory video*, Plymouth, UK: AltaMira Press, 1–15.

O'Brien K, Eriksen S, Nygaard LP and Schjolden ANE (2007) Why different interpretations of vulnerability matter in climate change discourses. *Climate Policy* 7(1): 73–88.

Pepermans Y and Maeseele P (2014) Democratic debate and mediated discourses on climate change: from consensus to de/politicization. *Environmental Communication* 8(2): 216–232.

Plush T (2015) Interrogating practitioner tensions for raising citizen voice with participatory video in international development. *Nordicom Review* 26(Special issue): 37–70.

Ribot JC (2010) Vulnerability does not just fall from the sky: toward multi-scale pro-poor climate policy. In: Mearns R and Norton A (eds.) *Social dimensions of climate change: equity and vulnerability in a warming world*, Washington DC: The World Bank, 47–75.

Rowlands J (1995) Empowerment examined. *Development in Practice* 5(2): 101–107.

Scollon R (2010) *Analyzing public discourse. Discourse analysis in the making of public policy*, New York: Routledge.

Shaw J (2012) Interrogating the gap between the ideals and practice reality of participatory video. In: Milne E-J, Mitchell C and de Lange N (eds.) *Handbook of participatory video*, Plymouth, UK: AltaMira Press, 225–241.

Smucker TA, Wisner B, Mascarenhas A, Munishi P, Wangui EE, Sinha G, Weiner D, Bwenge C and Lovell E (2015) Differentiated livelihoods, local institutions, and the adaptation imperative: assessing climate change adaptation policy in Tanzania. *Geoforum* 59: 39–50.

Sugden F, Maskey N, Clement F, Ramesh V, Philip A and Rai A (2014) Agrarian stress and climate change in the Eastern Gangetic Plains: Gendered vulnerability in a stratified social formation. *Global Environmental Change* 29: 258–269.

Swyngedouw, E (2010) Apocalypse forever? Post-political populism and the spectre of climate change. *Theory, Culture and Society* 27(2–3): 213–232.

Wheeler J (2012) Using participatory video to engage in policy process. Representation, power and knowledge in public screenings. In: Milne E-J, Mitchell C and de Lange N (eds.) *Handbook of participatory video*, Plymouth, UK: AltaMira Press, 365–379.

Wittmayer JM and Schäpke N (2014) Action, research and participation: roles of researchers in sustainability transitions. *Sustainability Science* 9: 483–496.

Yates JS (2012) Uneven interventions and the scalar politics of governing livelihood adaptation in rural Nepal. *Global Environmental Change* 22(2): 537–546.

Young IM (2000) *Inclusion and democracy*, Oxford New York: Oxford University Press.

Co-inquirer reflection

Damakant Jayshi

Kathmandu, the capital of mountainous Nepal, suffers from very severe air pollution.[1] One might add water and sound pollution in the mix as well, since those who live in Kathmandu have to grapple with these problems every single day. Politics, economy, and development discourse in Nepal mainly happen in the capital. It is, therefore, not surprising that any discussion about politics, economy, and climate change and its effect on people is dominated by what happens in the Kathmandu valley. The discussions are also mostly urban-centric.

So, when International Water Management Institute (IWMI)'s Nepal office approached Panos South Asia (PSA), a non-profit devoted to facilitating dialogue on various subjects, including environment and climate change, to partner on a project focused on vulnerabilities of farmers in Nepal's southern plains or Tarai due to political, economic and climate-related changes, I accepted the opportunity immediately. Our involvement was to coordinate two candid discussions between farmers from Tarai and government officials – one in Janakpur in Tarai and the other in Kathmandu. Our responsibility also included broadcasting of the discussions over radio and televisions.

Compared to projects that PSA usually engages in, the IWMI-initiated farmers-policymakers' roundtable project was small in scale and engagement for Panos. But I was more than keen to make PSA part of this IWMI initiative. Here's why.

This was an opportunity for us to promote discourse and debate where, for once, the people at the grassroots level were at the centre stage. Besides, they were getting an opportunity to question government officials in full public glare about the impact of their decisions on their life and livelihoods.

While working on projects, we encountered all kinds of unexpected events, given Nepal's fluid political situation. In this context, a critical element in our relationship with IWMI was the co-operation of Dr Floriane Clement, the IWMI researcher leading the project. Her professionalism, understanding, and empathy made our work a lot easier. Sometimes we face interference in our work, which leads to misunderstanding. Dr Clement refrained from micro-managing. Through the many discussions we had before, during, and after the project engagement, it was clear to me that she meant to make the project as meaningful and impactful as possible. I was determined to do our bit to make that happen.

The roundtable was going to be challenging for a variety of reasons. Language barriers was one. Most farmers spoke only Maithili (Lingua franca of Dhanusha). However, the biggest of them all was to ensure the participation of government officials. As Dr Clement notes in her contribution, there is a lot of rhetoric around participation of vulnerable people in climate adaptation programmes, but their "voices ... have had a limited inclusion in national or international policy arenas." This is very much true for Nepal.

During my journalism days, I faced reluctance by many government officials to speak on the record. Moreover, they are not used to being challenged on government policies or how they work. Like many bureaucrats around the world, they defend or justify any state action or inaction, either by training or out of habit. Besides, the very idea that it was to be a candid and on-the-record deliberation and to be broadcast on TV and radio stations was received with much surprise.

But Panos South Asia and the Janakpur-based dialogue facilitators it engaged were able to convince them that it was a worthwhile dialogue. In some cases, we had to tell them that this was the opportunity to get their side of the story out since the discourse was going to be broadcast locally and nationally. Their absence from the deliberations or silence might be construed as tacit acknowledgement of charges of red tape and inaction levelled by farmers in the videos. I also believe that the very idea of being challenged by farmers intrigued them and thus they agreed to participate and we got a healthy number of government officials for the two roundtables.

The roundtables were a revelation. One novelty used during the program was the sharing of a short film made from 12 videos shot by farmers – male and female – after they were trained by IWMI-engaged trainers. Those videos were yet another reminder of the chasm between policymakers' promise and reality. Here we were witnessing a first-hand account of the hardships faced by the farmers. It was straight from the heart, not some filtered narration, and it hit home.

Besides the two roundtables, we also organised an interaction involving Ganesh Sah, a former minister, Kunda Dixit, an editor who has written extensively about the impact of climate change, and government officials. Mr Sah suggested that farmers do not trust government officials, which discourages them from participating in any policy or programme implemented by the government. Mr. Dixit said the agriculture sector was not adequately covered by the media in Nepal.

There were other noteworthy moments. In one instance, a farmer shared a very positive outcome after the video stories were shared with high-level government bureaucrats (but before the Janakpur roundtable). Some farmers interviewed in one of the videos rued the lack of a very-much needed culvert in their locality. The culvert was built soon after the sharing of the video. It was a clear demonstration of the impact of the power of storytelling.

For me and Panos South Asia, that was one of the biggest takeaways from this project. It was the vindication of our approach to initiating debate and creating impact. It was also a reminder to keep doing what we have done throughout: finding ways to disseminate the voice of the vulnerable.

Note

1 http://nepalitimes.com/article/nation/Sick-city,108.

11 Really imagined

Policy novels as a mode of action research

Sonja van der Arend

One day, in the office

'Okay, it's time to get your fingers out of your hair now and onto the keyboard. Start writing that thing, woman!' Her voice echoes in the empty office. Never mind. There's no one but her to hear. And she doesn't even listen to herself. For three hours she's been sitting at her desk, typing and deleting, and the only result is a blank Word document saved under the name Chapter Action Research. Oh, and a folder with that name, too, with the blank document in it. She grins at the empty computer screen, sarcastically. How time flies when you're having fun.... Stop, she thinks, no more mucking about now. With her back straight in the chair, she opens the mail with the abstract she submitted months ago, copies the entire text into the blank document, makes some minor changes on the go and then rereads it.

Abstract

While citizens and stakeholders are increasingly expected to actively participate in policymaking, it is unclear where they should acquire the knowledge to do so effectively. Useful, practical accounts on the work of policymaking are absent in public discourse and popular culture. Several decades of research on public participation and democratic governance have hardly reached an audience beyond fellow students and policy professionals. The research methods of policy science prevent it to address its own role in maintaining top-down, expert-based, one-way relations in the policy domain (Bevir, 2010). This chapter introduces policy fiction, specifically the policy novel, as an alternative mode of research that may foster civic knowledge and open up policy research to the wider public. It describes this new genre as a co-creative method in policy research, through a reflection on the making of three such works of fiction on policy (Van der Arend, 2013, 2016a, 2016b; also see Van der Arend and Behagel, 2012). I will elaborate on roles and relations in the making of policy novels, and their criticality. The goal of the chapter is to deepen our understanding of how the use of fiction may generate relational, diverse and empowering knowledge practices in policy.

The same pretentious jabber as ever, she mutters to herself, and then shrugs her shoulders. Not too bad, actually, for an abstract. She puts her fingers on the keyboard, eagerly awaiting the sentences that will begin to flow.... Still, nothing comes. Why on earth did she promise to participate in the Action Research book? She is struck by the complete absurdity of writing about policy fiction *in an academic volume*. In the scholarly prose she has come to hate. Scientific writing is tedious and produces ugly texts, which no one you would want to read will ever see. Plus, it doesn't pay. She sighs, leans back in her chair, and recaps the motives she enunciated last week in an effort to convince her accountant (Why him? I hire the man): it's good to claim policy fiction as a creative research method; it's a good chance to elaborate the philosophy behind it; it's a good way to reflect on what I am doing, to link it to related approaches, to make it better. Good, good, good, better, she mutters. Gosh, I must have sounded like I was stuck in an echo well. While he had raised his eyebrows, she had continued her rant. It may, someday, somehow, lead to a new project or assignment. You never know, she had concluded hopefully. "Sure", the digit guy had replied in his dullest tone of voice.

She leans forward and puts her fingers back on the keyboard. Her last real job was a four-year post-doc position. The good thing was that it had made her realise that her academic career was coming to an end, finally. One cause for the breakup was that over the years, doing policy science felt less and less meaningful. Early on in her education as an environmental engineer, she had chosen to switch to social sciences, because she did not believe that environmental problems could or would be solved with simple technical fixes. She was happy to find other students who believed that social and political aspects were the key to understanding the ecological crisis. Her goal had always been to make a contribution, however small, to enhancing environmental governance through critical reflection. But she never saw much proof that policy science actually worked that way – certainly not in her own work. Early in her study, the manifold relations between government and society became her main topic. She researched policymaking practices in the fields of agriculture, water management, spatial planning, sustainability, etc. Everywhere, the participation of citizens and stakeholders was celebrated as the solution to the many ills in environmental policy. Participatory policy would raise its quality, acceptance, legitimacy, and efficacy. Most scholars hardly questioned these expectations, concentrated as they were on advising policy professionals and managers to effectively organise and manage citizen participation. The principles and outcomes of participatory governance were hardly ever debated or challenged. And the intricate role of power in the interactions between government and society was generally neglected. She was surprised to find that – despite all the talk of a shift from government to governance and of the importance of citizen participation and deliberative democracy – policy science was still almost exclusively done with, about and for policy professionals. In the process of her PhD research, she experienced that scientific institutions and academic culture themselves worked in many little ways to maintain this state-centred or managerial view on policymaking. The paradox in this seemed to elude most policy scientists, while participating and non-participating citizens understood all too well that 'they say they listen, but they will do as they want anyway'. Thus, the possible value of citizen participation got crushed between all too naïve hope and all too cynical realism – deepening rather than relieving the legitimation crisis in environmental governance. Sometimes, this made her more than professionally angry. She worried that, more generally, the role of social scientists as critical observers of vested powers was waning. In this institutional setting, it seemed impossible to spark a critical, informed debate on participatory governance that would actually include and benefit citizens and other potential participants.

The second cause for her breakup with university was that she wasn't achieving all the demands of the trade, also because these demands mainly seemed to reinforce academic institutions rather than served to promote interesting and meaningful research. Especially writing scientific articles, and getting them published, was a skill she never fully mastered or enjoyed. And then her four-year post-doc assignment was coming to an end, in the midst of the economic recession following the financial crisis of 2008. She had never had problems finding a job, but in the overloaded labour market no university would hire a scholar without an impressive track record in international journals. What to do, what to be? Although she had worked as a chef and some other trades, she had never seriously considered becoming anything but a researcher.

But in the last months of her postdoc assignment, something new came her way. The research project she took part in studied the governance approach in the EU Water Framework Directive (WFD, in short). Her last study in this research project was an inquiry on how the implementation of the WFD affected the position of aquatic ecologists in Dutch water management. To avoid producing a hermetic piece of social science prose hidden behind a paywall, she and a colleague in the project decided to use an interactive, narrative approach. They would organise two workshops, where the ecologists would share their experiences with the WFD. Their stories would be combined into a factual but easy-to-read account with both scientific and practical value – to be written by an experienced novelist or journalist. She and her colleague failed, however, to find funding for a professional writer. So, at some point, she proposed that she herself would write the story. She would also organise and guide the workshops. Somewhere in the process, the original idea to write the report in the form of 'faction' – a non-fiction text with literary features – evolved into the plan to concoct a fictional story, together with the workshop participants, which she would convert into a full-fledged novel. This is how she almost accidentally made her debut as a writer of policy fiction, with a short novel on the EU WFD. Could this be the first of a new genre?

Sitting in the silent office, she smiles in memory of her bold, unsubstantiated confidence at the start of the project. It was not that easy. After the workshops, it took her almost one and a half year to finish the novel. She couldn't have done it without the help of a very patient writing coach. But it restored the love for writing she had doing her dissertation. No, it excelled it. At last, she was allowed, required to use her imagination; plus poetry, humour, empathy, ambivalence, suggestion, imagery.... The novel was published, with a beautiful cover, and even got a second print. Many people said they liked the story, professional readers said they found the portrayal of water management in it deeply familiar.

Looking back, she realised that the novel wasn't just research outcomes wrapped in a story. The process of inventing, crafting and writing the story itself had generated new insights with her, the workshop participants, and hopefully the readers. Could it be that policy fiction was actually a mode of research? And if so, could policy fiction become a continuation of her career by other means?

Somehow, time went by. At the end of 2015, she got an assignment for a second policy novel from someone who had read the first. Again, the topic was water policy, but now the question came from a group of citizens who had participated in a flood prevention project. The novel was published mid-2016. And then, in the same year, she wrote a third, on zero energy renovation of office buildings. The process of organising workshops, inventing a plot and writing a story became more predictable, but never easy or straightforward. She always had to delve deep to get it done; to put herself on the line to make the story genuine and meaningful. But more importantly, every time, inventing the story and writing the chapters gave immense joy: the participants gaining new perspectives, their candid stories in which they gave a vivid insight in their worlds, the characters coming alive, the pieces falling in place, and the feeling of flow when the story seemed to write itself. How nice would it be to share that joy, she thinks. A second later she slaps herself on the forehead. *That*, of course, is the main reason to contribute to the Action Research book. But then she frowns. I can't write that in a scientific paper, she thinks. I will have to define some serious goal or research question, otherwise the reviewers will fry me. Oh well, I'll just write something like: *In this chapter, I want to convey that fiction has a contribution to make to the public understanding of policy, and possibly to academic knowledge as well.* She types it, reads it out loud, and laughs. Really convincing. So, come on now, she thinks, make yourself a coffee and write that chapter. It may even be something worthwhile to do, after all. Surely, it's not a novel, but it may have a happy end.

Fiction in research

The aim of this chapter is to convey that fiction has a contribution to make to the public understanding of policy. The story above is a short illustration of how policy fiction works as an action research method: inventing and writing a story with those involved as a means to reflect on and make sense of the situation they find themselves in. I have applied this method in three policy novels, the creation of which will serve as three case-studies of relational and critical action research, to find principles that make fiction a meaningful method in policy analysis. But first, this section very briefly points at some of the theoretical backgrounds to applying fiction in social scientific research, namely: fiction-based research, writing as inquiry, and narrative research. I focus on two issues: how does fiction generate knowledge, and how to deal with the tensions between fiction and research?

With her volume "Fiction as research practice" (2013), Patricia Leavy champions fiction-based research, a term she coins as a subsection of arts-based research (Leavy, 2009, 2013; Barone and Eisner, 2012). Fiction-based research embraces two types of research, in which either "the act of writing is the act of inquiry" or "data are collected in traditional ways and then written up using the techniques of fiction" (Leavy, 2013: 12). The first type applies the principle of writing as "A method of inquiry", as elaborated by the ethnographers Richardson and St. Pierre (2005). They see writing not as the representing of knowledge that is collected and analysed before fingers touch a keyboard, but as a dynamic "creative analytical process", in the act of which data are found and analysed and a situated interpretation of social life is created. The second type of fiction-based research, which basically uses literary devices to write up 'traditional' data, relates to a wealth of pleas for more creative and narrative writing in the social sciences, such as Czarniawska's in "Narratives in social science research" (2004; cf. Banks and Banks, 1998: 12).

How can fiction be a mode of research and generate knowledge? One of the key benefits of both applying creative literary devices and writing fiction as a method of inquiry is the ability to portray the complexities of "people and settings realistically, truthfully, and authentically" (Leavy, 2013: 38). This then helps to promote empathy and reflection, reach out to new audiences, introducing these to unknown social worlds, and disrupt stereotypes and dominant ideologies (Leavy, 2013: 47–52). Czarniawska points at narrative structure (plot) in fiction rather than imaginary elements as a source of knowledge. Narrative structure supplants causality – the logico-scientific mode of explanation – with "a scheme assuming the intentionality of human action" that helps to organise experience. Narrative allows for an openness in interpretation: "the same set of events can be organized around different plots" (2004: 7). Rather than writing an authoritative text that closes off the multiplicity of meanings typically found around an issue, "fiction-based research involves a process of weaving meanings, creating subtexts, and offering one of more points of view" (Leavy, 2013: 84). Enhancing the quality of writing is another important goal (Banks and Banks, 1998: 12; Czarniawska, 2004: 136). Writing appealing and accessible texts is vital to the value of qualitative research, because:

> unlike quantitative work that can carry its meaning in tables and summaries, qualitative work carries its meaning in the entire text. Just as a piece of literature is not equivalent to its 'plot summary', qualitative research is not contained in its abstract.
>
> (Richardson and St. Pierre, 2005: 960)

How researchers choose their words determines the type of knowledge they generate. In this way, artistic methods promote reflexivity (Richardson and St. Pierre 2005: 962).

When creative and logical genres meet and mix, a blurring of boundaries between fact and fiction may occur. And this blurring raises critique, even among supporters of arts-based research (Barone and Eisner, 2012: 101), let alone with defenders of the norm of scientific objectivity. This disruption may be exactly what some fiction-based researchers aim for, by way of undermining the objectivist pretensions of modernist science (e.g. Richardson and St. Pierre, 2005). Indeed, one may argue that all scientific facts are to some extent human constructions and thus representations (Leavy, 2013: 25; Frank, 2000: 485). The distinction between fact and fiction is not absolute, but scalar. Moreover, this scale between fact and fiction is not simple, but multi-dimensional: factual does not equal true and fiction is not identical to false or erratic (Banks and Banks, 1998: 12–13). So, how do fiction-based researchers deal with these multiple tensions? They try to get beyond the dichotomy. For instance, rather than splitting hairs over the accuracy of a text, they find it more fruitful to consider its value in the light of the "purpose for which the text is composed, the context for publication, and the way it is used by readers" (Barone and Eisner 2012: 103). In other words: "The difference is not whether the text really is fiction or nonfiction; rather, the difference is the claim that the author makes for the text" (Richardson and St. Pierre, 2005: 961). Czarniawska calls such a claim the *contract* between the author and the reader. She distinguishes two types of contracts. In a fictional contract, the author asks to "suspend your disbelief, as I am going to please you", while in a referential contract, the request is to "activate your disbelief, as I am going to instruct you" (2004: 9). She trusts readers to be able to manage both contracts at the same time (2004: 136). Accordingly, "fiction-based research has to be evaluated on its own terms"; "[t]here should be a tight fit between the research purpose/goals and the standards by which we evaluate the research outcome" (Leavy, 2013: 25; 78). An example of a set of such standards or evaluative criteria is: substantive contribution, aesthetic merit, reflexivity, and impact (Richardson and St. Pierre, 2005: 964). Leavy proposes a more elaborate, yet similar combination of literary and functional (i.e. research related) criteria, such as: creation of a virtual reality, sensitive portrayals, empathy, narrative coherence, ambiguity, substantive contribution, aesthetics, personal signature, and audience (2013: 71–90).

In short, the benefits of fiction in research can be enjoyed safely if the context of creation, publication and consumption of fictional knowledge is considered carefully and evaluated on relevant terms.

Is it a report? Is it fiction? No, it is a policy novel!

Up to now, I have written three policy novels, each by more or less the same approach. This section describes how the novels came about, so the next section can relate the approach to the guiding framework of this volume.

Case-study 1: An otter in Brussels

The making of the first policy novel started in 2013. It was one of the last endeavours in a four-year research project on the EU Water Framework Directive (Arts *et al.*, 2013). Together with the knowledge centre of the Dutch water boards (STOWA), the client, I wrote a short research proposal. The data for the story were yielded in two workshops with ten aquatic ecologists from various organisations including the client. All had been directly involved with the implementation of the WFD in the Netherlands. Additionally, four academic water policy researchers, and a writing coach the client had hired to support my writing process, participated. Aquatic ecologists monitor the biological quality of surface waters. As traditionally flood prevention and controlling water supply for agriculture are the key tenets of Dutch water management, their position has always been quite marginal (Disco, 2002). When the WFD was implemented, aquatic ecologists all over Europe hoped to gain much more influence on water policy and management. But after a few years into the implementation, they were not so sure their hope would be met (Winfield, 2006). So, my question was how the WFD had affected the role and position of aquatic ecologists in Dutch water management. Had their dream indeed turned into a nightmare? Two research

---

Box 11.1 A policy novel "An otter in Brussels"

Research question: How does the Water Framework Directive affect the roles and positions of aquatic ecologists in Dutch water management?

Research goals:

- Re-energize the people working on the Water Framework Directive (WFD).
- Make an accessible study on this complex case of EU environmental policy for a professional readership and the wider audience.

Story outline:

Henk Vleugel works at a regional waterboard as an aquatic ecologist. When his superior asks him to manage the implementation of the WFD, he is honoured but hesitant. Is he the right person to do this complicated policy job? Then, by accident, he meets Katelijne van Zwaay, a legal expert with the EU. Within a few weeks, his new life as a policymaker accelerates. She seems to know everything about European environmental policies. In preparation of a presentation for the managers of the waterboard, he visits her in Brussels.

Henk expects much of Katelijnes advice, and then she seems to expect more of him... Inspired, Henk starts building a website that should help a bottom-up implementation of the WFD. Within a few weeks, Katelijne returns the visit. This development does not bother his wife Dafne, but his new career move does. He delves deeper and deeper into the intricacies of the directive and risks losing touch with the values he and Dafne share. Then Henk finds out that Katelijne has been manipulating him and he must make a difficult choice: terminate his website or co-operate with the EU.

Moral of the story:

The meaning of the Water Framework Directive is not what it does to you, but what you do with it.

goals were formulated in the proposal. The client, STOWA, wished the novel would re-energise the people working on the next round of river basin management plans. As researchers, we wanted to make an accessible study on this complex EU environmental policy for a professional readership and the wider audience. The experimental workshop design was remotely inspired by 'learning history', a participatory storytelling method for organisational change developed at MIT (Kleiner and Roth 1997).

The first workshop took a full day: six hours of alternately telling practice stories and thinking up elements for the fictional story, plus short breaks in between every hour. It was about ten years after the EU had issued the directive, so there were plenty of stories to tell. My idea was that the alternation between storytelling and 'storymaking' would give the feel of a tidal movement, with an outgoing, empathic phase and an incoming, expressive phase. The three hours of storytelling were all plenary, and guided by three consecutive, narrative questions: (1) How did you first come in touch with the WFD? (2) What were the main ups and downs you experienced in the implementation process? (3) How has the WFD impacted you and your work? In the three hours of story-making, the participants – alone, in groups and plenary – worked on creating the main characters and inventing events for the plot. Interestingly, when the participants were asked to imagine an antagonist, they came up with all sorts of bad guys, who remarkably had not played any role in their own experiences. When this was pointed out, a vivid conversation followed that soon delivered the conclusion that perhaps they themselves were their own biggest enemy. Of course, this realisation was taken up in the novel as a key development for the main character.

The aim of the first workshop was to generate the basic outline of a fictional story on the WFD. However, I had no adequate procedure to converge two different ideas the participants had for the story. We spent some valuable workshop time working on both ideas, although looking back only one idea was useful. All participants agreed with this choice in the second workshop. Luckily, my writing coach had made extensive handwritten minutes, as the recording equipment was not good enough to capture the exchanges in a group of 15. As a part of the group assignments, the participants themselves had also produced notes. As a help in making the outline, I bought a handbook on plot-building (Bouma, 2010). Because I had never written fiction, I decided to stick to the handbook, initially. Together with the protagonist and his goal, the antagonist and some other characters, it gave enough guidance to produce a six-page synopsis of the story, based on the written recordings only. 'Emplotment' – the creation of a narrative structure – proved of great value as an analytical tool. Every step in the handbook called to mind episodes, observations and images from the practice stories. Before the second workshop, a few weeks later, the participants read the synopsis. The goal of this second workshop was to elaborate the synopsis. In about five hours we further developed the characters and important scenes in the story; made an inventory of the different 'tribes' working at the office of a Dutch water board; talked about the moral of the story; etc.

With the input from the two workshops and some additional interviews, I reworked the synopsis into a longer, chapter-by-chapter outline and started writing. Finished chapters were commented on by the writing coach and a few other proof-readers. Along the way, the story itself overgrew the structure in the handbook. Surprisingly, though, I did not have to make significant changes in the original sequence of events. During the writing of the chapters, the plot became denser, as the characters became more complex and more links developed between the events. In the process, the fictional story and the practice stories kept on feeding each other. Like emplotment, the actual writing of the chapters worked as an analytical tool: finding the right tone of voice for each of the characters, elaborating their motives and their relations, adequately depicting their world. Apart from comments from my writing coach and the proofreaders, writing was mostly a solitary activity. On a few occasions, when an episode required specific professional knowledge, I would ask one of the participants. The writing was not going very fast, also because the client had not set any deadline. After a year or so, I was halfway the outlined chapters. In an effort to speed up, I booked a stay in a hotel. In four days, I completed the second half of the story. When the text was finalised and approved by the client, a publisher was found in a small communication consultancy with a publishing branch. They took care of final editing, layout, printing, and sales. *An Otter in Brussels* became available in bookstores online and offline (Van der Arend, 2013). After about a year, the first 600 copies were sold and a second print was issued.

Case-study 2: The side-channel of Kampvoort

The assignment for the second policy novel came at the end of 2015, from an independent project manager who received and read the first. He was working with a group of citizens and farmers from the vicinity of a newly created, ten-kilometre-long, high-water channel along the river IJssel. This was one of some 30 projects in a major national flood protection program called Room for the River. The high-water channel required building two new dikes and some major hydraulic works, mainly through farmland. In case of high water, a small village would be enclosed by the channel and the river. In the process of planning and building the high-water channel, the responsible governments had organised many occasions for participation. However, the way they dealt with the local involvement only seemed to infuriate citizens and farmers more than the channel itself. When I got involved, some 100 people in the area were already in the midst of preparing an open-air community theatre production showing their experiences over the previous ten years. But the project manager also wanted something more permanent than a theatre production, a sort of a study that could go deeper into the matter and could reach a wider audience. The idea of a policy novel was new to him, but was exactly what he thought he needed at that point. For me, this was the perfect assignment to further develop the notion of the policy novel as a sort of 'policy analysis for citizens'. Or rather: by and for citizens. From a participatory research perspective, I wanted the IJssel dwellers to use their experiences to help and inform other citizens in similar situations.

Box 11.2 A policy novel "The side-channel of Kampvoort"

Research question:

How have citizens participating in Room for the River projects along the river IJssel experienced the actions of policy professionals, how have they reacted, and what were the consequences?

Research goal:

Share the experiences and knowledge of participants in Room for the River projects along the IJssel, to prepare other citizens and policy professionals in similar current and future projects.

Story outline:

In a terrible rainstorm, a person walking along the river IJssel finds shelter in a house in a small hamlet called Kampvoort. Strangely, this place is not on the map, and neither is the new side-channel that blocks the way to the ferry that connects this side of the river to the city on the other side. The walking person – a civil servant on sick leave – is forced to spend the night at a local inn, run by a former farmer and her son. Over the next few days, the walking civil servant somehow fails to leave Kampvoort, and meets the other inhabitants of the hamlet. One after another, they tell how the planning and building of the side-channel has affected their lives and the community, which has nearly fallen apart. Most of the inhabitants left Kampvoort and many still hold a grudge against the responsible governments. After hearing their partly opposing stories, the civil servant feels inclined to leave the outsider position and tries to reconcile two conflicting neighbours. In the meantime, interactions with the innkeeper have taken a romantic turn. Promising her and her son to come back soon, the civil servant finally leaves Kampvoort, using the new dike. Escaping another fierce shower, the civil servant accidentally meets the area manager of the side-channel project. She tells her side of the events, which seriously confuses the civil servant. But that is nothing compared to the shock of the story told on the ferry. Will the civil servant ever see the innkeeper again?

Moral of the story:

Many things that happen in policy are not caused by good or bad intentions; they are contingent, and perceived very differently by different people. Policymaking is storytelling.

Together we decided to stay close to the way the first policy novel was made, with two consecutive storytelling/story-making workshops as the main research activity. We did not only invite the people in the local project, but citizens actively involved in each of the ten Room for the River projects along the river IJssel. Thus, the workshops would have an end in themselves; as a meeting between people who had been participating in similar projects, sharing similar positions, but with very different experiences – all along the same river. Perhaps the IJssel itself could become a character in the story. Also, collaboration between people involved in ten different projects would make the resulting story much more fictional, rather than a direct translation of this one high-water channel project. The novel would be made and published on a minimal budget, to be covered by a crowd-funding campaign organised by the client. To avoid the time pressure, I had felt during the workshops for the first novel, I made a more realistic planning. I reserved more time for creative exercises. I hired someone with the only task to take notes of everything that was said.

Talking with the client and the workshop participants, I found that their most 'significant other' was the so called 'area manager' (*omgevingsmanager* in Dutch). This is someone working for the responsible governments with the task to organise and manage the local participation in Room for the River projects. Therefore, I interviewed two area managers before the workshops, one from the clients' area, and one working on two other IJssel projects. The first was initially quite wary to cooperate with the citizens' initiative to have me write a novel on their experiences. Before the interview started, he expressed the ministry's concern and their wish to leave what had happened behind and look forward. I made clear that the citizens would do as they wanted. I explained that the aim of the novel was not to recount this one particular project, but to combine the experiences of many different citizens along the whole of the river IJssel, so that other citizens could learn. After that, we had a long and interesting interview. However different, the two area-managers proved to be people with a heart for the project as well as for the local communities. Their position in-between was full of tensions and difficulties. They both gave examples in which they had gone a long way to satisfy the citizens needs and interests, sometimes succeeding and sometimes failing. The participants in the workshops recognised what these people did, but they remained critical. They felt deeply affected by the flood prevention project and the way it was done, and the area managers had played a dual role in it. When I started composing the plot after the first workshop, I was concerned about how to represent these contrasting perspectives. Should I just take the side of the client and the participants, or leave the issue open? This was a tough puzzle. I wanted to do justice to the different perspectives and motives, and not simplify all that had happened to a good guys vs. bad guys script – citizens vs. governments, local interests vs. the so-called general good. Reflecting on the stories the participants told helped solving the issue. Rather than a focus on the conflict between governments and citizens, I wanted to let the story evolve around the conflicts within the community, which had actually occurred in some of the project areas. When I proposed this idea at the start of the second workshop it immediately triggered a lot of new stories, now focusing much more on life and culture in the rural communities along the IJssel, than on the flood prevention projects only. This really gave a lot more depth to the experiences of the workshop participants. We chose four different main characters for the story, who would each have their own perspective on the fictional project that would upset the fictional community in the book. The perspective of the area manager was just one more.

The crowd funding campaign raised another, related issue. The client and one of the local farmers working in the high-water channel made a short film to promote the theatre project and raise money for the novel. In it, they prospected the novel as an allegation against the responsible governments. Government officials and civil servants should read it in order to learn to never do it like this again. This was not the story I was busy writing. I was writing a policy novel primarily for citizens, not for government people – although they might be eager to read a novel made by and for citizens. Most policy research is written specifically for managers, governors and civil servants (and for other scholars), confirming their agency and key position in policymaking. If we want citizens and their organisations to be more active and empowered, we need a discourse on their agency in policy processes. The crowd funding film risked creating an image of citizens as victims. Not as people who had been through a rough time, found a way to deal with it and had thus learned things other people could use to their advantage. I convinced the client to change the text in the film, also hoping this would indirectly influence their self-image. In the workshops, I had already taken up the issue of self-perception, for instance by asking the participants how the project had changed them and what they had taken from it. Now I realised that the research process itself could affect the identities of the participants in unexpected ways, and that I should definitely include these process developments in the story. This example shows how the research process, the novel as its outcome, and social change can reinforce each other.

The novel (Van der Arend, 2016a) was produced by the same publisher and presented at the first night of the open-air theatre production. Apart from promotion for professional target groups, specific efforts were made to reach a wider audience in the region, through newspapers, local bookstores, and libraries. A few of these agents picked up the news, but overall, their response was limited. Perhaps it was hard for them to categorise the novel. Some weeks after publication, the client organised a reading-group night to discuss the novel with some people from the workshops and some from the theatre production. Interestingly, one person found the story too much in favour of the citizens and another thought the image of the area manager was too positive. Later, I was invited to speak to people from a community along the river Rhine, who were confronted with a similar flood prevention project. Other than this, follow-up was limited, also because I was immediately asked to write another policy novel.

Case-study 3: Better than zero

The third assignment came from a government program promoting zero energy renovation of office buildings. The contact with the client was mediated by a former fellow student in Environmental Sciences who works in real estate. It helped a lot that I now had a small portfolio to present. The client wanted to learn which barriers are impeding the use of available measures to radically reduce energy use in office buildings, and how they can be overcome. The novel should present their knowledge on zero energy renovation in an attractive, innovative and accessible way for professionals in the field of office real estate, building and renovation, finance, commissioning, accreditation, consultancy, etc. After the slightly introvert aquatic ecologists and the modest IJssel dwellers, this seemed a completely different research population. With the financial crisis, real estate had been exposed as a world of arrogance, greed, intimidation, fraud, and other white-collar crimes. The list of potential workshop participants handed by the client was littered with CEOs, deputy directors, heads, and managers. It

---

Box 11.3 A policy novel "Better than zero"

Research question:

How can individual actors further zero energy office renovations by working with and against established institutions in office real estate?

Research goal:

Share, develop, analyse, and spread the experiences and knowledge of pioneers in zero energy offices.

Story outline:

Tilly van Deurnen is 59 years old and the owner of a building company employing 172 people. Her deepest wish is to build zero energy offices and help fight climate change. The new university's head office was her big opportunity. Unfortunately, everything went wrong, and now she finds herself in an orange suit, picking trash in a park, by way of community payback. Working irritatingly close behind her is a roughly built, coarse guy, who seems to know more of her history. Against her will, he introduces himself as Olivier de Rover. Somehow, this impertinent real estate agent convinces her to take revenge on the people who made the university project fail. In his pompous Maserati they visit her adversaries in the university project and try to make them invest in a fake plan to build a huge solar power plant in Africa. She tells herself her motives are clean – she wants to test their integrity and find out what made the university project fail. Meanwhile, her companion is clearly in it to get their money, as he thinks everyone in the business is corrupt. During the visits, Olivier and Tilly get to know each other, but when he finds out she was secretly making phone calls with his father, he explodes and they break up. A few weeks later, in the depth of her despair, he shows at her door again, with a young woman called Robine Labrise. Together, they concoct a plan that should make a change in office real estate, teach Tilly's adversaries a lesson, get Robine a job, put Olivier on the right track, and find Tilly a new purpose in life.

Moral of the story:

Innovation is not about overcoming barriers, it is about making the most of your profession.

would be tough to convince them to spend two full afternoons on something as whimsy as making up a novel. For some of them, this proved to be true: "Here, we measure our time by the hour, not in afternoons." But most people on the list appeared happy to participate in what many saw as an innovative project. I realised that especially with this populace, I needed a chairperson to run the meetings, so I could focus on facilitating the storytelling and storymaking exercises. Combining these two tasks had been demanding in the earlier workshops, with the effect of running out of time. At the actual workshops, of course, the invited CEOs and directors appeared to be quite ordinary people – willing workshop participants and avid storytellers. Moreover, they were the exceptions in their field, the ones who go against the routines and traditions, trying their utmost to realise fundamental changes, ahead of current laws and policies. This time, using fiction proved useful as a safe way for the participants to talk about the sensitive things going on in their work; to give details without being too specific.

The time between the workshops and the publishing deadline was short, again. Despite a background in environmental sciences, I was unfamiliar with much of the knowledge involved. It was very specialised in several domains: building and renovation, energy policy, the office real estate market, finance, energy technology, sustainability assessment, facility management, etc. All this knowledge had to be brought together in the plot of the story. The workshops had yielded an interesting protagonist-antagonist duo, and a lot of side characters representing the variety of actors involved in office building projects. I was used to construct the plot on my own, but this time it proved too complex to combine the motives and actions of all the different characters with the specificities of the field. A bit to my surprise, the client had not expected I would do it all alone. So more than before, we co-operated in developing the characters and the plot. The client wrote a document describing the parties involved in a large building project. Interestingly, in this text one could see the functional descriptions of the roles of actors slowly evolving into more fictional 'living' characters. Another issue to solve in the writing process was finding an inspiring way to write about climate change and the energy transition. Typical stories on the topic follow an apocalyptic script, which has about the same effect on fossil fuel users as nasty pictures on tobacco packages have on smokers: denial and apathy (Lertzman, 2015). I found an alternative script in the stories of the participants, and this also reframed the clients' research question. In the end, the novel is not about barriers impeding zero energy renovation, but about how great it is to build the best offices possible.

The client ordered 1500 copies of the novel (Van der Arend, 2016b). People in their network could request it for free. In one organisation, the novels were spread through a new method: by handing them over one by one, with a personal invitation to read it. The publisher printed another 500 copies to sell to a wider audience.

Policy novels as fiction-based action research

The theory section above, Fiction in research, argued that fact and fiction are not perfect opposites. Indeed, in my experience as a policy scientist and a policy novelist, the contrarieties between doing research and writing fiction are greatly surpassed by their commonalities and complementarities. Research and fiction share a need for curiosity, creativity, imagination, precision, authenticity, and perseverance. The opposite – the absence of the qualities of both research and fiction – would be a total lack of awareness and attention for others and the world we live in. Advocates of fiction-based research propose to carefully position it as both functional and literary texts that have to be evaluated on their own, multiple terms. Indeed, my three policy novels are clearly labelled as research-informed works of fiction that aim to promote learning and action upon policy issues. Furthermore, concerns with the lack of facticity are surpassed by always combining experiences from different cases, places or organisations. The resulting story should not be evaluated as a more or less inaccurate translation of one particular situation, but as an authentic, engaging and informative representation of several similar cases. So, policy novels seem to be open for testing against the type of criteria proposed by fiction-based researchers. But in the making of the policy novels I see another way to deal with the tension between fact and fiction, or rather, to make the most of this tension. This is through the active participation of people in the field of study. Their input is what makes a policy novel 'really imagined': fictional, yet full of truth and realism.

This section further develops this idea of employing the tensions between fact and fiction by participation, or action research. I first argue that the cases illustrate that policy novels are preferably created through an action research approach. Then, I discuss the issues of roles and relations and criticality respectively, as two of the key action research elements in the guiding framework of this volume.

Really imagined: the value of co-creativity in fiction-based policy research

A familiar notion in education is that students retain more knowledge from what they do themselves, than from reading or listening to a teacher.[1] In a policy novel, experienced practitioners – be they professionals or 'amateurs' – inform and invent the story. It is this action research approach that puts the policy knowledge into policy fiction. When the workshop participants convert their own experiences and each other's stories into fiction, they actually perform an implicit comparative case-study. They draw out the things that appear most meaningful for the understanding of this particular policy. Seeing this happen on three occasions has convinced me that policy novels are most relevant, reliable and viable as a mode of action research: practice based, applied, and participatory. Practice-based means, inter alia, that research questions derive from the problems encountered by people actually involved in a particular policy. Applied means that the outcomes inform practical action in the field. Participatory, in this case, means based on 'co-creativity': when the people who have direct experience with the policy under scrutiny contribute to the invention and/or writing of the story. By doing so, they practice a particular type of knowledge, which could be called 'imaginative knowledge'.

Imaginative knowledge enables us to see the truth in fiction and the possible in reality. It is the way we understand the world in our mind's eye; by seeing how things *could* be, how people *could* act. It is related to experiential knowledge, embodied knowledge and other variants of what is called tacit knowledge (Polanyi, 1966). As the workshop participants invent the characters – give them a name, physical and mental features, a family, a job, a house, actions – they imbue them with everything they tacitly know from doing their job and living in their world, including the possible. The particular added value of policy novels as a mode of action research is based on this co-creative interchange between storytelling and 'storymaking' – between recounting facts and creating fiction. As shown above, the conversion from experience to fiction allows for anonymity, which may make it easier for participants to stay close to how they actually experience the policy studied and act upon it.

The alternation between storytelling and storymaking also works as an important reflective tool of the method. In the making of a policy novel, practical experiences and stories are reworked into a fictional story, while the fictional perspective informs and transforms the interpretation of past experiences. Viewing their own actions and experiences through a literary lens gives participants new ideas about their roles and possibilities, and may even change them. As a researcher/author I want to incorporate as much of these reflections, insights, and changes as possible into the story to make the most of the imaginative knowledge available. More generally, I look for ways in which the process and the product of policy fiction can inform and reinforce each other. Therefore, the workshops have an end in themselves for the participants, as events to meet and learn.

Furthermore, imaginative knowledge also originates from the actual writing of the chapters; in the dialogues and thoughts, in the setting of the story and the world that is built, in the scenery, the humour, and the imagery used, etc. Like a designer developing a new object, creative writers encounter many little problems, such as when something that the protagonist needs to do in the story is out of character. New ideas, insights, and links are born as solutions to such little problems. Therefore, clients and participants would ideally co-create the actual text as well, or at least contribute by proofreading. Then, the story profits even more from their tacit knowledge, and vice versa.

Like mixing oil in vinegar: roles and relations in co-creating policy novels

Like most research projects, a policy novel is made in cooperation between people in several different roles: a researcher/writer, a client, workshop participants, interviewees and specifically, I may add: readers. Based on their so-called referential contract, scientific and other factual texts demand a binary reading: do I buy into the argument or not? I think the attitude of fiction readers is more active and engaged. When they read fiction, readers absorb the novel's elements in coherence, and through their imagination they (re)create tacit knowledge. The fictional contract invites them to envision the story, to sympathise with characters, to think what they would do in their shoes, to feel sorry, happy, excited, or relieved. In their mind's eye, they make the conversion from fiction to experience, without (necessarily) going into abstractions. Thus, the process of co-creativity continues after publication. This is how policy fiction is relational: it activates writers, clients, participants, and readers to be co-creators of meaningful policy knowledge.

Like the role of readers, other roles and relations are also impacted by the use of fiction as a research method. As an action researcher, the work of a policy novelist is to continuously make the most of the imagination, creativity, aesthetics, interpretations, experiences, intelligence, stories and information from the client, participants, interviewees and others involved. The primary responsibility is to connect and balance the research questions and goals on one side and the creative and literary quality on the other. To underline the importance of a good mix, my company is called SenF. Of course, this stands for science and fiction, or perhaps study and fantasise. But *Senf* is also the German word for mustard, a condiment with the capacity to sustain a salad dressing, i.e. an emulsion of oil and vinegar. These are two substances that normally do not mix – like policy research and fiction. The nuts and bolts of mixing research and fiction are hard to spell out in a detailed methodology, but the principle is to 'love both, and treat fiction as the medium'. As fiction is the research method, it is vital to let imagination, creativity and aesthetics do their work: to stop, at some point, thinking analytically about the research question and possible explicit answers, to let the story develop, and try and interpret it as the implicit answer. Doing so is partly a question of research design. But mostly it is done on a daily basis throughout the research process, from defining a research question with the client up to communicating with readers after publication.

The roles and relations of participating policy practitioners may change too. In a 'normal' academic research project, or even in a non-fictional action research project, they would be primarily expected to provide information and opinions. This places an emphasis on their credibility, expertise, and key position in the field. In a fictional research project, they are mainly asked for their personal experience, their creativity, and their ability to reflect on the routines and values in their daily lives.

Co-creativity develops between the client, participants, readers, and writers of policy fiction. In this respect, one of the disadvantages of creative writing is that it is a lonely art form, both in production and in consumption. This has advantages too, as the writer/researcher is 'allowed' to retreat and gets some (creative) autonomy. Another good thing about written fiction as opposed to theatre and film, is that it is lo-tech and cheap. On the downside, the solitary character makes it hard to organise an effective follow-up, such as a public discussion after a political play. I have tried reading groups, but the results were not yet very convincing as a way to further co-creativity and imaginative knowledge. As said above, including collaborative writing in the project or organising writing lessons may be a step forward. Using policy novels in education seems a worthwhile option as well. This is just to say that co-creativity is not always easy or uncontested, which includes the position of the writer/researcher. But as illustrated in the cases above, many of the troubles along the way can be made productive by thinking about their meaning in the policy practice the action research project engages in.

Critical knowledge: recounting policymaking as human practice

In this volume, relationality and criticality are seen as possibly conflicting aspects of action research. In my view, policy novels are critical, just because they are co-created in a relational context – in an alternative knowledge practice between storytellers, storymakers, writers and readers. Like any scientific discipline, policy analysis is typically based on the idea that its object of knowledge – policies, in this case – can be known and controlled from the outside. This is why policy analysis typically generates managerial knowledge, which supports and informs those who can define themselves as overseeing a policy as a whole, like scientists and managers. Thus, policy analysis is performative: it produces, changes, and reinforces (hegemonic) explanations, roles and relations in policy practices (Bevir, 2010). As commentators and analysts, policy researchers are vital in making the accounts that render myriads of largely uncoordinated activity into a structured policy process (Colebatch, 2014: 313). Of course, the same counts for policy fiction as a mode of action research: it is a knowledge practice connected to policy practices (and other social practices). But "academic discourse, [...] prefers universal, systemic explanations of practice" (Colebatch 2014: 313).

In contrast, the way a policy novel portrays policymaking seems more relevant for those not in positions to (think they can) manage policies. A fictional account of a policy process gives an ambiguous, multifaceted, layered description of events rather than a single, univocal systemic explanation of outcomes. It can convincingly and intimately present policy practice as the work of people. As such, it allows for the key role of emotions, contingency, uncertainty, opacity, non-linearity, relations, personality, etc. All this makes fiction fit to recount the fundamentally decentred, contested, emergent conditions of policymaking in the real world. Rather than speaking to scientists and policy professionals only, such stories may confirm and inform the agency of citizens and other (non-)professional actors with a marginal position in policy networks. Combined with its accessibility, policy novels thus may help all those involved or implicated in a policy (including managers, civil servants, governors, and citizens) to make sense of the situation they find themselves in and to support them to act upon it. By co-creating new accounts of policymaking that open up the work of policy professionals and emphasise 'ordinary people's' agency – however small –

experienced and new readers of policy accounts may get some grip on policy practices.

Conclusion

Next to its advantages in social science generally, as a way to approach the complexity of lived experience, fiction seems specifically useful in policy analysis as a mode of action research. Policy novels work not (only) because of their fictional properties, but because they are relational in the process and as a product. Fiction is not only an accessible way to write about policy, it creates an image of policy-making that is more activating and empowering for people in policy practices. Provided it is seen and done as a mode of action research, policy fiction is able to generate more relational, diverse, and inclusive knowledge practices. For evaluating policy novels some process-related criteria may be added to the sets of functional and literary criteria quoted in the section 'Fiction in research'. Transparency may be the key requirement here, although the policy novel itself is not always the best place to take up non-fictional texts describing the research process.

In this light, it is relevant to be aware that novels may also have exclusionary effects. First, although not as narrow as those of scientific articles or policy documents, the readership of fiction is still concentrated in specific social strata. Second, the typical narrative structure of the modern novel with its Hollywood-like plot may not be culturally neutral. For this reason, fiction writers experiment with post-modern plots or plotless stories, but these are not necessarily less exclusive than average novels. This is something to consider within the specificities of each policy fiction project. Third – as far as I can judge, and that is hard – my policy novels are still mostly read by policy professionals and people who know me personally, and less by a wider, general audience. In any chosen form, policy may remain a topic for experts. This situation is reinforced by the fact that 'ordinary' citizens are not the most likely clients of a policy research project, although my second novel was a notable exception.

To overcome such shortcomings, it is wise to enhance co-creativity in future policy fiction projects. Workshop participants could contribute more to the synopsis and the writing of the chapters. Also, their role could be enhanced as advocates and distributors of the novel in their professional, local, and personal networks. I aim for assignments that allow me to develop other possible ways to use fiction as a method in action research: e.g. writing sessions, creative workshops, fictional interviewing. Trying a wider variety of genres, such as comic books, thrillers and detectives, short stories, fantasy, or science fiction (!) may broaden the readership of policy fiction. As my versatility as an author is limited, these may be ventures open for other disappointed policy analysts.

Note

1 See references to the so-called 'Learning Pyramid' and to Confusius: "I hear and I forget; I see and I remember; I do and I understand".

References

Arts B, Behagel, J, van Brommel, S, de Kroning, J and Turnhout, E (eds.) (2013) *Forest and nature governance: a practice based approach*, Dordrecht: Springer.

Banks SP and Banks A (1998) *Fiction and social research: by fire or ice*, Walnut Creek, California: AltaMira Press.

Barone T and Eisner EW (2012) *Arts-based research*, Thousand Oaks, California: Sage.

Bevir M (2010) *Democratic governance*, Princeton, New Jersey: Princeton University Press.

Bouma M (2010) *Storytelling in 12 stappen. Op reis met de held*, Antwerpen, Amsterdam: Augustus.

Colebatch HK (2014) Making sense of governance. *Policy and Society* 33(4): 307–316.

Czarniawska B (2004) *Narratives in social science research*, London: Sage.

Disco C (2002) Remaking "nature". The ecological turn in Dutch water management. *Science, Technology and Human Values* 27(2): 206–235.

Frank K (2000) "The management of hunger": using fiction in writing anthropology. *Qualitative Inquiry* 6 (4): 474–488.

Kleiner A and Roth G (1997) How to make experience your company's best teacher. *Harvard Business Review* 75(5): 172–177.

Leavy P (2009) *Method meets art. Arts-based research practice*, New York: Guilford Press.

Leavy P (2013) *Fiction as research practice. Short stories, novellas, and novels*, Walnut Creek, CA: Left Coast Press.

Lertzman R (2015) *Environmental melancholia: psychoanalytic dimensions of engagement*, New York: Routledge.

Polanyi M (1966) *The tacit dimension*, Chicago: University of Chicago Press.

Richardson L and St. Pierre EA (2005) Writing: a method of inquiry. In: Denzin NK and Lincoln YS (eds.) *The Sage handbook of qualitative research* (3rd edn), 959–978, Thousand Oaks, California: Sage.

Van der Arend SH (2013) *Een otter in Brussel. Waterkwaliteitsroman*, Wageningen: Landwerk.

Van der Arend SH (2016a) *De nevengeul van Kampvoort*, Participatieroman. Wageningen: Landwerk.

Van der Arend SH (2016b) *Beter dan nul. Innovatieroman*, Wageningen: Landwerk.

Van der Arend SH and Behagel J (2012) Het falen van deliberatie. *Bestuurskunde* 2012 (1): 61–69.

Winfield IJ (2006) Fishes, wishes, curses and directives. *Aquatic Conservation: Marine and Freshwater Ecosystems* 16: 549–553.

Co-inquirer reflection

Martine de Vaan

In the hallway of the ministry I work for, next to the energy label that every government lawfully has to display in their public buildings, I stand waiting for Sonja. My financial colleague André walks by – a pain in the ass when it comes to sustainability projects. Some time ago I heard he has had solar panels on his own roof for years. When I shared my surprise, he replied: "Of course, as a grandfather I want to contribute to the energy transition". The conversation still puzzles me.

Two weeks ago, Sonja asked me to contribute to a book chapter on her policy novels. As a practitioner in zero energy office buildings, I was actively involved in the making of her novel *Better than zero*. I told her what readers tell me: "It's exactly like that." She was happy to hear this, but she seemed even happier that the project also gave me some new insights. Although I am really busy, I agreed to a walking meeting to reflect on the novel project together. We thought it fun to meet in front of the energy label, as the novel also showed how, ironically, such labels do not say much about the actual energy use in a building. I think about the novel and how it came about. What is its meaning for my work, for office real estate, or for the energy transition?

"It's exactly like that." Most readers say it with a smile, as if they are finally understood. As if they finally get recognition for the hardship of trying to realise energy neutral buildings. Dealing with the endless list of parties and people involved: builders, engineers, controllers, lawyers, banks, appraisers, architects. All of them can make the project fail, by a lack of knowledge, curiosity or vision. Or all three. Like those readers, I was getting increasingly impatient. When I started studying environmental science in 1990, climate change was already a big issue. Sufficient measures still have to be taken. Now and then, people ask me how I survive in this big bureaucratic organization, where most colleagues don't feel they have a role to play in the climate policies when it isn't in their job description. My reply is that I work at the largest Dutch real estate organisation, which can completely change the market standard, for example when it decided to rule out offices with an energy efficiency below 'label C'. Such changes are a crucial piece of the puzzle towards a sustainable world and I'm convinced we can do it again. Several colleagues advised me to lower my profile on sustainability. But what then is the point of working here? Luckily, the number of people who co-operate is growing by the day.

I've known Sonja since we studied environmental science and I really believe in the power of her policy novels. I brought her in touch with Eelco Ouwerkerk, program manager of "Office Full of Energy", an independent innovation program focusing on the intractable energy transition in the utility building sector. He was looking for an innovative way to present their lessons learnt to their target group. He liked her first two novels and there was a match, so I could reassume my role as 'just' one of the workshop participants.

The workshops enabled me to contribute to the book in ways that an interview never could have. Because you create fiction, you can tell the truth. I think this also held for the other participants – a blend of people from public and private parties. It was a challenge to get them together for two full afternoons, but once there, it was extraordinary to see how quickly and naturally they exchanged their deepest motivations. We were able to talk on an emotional level, about how we try to change things, how hard it is as an individual in a conservative environment, but also how fantastic when you achieve things. The stories gave us new insights; something I had not expected. It became clear why different people in the business behave the way they do. We came to understand that it is too easy to blame people personally, but you can't only blame 'The System' either. We came to realize that when everybody simply follows their job description, nothing will change. I thought the system in which to create the energy transition in the built environment would be too complex for outsiders to understand. But the great thing about fictional characters is that they are complete persons, with their work and private lives as intertwined as in real life. They draw readers into the story and help convey the complexities of the topic.

One evening of reading a novel saves a lot of time and frustration for people new to the field. I receive many positive reactions. Practitioners recognise the larger patterns behind incidents in their daily work, and feel readier to deal with them. Some asked for copies to distribute themselves. Fortunately, I get critical feedback too. Some readers dislike the somewhat hyperbolic storyline. Others think the 'happy end' comes out of the blue. In response, I would like to issue a writing challenge for 'the missing chapter'.

After picking up his guest at the reception, André passes again. Now he sees me. "Ah good, Martine may tell us: what will be our next energy neutral building?" And to his guest: "Did you know? We need to do more than one every single workday, until 2050!" I watch him move on immediately.

Then, another voice. "Hey, you seem happy! What are you smiling about?" Without me noticing her arrival, Sonja suddenly stands before me.

"Nothing ...," I say. "Let's go walking. I think I have an idea what to write for the book."

12 Conclusion

Critical and relational action research for policy change and sustainability transitions

Julia M Wittmayer and Koen PR Bartels

The ecological, political, social and personal crises we confront at this time need no rehearsing here; fundamental to all these crises is the way we think and how the way we think separates us from our experience, from each other, and from the rhythms and patterns of the natural world.

(Reason, 1994: 9)

Over two decades ago, Reason (1994: 9) stressed that the "ecological, political, social and personal crises" of the time begged a different way of thinking and doing research. This book shows that contemporary sustainability crises and unprecedented scales of policy change, along with structural inabilities to govern these, have only deepened the need for actionable knowledge and research. We therefore believe there is a strong need to share, reflect on, and promote a diversity of research approaches to and experiences with generating actionable knowledge, cultivating interdependencies, and transforming the status quo. By providing an overview of the state-of-the-art in our fields, this book demonstrates that action research offers a wide range of approaches to dealing with the critical-relational dynamics of generating policy change and sustainability transitions.

In this final chapter, we first reflect on the diversity in approaches to action research and the ways in which criticality and relationality are interpreted and enacted across chapters. We then discuss what we can learn from the chapters about the different elements of our guiding framework for critical and relational action research: starting point; multiple roles and relationships; hegemonic structures, cultures, and practices; and reflexivity, impact, and change. Finally, we assess the overall contribution of the book and identify key issues for future action research in policy analysis and transition research.

Criticality and relationality in action research

We define action research as *critical and relational processes through which researchers and their co-inquirers aim to collaboratively produce scientifically and socially relevant knowledge and transformative action.* This definition is intended to be inclusive of the diverse family of action research, including such approaches as collaborative research (Demeritt, 2005), co-operative research, (Stirling, 2006), participatory research (Pain and Kindon, 2007), co-production (Richardson and Durose, 2006) and transdisciplinary research (Hadorn *et al.*, 2008). These various labels are testimony to important differences in philosophical traditions, field-specific histories, and actual methods, but also carry a certain risk of getting stuck in semantics. Without negating their disparities, we are committed to a shared, inter- and transdisciplinary, and reflexive approach to learning from the contingent ways in which we develop local responses to our global crises through diverse actionable research methods and experiences.

Table 12.1 highlights this *diversity in approaches* as well as their fields of origin, applications, and methods. It is worth highlighting that some contributors mostly draw on existing action research approaches, while others developed more of their own approach within the context of their research project, institute, or partnership. Compare for instance Clement's use of audiovisual media and deliberative meetings within a Participatory Action Research tradition with Van der Arend's pioneering efforts at establishing Policy Fiction. Another important feature is that all these approaches originate from different fields, ranging from organisational development (Appreciative Inquiry in Gardner's chapter) through territorial development (Action Research for Territorial Development in Arrona and Larrea's chapter) to science and technology studies (Cooperative Research in Balázs and Pataki's chapter). A final key issue is that the methods some contributors use are primarily aimed at producing collaborative knowledge (e.g. Westling and Sharp's collaborative partnership meetings) whereas those of others place greater emphasis on joint action (e.g. Jhagroe's participation in a local space).

A common thread through this diversity is a *shared emphasis on the critical-relational dynamics* of action research. Action research is *critical* towards power inequalities, social injustices, and mainstream research philosophies, as well as *relational* in engaging with the interactive processes through which we co-create the world. On the one hand, there are tensions between striving to transform the status quo based on counter-hegemonic aspirations *and* trying to cultivate trustful and meaningful relationships through collaborative sense-making processes. On the other hand, action research is more likely to generate change when it is grounded in shared critical awareness of local and wider relational interdependencies. Hence, engaging in such critical-relational action research is inherently challenging yet necessary for policy change and sustainability transitions.

To be sure, we do not propose criticality and relationality as black-or-white normative ideals but take an ideal typical approach in which they serve as analytical yardsticks that help to unpack the diversity of interpretations and methods employed in action research approaches (see Stout, 2010). In this way, we can appreciate how, for instance, Kuitenbrouwer emphasises relationality through 'reconstruction clinics' that raise awareness of relational interdependencies, dynamics, and patterns in Dutch policy conflicts, Clement focuses on criticality to empower Nepalese farmers to challenge hegemonic climate change discourse,

Table 12.1 Overview of different approaches to action research used in this book

Ch.	Topic	Approach	Field(s)	Key methods
2	Clean water in the UK	Critical-Applied Social Research	Collaborative research in geography	Partnership meetings
3	Food sovereignty in Hungary	Co-operative Research	Science and technology studies	Scenario workshop Network building
4	Urban gardening in Dutch city	Transition Scientivism	Transition research	Participatory co-production of glocal spaces and visions
5	Collaborative governance in Scotland	Collaborative Action Research	Network governance, education	Group-based inquiry Working within existing spaces
6	Civil society network for sustainability transitions in Flanders	Mix of action research approaches	Sustainability science, transition research, community action research, action science	Mind mapping Learning history
7	Territorial development in the Basque Country	Action Research for Territorial Development	Territorial development	Arenas for co-generating knowledge
8	Austerity in British local governance	Appreciative Inquiry	Organisational development, local governance	Visioning workshops Co-producing policy
9	Policy conflicts in the Netherlands	Reconstruction Clinic	Conflict resolution	Reflective workshops Narrative braiding
10	Climate change and farmers in Nepal	Participatory Action Research	Rural development in the Global South	Audiovisual media Deliberative meetings
11	Environmental sustainability in the Netherlands	Policy Fiction	Fiction- and arts-based research	Participatory workshops Fiction writing

and Arrona and Larrea strive to balance both principles by enacting 'soft resistance' to institutionalise new governance arrangements for territorial development in the Basque Country.

Many contributions affirm that *criticality and relationality are highly intertwined and mutually constitutive*. Gardner for example explains that the relational nature of 'appreciative inquiry' helped to build trust and create space for reflecting back unspoken critical views of the impact of austerity on local public services. Arrona and Larrea argue that being relational by building trust and collaborating pragmatically can facilitate action researchers in being critical of hegemony and transforming disempowering systems. Henderson and Bynner make a similar argument and add that 'holding steady' to principles, expectations, and accountability is important for having clear and robust relationships. In turn, Balázs and Pataki emphasise that critical change is only possible if there are strong relationships, as these generate transformative agency that cannot be created individually.

The book also showcases the plurality of ways criticality and relationality are interpreted and enacted by contributors. In Jhagroe's 'transition scientivism', criticality means joining a group of urban gardeners to co-develop their innovative practices and counter-hegemonic vision, while for Balázs and Pataki it takes the shape of 'cooperative research' with a wide network of Hungarian small-holder farmers, NGOs, and activists to formulate a bottom-up policy proposal for food sovereignty. For Van der Arend, an explicit relational worldview is fundamental to appreciating how 'policy fiction' can activate those involved in co-creating new knowledge and imaginations of environmental governance, whereas Westling and Sharp argue that a more modest interpretation of relationality focused on the applicability of critical action research is better suited to working in a technical field like the UK water sector.

Crucially, Paredis and Block stress that reflexivity about how critical-relational dynamics play out in local contexts is fundamental to producing socially relevant and usable knowledge. In the next section, we therefore reflect on the diversity of contingent approaches to critical-relational action research along the four dimensions of our guiding framework.

Reflections on doing critical and relational action research

We developed the guiding framework as a heuristic that can enhance the sensitivity of action researchers and all those involved in the main issues, tensions, and possibilities they are likely to face. For each element, we (1) highlight the diversity in experiences and issues, (2) compare different approaches and perspectives, and (3) outline shared insights on engaging in its critical-relational dynamics. See Table 12.2 for an overview.

The starting point

The starting point of action research can be as simple as in Jhagroe's case: a researcher walks into a space that interests him and starts doing things together with those present. It can also be intimately tied up with a personal journey, as illustrated by Van der Arend's story of disillusionment with academia or Paredis' previous involvement with civil society organisations and interest in sustainability. For others, it starts with partnerships or research institutes, such as TWENTY65 (Westling and Sharp), What Works Scotland (Henderson and Bynner), Orkestra (Arrona and Larrea), the Public Mediation Programme (Kuitenbrouwer), and the International Water Management Institute (Clement). Such institutional commitment to the co-production of knowledge and action has significant potential to enhance the legitimacy of action research amongst policy actors. However, McPherson and Digman reflect that even in such institutional infrastructures, action researchers and co-inquirers need to navigate the starting point by finding sufficient time, bridging different 'languages', and juggling with divergent habits and expectations.

All chapters show that *(understanding) the (international, national, regional, local) context* is crucial to how an action research project unfolds and what effects it has. For instance, Kuitenbrouwer describes how the Dutch governance tradition of collaboration and consensus-seeking created a favourable context for collaborative learning but also inhibited systemic changes in conflict resolution practices. In turn, Jayshi explains that, in Nepal, empowering rural farmers was necessary as they are marginalised in climate policy focused on the capital city and dominated by 'expert' officials. In contrast, Arzelus highlights how action research can change a governance context of top-down and compartmentalised relationships by reorienting actors and arrangements towards co-generative learning.

A shared insight across chapters is that it is vital to *treat the starting point as a fluid and relationally co-created context* subject to ongoing critical reflection. As Paredis and Block explain, action research does not 'just happen'; space and support are actively crafted through interaction with policy developments, funding opportunities, relationships between researchers and policy actors, and, crucially, glocal challenges and requests for help. Henderson and Bynner argue that the starting point is not a static point in time/space but results from ongoing efforts at cultivating 'sanction and sanctuary'. As the research develops, action researchers need to constantly sustain organisational commitment and safeguard time and space for learning and change. Hence, the starting point produces specific critical-relational dynamics for action research but is also reshaped through these.

Multiple roles and relationships

Action research can be born out of existing relationships: De Vaan already knew Van der Arend and asked for her help with a specific problem. But action research can also give birth to relationships: Jhagroe and Henneman developed a friendship whilst gardening and reflecting on shared values. According to Henderson and Bynner, these relationships always involve a certain degree of 'mutual instrumentalisation' (or, framed differently, 'reciprocity') to each

Table 12.2 Cross-contribution analysis of the guiding frameworks' four dimensions

Chapters/contributors (authors/co-inquirers)	The starting point	Multiple roles and relationships	Hegemonic structures, cultures and practices	Reflexivity, impact, and change
2 Westling and Sharp *Digman*	Major interdisciplinary collaborative partnership	Trying to bridge critical and applied roles	Creating legitimacy and space for critical action research and eliciting issues of power and social justice	A priori limited impact of a critical approach in the technical field, moderated by efforts at enhancing applicability
3 Balázs and Pataki *Kiss and Sarbu-Simonyi*	Existing interests and methodological preferences	Division of responsibilities for the cooperative research process; strong relationships generate transformative agency	Empowering marginalised local farmers and civil society organisations	Change agricultural policy through jointly developing the capacities, vision, and influence of a bottom-up network
4 Jhagroe *Henneman*	Walking into a space and start doing things together	Developing friendships whilst doing and reflecting together	Experimenting with innovative practices and helping to develop counter-hegemonic vision	Personal transformations and small-scale interventions in evolving practice
5 Henderson and Bynner *McPherson*	Ongoing efforts at cultivating 'sanction and sanctuary'	Mutual instrumentalisation; 'holding steady' to principles, expectations, and accountability	Research subject to existing hegemonic forces	Building new relationships and creating time for reflexivity
6 Paredis and Block *Barrez*	Previous involvement and interests, policy developments, funding opportunities, relationships between researchers and policy actors	Mutually adjust to the rhythm of the process	Engaging in 'mild interventions' to co-produce new sustainability narrative	Creating a common vision, facilitating learning and strategic dialogue, but limited direct external impact

Case	Context	Roles/Relationships	Approach	Aim/Outcome
7 Arrona and Larrea *Arzelus*	Governance context of top-down and compartmentalised relationships	Building trust and collaborating pragmatically	Enacting 'soft resistance' in practice (versus being critical at an ideological level)	Institutionalisation of new governance arrangements for territorial development
8 Gardner *Jones*	Collaborative partnership between university and local authority	Time-consuming and frustrating process of dealing with role expectations, ethical boundaries, staff turnover, and the legitimacy of the research(er). Dialogical vs. monological relationships	Appreciative inquiry to reflect back unspoken critical views; more than putting lipstick on a pig	Action researchers have limited potential to realise transformation on their own terms because they are only one voice amongst many
9 Kuitenbrouwer *Arichi*	Dutch governance tradition of collaboration and consensus-seeking	Researcher as facilitator Division of critical and relational roles	Disentangling policy conflicts	Helping stakeholders in 'getting unstuck' and moving forward and enhancing critical awareness of the need for structural change and capacity-building
10 Clement *Jayshi*	Marginalisation of rural farmers by urban-focused policy and 'expert' officials	Dividing roles for filming, editing, facilitation, and analysis	Empowering marginalised local farmers via audio-visual media and changing power relationships through deliberation	Challenging hegemonic discourses by increasing consciousness, emancipation, and counter-framing and changing relationships
11 Van der Arend *De Vaan*	Disillusionment with academia and request for help	Existing relationships; co-producing stories; researcher as solitary writer	Critical knowledge of and reflection on policymaking as human practice	'Practice what you preach' by co-producing non-conventional knowledge that stimulates relational imagination

other's purposes, as co-inquirers and researchers inevitably both seek to benefit from their collaboration. However, the risk is that it turns into 'institutional instrumentalisation' of endorsing pre-held views and hegemonic interests rather than engaging in mutual learning and transformative change (see also Bartels and Wittmayer, 2014).

In all chapters we can observe *a struggle with positionality*. Gardner shows in much detail how building productive relationships and mutually acceptable roles is a time-consuming and frustrating process of dealing with role expectations, ethical boundaries, staff turnover, and the legitimacy of the research(er). For both researchers and co-inquirers, this means learning how to collaborate with different people, including dealing with resistance and contestation. It is not possible to stay 'neutral' in this process; co-inquirers and other stakeholders will 'push and pull' action researchers in a certain position. Compare for instance how Gardner strives to create dialogical relationships of shared inquiry and learning while Jones values an objective researcher with no 'loyalties'.

A shared insight is that it is important to *reflexively engage with the multiple relationships and roles* of action researchers and co-inquirers. Kuitenbrouwer recommends positioning the researcher as facilitator who helps co-inquirers in understanding what happened and how they could collaborate more productively, and, second, to divide critical and relational roles between facilitator and reflectants. Arichi values how this creates a non-judgmental and non-threatening space for joint learning, yet also emphasises that confusion about role divisions is nevertheless possible. Similarly, Kiss and Sarbu-Simonyi appreciate the division of responsibilities with the researchers but also stress that they were unfamiliar with methodological options and their consequences at the time of the research design. Ideally, the research design should cater for the ongoing negotiation of relationships and roles and for necessary changes because of unforeseen developments and emergent ambiguities. Multiple roles and relationships evolve according to critical-relational dynamics, requiring researchers and co-inquirers to, as Paredis and Block note, mutually adjust to the rhythm of the process.

Hegemonic structures, cultures, and practices

Challenging the status quo can take many shapes, such as eliciting issues of power and social justice (Westling and Sharp), experimenting with innovative practices (Jhagroe), or co-producing new sustainability narratives (Paredis and Block). The problematic nature of the status quo can be explicitly recognised, as in the case of Dutch stakeholders stuck in policy conflicts (Kuitenbrouwer), or hidden or ignored, as the vulnerabilities of the Nepalese farmers excluded from hegemonic climate change discourse (Clement). In either case, as Gardner's experiences with appreciative inquiry in a setting of harsh spending cuts demonstrate, the key question is whether action research is doing more than 'putting lipstick on a pig'.

Each chapter shares experiences with trying to *meaningfully engage with the status quo and effectively challenge it*. This often involves working in organisations, systems, or fields dominated by technologies, discourses, and power relations unconducive to criticality and reflexivity. See for example Westling and Sharp's struggle to create legitimacy for critical thinking and qualitative-interpretive research in a research project dominated by engineers and for-profit utility companies. The tensions around translation and integrity, applicability, and influence they identify come to show that challenging hegemony also involves breaking through engrained patterns and expectations of what research is and how knowledge should be produced. However, also fields with seemingly conducive rhetoric of co-production and change are rife with resistance to transformation. Henderson and Bynner's action research in collaborative governance networks reveals how their transformative ambitions were inhibited by the very forces that kept actors from critically looking at hegemonic structures, cultures, and practices below the surface of benign policy ambitions.

A shared insight is that *challenging hegemonic structures, cultures, and practices involves carefully threading the tightrope of criticality and relationality*. Clement sought to empower local farmers to communicate their views and influence policymakers by balancing her counter-hegemonic stance to climate change discourse with relational processes of joint deliberation and mutual acknowledgement. In turn, Paredis and Block engaged in 'mild interventions' in the transition movement of civil society organisations in Flanders by reframing its vision in 'this direction and not that direction'. Finally, Arrona and Larrea enacted 'soft resistance' by building up relationships of trust and pragmatic collaboration that served as buffer for exerting critical pressure for change. Crucially, they add, challenging hegemonic structures, cultures, and practices should not be done on a level of ideological positions but by negotiating critical-relational dynamics in practice.

Reflexivity, impact, and change

Action research can have many different effects: policy change, new practices for addressing a societal need, changes in social relationships and worldviews, integration of knowledges, and empowerment through stronger motivation and sense of control, just to name a few. At the same time, ideals of generating reflexivity, impact, and change can turn out to be so hard to achieve that action researchers can struggle with a sense of failure. Gardner for instance reflects on her personal desire to be more useful and concludes that action researchers have limited potential to realise transformation on their own terms because they are only one voice amongst many. And Westling and Sharp wondered right from the start how much of an impact their critical-applied approach would have on their technically minded partners.

The chapters showcase *a wide range of impacts on policy processes and sustainability transitions*. A clear and tangible outcome is the adoption of a new policy. The co-operative research of Balázs and Pataki managed to change Hungarian agricultural policy by jointly developing the capacities, vision, and influence of a bottom-up food sovereignty network. Other outcomes are more intangible and process-oriented. As Kuitenbrouwer argues, when facing an intractable conflict, action research can already make a huge difference if it helps stakeholders in 'getting unstuck' and moving forward. Drawing on classical pragmatism, she emphasises the value of enhancing the quality of (democratic) relationships and capacities for joint inquiry. Working in a Participatory Action Research tradition, instead, Clement argues that hegemonic discourses and powers can be, if not immediately overthrown, at least significantly challenged by increasing critical consciousness, emancipation, and counter-framing. Yet, Kuitenbrouwer also emphasises how critical awareness of the need for systemic change and capacity-building was enhanced, while Clement highlights changes in relationships between farmers and officials.

Hence, we can *evaluate reflexivity, impact, and change in terms of critical-ity and relationality*. McPherson's perspective is that building new relationships and creating time for reflexivity are already tremendously valuable to thinking and doing differently. Arzelus reflects that relational capacities for explicating and managing conflicts can create novel solutions and even change the 'rules of the game'. More fundamentally, both Barrez and Westling and Sharp argue that creating space and legitimacy for critical action research is imperative to more socially and environmentally progressive futures. For Van der Arend, this requires that academics more self-critically 'practice what they preach' by co-producing non-conventional knowledge (fiction, but also photo and video, art, social media; see also Beebeejaun *et al.*, 2014) that stimulates the relational imagination of co-inquirers and wider publics. Therefore, generating reflexivity, impact, and change means enhancing the quality of critical-relational dynamics.

Into the future

The overarching aim of this volume has been to provide an overview of action research in policy analysis and transition research in order to understand what forms of knowledge and research might better contribute to policy change and sustainability transitions in an era of unprecedented turbulence and crises. We have gathered a great diversity of approaches and settings in which researchers and co-inquirers produce scientifically and socially relevant knowledge and transformative action. Moreover, we have homed in on the 'critical-relational dynamics' underlying these processes and explicated a range of practices for negotiating 'the starting point', enacting 'multiple roles and relationships', addressing 'hegemonic structures, cultures, and practices', and evaluating 'reflexivity, impact, and change'. This four-tier guiding framework contributes to the theoretical foundations of action research and can also serve as a 'boundary object' for facilitating further sharing of approaches, practices, and experiences involved with fostering policy change and sustainability transitions.

The contributors to this book are optimistic about the potential of action research to galvanise ambitions and opportunities for greater democracy, social justice, economic prosperity, and environmental resilience. At the same time, they do not lose sight of the manifold practical barriers and structural inequalities inhibiting transformative change. To deal with this double-sided nature of co-producing actionable knowledge (Bartels and Wittmayer, 2014), they recommend researchers, citizens, policymakers, and practitioners to actively engage *in the practice* of navigating the contingent dynamics of critically challenging the status quo and strengthening relational interdependencies. As Westling and Sharp, Balázs and Pataki, and Arrona and Larrea emphasise, it is no longer enough to study or criticise hegemony; we need to engage with it by developing innovative practices with, against, and beyond it. This places great onus on what Jhagroe calls the performative role of researchers as co-producers of knowledge and action, reflexively monitoring how collaborative processes and outcomes take shape through many decisions, interactions, and contingencies. By focusing on practice rather than principle, we can deepen understanding of how much influence localised practices of action research can have on glocal sustainability crises and the radical transformations that are necessary.

Barrez recommends policymakers to dedicate much greater resources to action researchers. Indeed, we believe that action research offers an important and legitimate way to answer specific questions and do things that other methodologies in our fields cannot. Because of its emphasis on collaboration with stakeholders in co-producing knowledge and action, action research has significant potential to generate new scientific knowledge that simultaneously contributes to policy change and sustainability transitions. We therefore encourage researchers in our fields to more widely and reflexively adopt action research principles and practices. Most 'mainstream' research primarily focuses on producing scientific knowledge for its own sake and is at best engaged in 'creating impact' based on the model of Mode-1 knowledge production. Most ethnographic and interpretive approaches do have a participatory nature and generate usable knowledge (see e.g. Schatz, 2009; Wagenaar, 2011), yet, tend to have more time and space for gradually coming to an understanding of a case through a posteriori analysis (cf. Rock, 2007).

At the same time, action research is not a panacea – it is suited to address specific questions and generate specific impacts and outcomes. It is only one approach (or, to be more precise, a family of approaches) among a great variety of critical, deliberative, interpretive, and process-oriented approaches to policy analysis and transition research (see our Introduction). Rather than simplifying or shutting down the debate on the nature, purpose, and meaning of actionable forms of knowledge and research (also in relation to other research approaches), we want to open it up by putting the diversity of action research approaches in the limelight. While action research has a long history, is applied in diverse contexts, and takes a wide variety of forms, it is only recently starting to get traction in policy circles and still operates in the margins of hegemonic academic systems (Levin and Greenwood, 2011).

This book cannot be more than a first seed in the process of growing action research and related approaches in policy analysis and transition research. We propose three directions for its development. First, in this book we have liberally drawn from the wider action research literature to develop a guiding framework for policy analysis and transition research. Further exchange and sustained dialogue with action researchers in other fields would help to clarify the wider contribution of our framework to the action research literature and to further improve our practices. Second, by incorporating reflections from co-inquirers in the book we have sought to provide a more comprehensive picture of such practices and enable a critical dialogue. It would be valuable to figure out how we can further enable joint reflection and mutual learning by researchers and co-inquirers – also using different means than writing. Third, we have included contributions from a variety of settings but, except for one chapter about Nepal, this volume focuses on Europe. We encourage action researchers and co-inquirers in other geographical settings to share their experiences so that we may learn from their contingent approaches to fostering policy change and sustainability transitions.

In these ways, we could further enhance the diversity and reflexivity of critical-relational action research approaches to address the current sustainability crises. Action research is more than a valuable alternative to conventional research and interventions; it is an increasingly unmissable approach for understanding and improving complex realities. But, as the contributions to this volume show, only when it is done in critical-relational ways and reflexive about its contingent potentials and limitations. Our hope is that this book makes some way in highlighting the usage and value of action research in policy analysis and transition research, enthusing researchers, citizens, policymakers, and practitioners to join forces in making a real difference. Crucially, we recommend them to engage in critical-relational action research processes in which "knowledge emerges only through invention and re-invention, through the restless, impatient, continuing, hopeful inquiry human beings pursue in the world, with the world, and with each other" (Freire, 2000: 72).

References

Bartels KPR and Wittmayer JM (2014) Symposium introduction: how usable knowledge means in action research practice. *Critical Policy Studies* 8(4), 397–406.

Beebeejaun Y, Durose C, Rees J, Richardson J and Richardson L (2014) 'Beyond text': exploring ethos and method in co-producing research with communities. *Community Development Journal* 49(1): 37–53.

Demeritt D (2005) The promises of collaborative research. *Environment and Planning A*, 37: 2075–2082.

Freire P (2000) *Pedagogy of the oppressed*, New York: Continuum.

Hadorn GH, Biber-Klemm, S, Grossenbacher-Mansuy, W, Hoffmann-Riem H, Joye D, Pohl C and Zemp E (eds.) (2008). *Handbook of transdisciplinary research*, Zurich: Springer.

Levin M and Greenwood D (2011) Revitalizing universities by reinventing the social sciences. In: Denzin NK and Lincoln YS (eds.) *The Sage handbook of qualitative research*, London: Sage, 27–42.

Pain R and Kindon S (2007) Participatory geographies. *Environment and Planning A* 39: 2807–2812.

Reason P (1994) *Participation in human inquiry*, London: Sage.

Richardson L and Durose C (2016) *Designing public policy for co-production: theory, practice and change*, Bristol: The Policy Press.

Rock P (2007). Symbolic interactionism and ethnography. In Atkinson P, Coffey A, Delamont S, Lofland J and Lofland L (eds.) *Handbook of ethnography*, London: Sage, 26–38.

Schatz E (ed.) (2009) *Political ethnography: what immersion contributes to the study of politics*, Chicago: The University of Chicago Press

Stirling A (2006) *From science and society to science in society: towards a framework for co-operative research*. Project Report. European Commission Directorate General for Research.

Stout M (2010) Revisiting the (lost) art of ideal-typing in public administration. *Administrative Theory and Praxis* 32(4), 491–519.

Wagenaar H (2011) *Meaning in action. Interpretation and dialogue in policy analysis*, Armonk: M.E. Sharpe.

Index

Page numbers in **bold** denote tables, those in *italic* denote figures.